THE COVENANT FORMULARY

TO MY PARENTS

Klaus Baltzer

THE COVENANT
FORMULARY

IN OLD TESTAMENT, JEWISH,
AND EARLY CHRISTIAN WRITINGS

Translated by
DAVID E. GREEN

FORTRESS PRESS
PHILADELPHIA

This book is a translation of *Das Bundesformular* by Klaus Baltzer. Wissenschaftliche Monographien zum Alten und Neuen Testament, No. 4, ed. Günther Bornkamm and Gerhard von Rad. 2nd rev. ed., with a bibliographical appendix. Neukirchen-Vluyn: Neukirchener Verlag, 1964.

Library of Congress Catalog Card No. 75–123504
ISBN 0–8006–0040–1

Printed in Great Britain
1–40

CONTENTS

Part Two

THE COVENANT FORMULARY IN JEWISH AND EARLY CHRISTIAN TEXTS

LIST OF ABBREVIATIONS

AfO	Archiv für Orientforschung (Berlin), Graz
ANET	*Ancient Near Eastern Texts Relating to the Old Testament,* ed. J. B. Pritchard, 2nd ed. Princeton, 1955.
ATD	Das Alte Testament Deutsch
BH	Biblia Hebraica
BKAT	Biblischer Kommentar. Altes Testament.
BWANT	Beiträge zur Wissenschaft vom Alten und Neuen Testament
BZAW	Beihefte zur Zeitschrift für die alttestamentliche Wissenschaft
FRLANT	Forschungen zur Religion und Literatur des Alten und Neuen Testaments
HAT	Handbuch zum Alten Testament
HKAT	Handkommentar zum Alten Testament
HNT	Handbuch zum Neuen Testament
ICC	International Critical Commentary
JSS	Journal of Semitic Studies
KAT	Kommentar zum Alten Testament
KHAT	Kurzer Hand-Commentar zum Alten Testament
SBT	Studies in Biblical Theology
ThLZ	Theologische Literaturzeitung
VT	Vetus Testamentum
ZAW	Zeitschrift für die alttestamentliche Wissenschaft

PREFACE TO THE ENGLISH EDITION

The present study goes back to my dissertation and *Habilitationsschrift* for the theological faculty at the University of Heidelberg. My teacher, Professor Gerhard von Rad, had originally encouraged me to make a form-critical study of the Testaments of the Twelve Patriarchs, the Damascus Document, and the Qumran texts, which had just been discovered. He supervised my work with great patience and kindness, even when discovery of the remarkably constant "covenant formulary" as a literary type necessitated following the historical trail backwards.

Since that time, a lively debate has sprung up among scholars studying the form, content, and significance of the "covenant" in the Old Testament as well as the relationship between the covenant and ancient Near Eastern treaties. The most important points are admirably summarized by D. J. McCarthy, "Covenant in the Old Testament: the Present State of the Inquiry," *CBQ*, XXVII (1965), 217–40; I refer the reader to this article and to his *Der Gottesbund im Alten Testament*, Stuttgart, Katholisches Bibelwerk, 1966, an English translation of which will be published by Basil Blackwell.

In the English-speaking world, more attention has been attracted by G. E. Mendenhall's study, *Law and Covenant in Israel and the Ancient Near East*, Pittsburgh, 1955. He and I produced our two studies quite independently. It is therefore all the more fascinating to note that completely different methodological and material assumptions could lead to similar results.

To facilitate an understanding of the present study, it may be well to emphasize once more that the approach is primarily form-critical. It is nevertheless my view that, when really comparable things are compared, the special content of the Old Testament texts can be worked out more precisely. Form criticism runs the dangers of depending too much on modern literary types as its point of departure. In its beginning stages, such an approach was perhaps possible. What is needed is comparison with the ancient types, to prevent over-hasty formalization.

The formal complexity of the "covenant formulary" in its details and its intimate association with specific legal conceptions make me doubt whether it is possible to assume an *ad hoc* origin within the

Old Testament. The many points of contact argue for a connection
with non-biblical treaty forms.

This is not to ignore the historical problems, but the conclusions
of form criticism have only limited usefulness for historical research.
Other arguments must be advanced. The geographical observation
that international treaties have been found in Syria and Egypt does
not suffice to prove dependence. Further archaeological discoveries
may give us a more precise picture on this point.

In the meantime, the textual material at our disposal has increased
somewhat, especially through additional attention to Assyrian texts.
It remains, however, a striking and historically unexplained fact that
the Old Testament texts resemble most closely the highly developed
formulary of the Hittite treaties. Both include an "antecedent
history" as an important element, as well as a statement of the mutual
treaty relationship. The Assyrian texts usually do not contain any
"antecedent history," and the elements of the curse are greatly
expanded at the expense of the blessing. These texts are therefore
more appropriately called "decrees" than "treaties." Unques-
tionably, of course, there were also treaties that did not include an
"antecedent history." It is a striking fact, however, that an historical
presentation could become a part of such treaties.

It is appropriate at this point to mention a difficulty in the English
translation that is due to divergent legal conceptions.

The "*Vorgeschichte*" ("antecedent history") is one of the presuppositions of the treaty relationship. It helps constitute the relationship. So far as we can tell, therefore, it is an integral part of the
treaty. The term "historical introduction" or "historical prologue"
does not express the situation clearly enough.

In the future, more precise legal distinctions will have to be made
in our analysis of the linguistic and legal usage of these treaties. The
statement that we are dealing with a treaty or covenant will no
longer suffice as an explanation; the precise nature of the treaty or
covenant must also be determined. The relationship between the
parties must be examined, together with the purpose of the treaty.
We must see whether—to use modern terminology—we are dealing
with civil contracts or international treaties. Only the latter are the
subject of the present study.

The date when this literary type was adopted still remains under
discussion. I would still consider the early period of Israel's history
likely. The literary form and the conception of a covenant between

God and people, with all its variations, are so intimately related that separate development is hardly conceivable. The rôle played by covenant terminology in the so-called Deuteronomistic tradition, especially if the Deuteronomistic tradition is associated with the period of Josiah, seems more a revival than an innovation.

Within the Old Testament, the conclusions of this study should be examined for their bearing on the question of the origin, function, and individuality of the historical works; the conclusions reached by literary criticism should also be re-examined. Theologically noteworthy is the "historicization" of the "blessing and curse" element. Especially in the prophets (such as Amos, Hosea, and Jeremiah), the rôle of these blessings and curses is increasingly illuminated by reference to the covenant between the God of Israel and his people.

Some critics have noted that the argument becomes "thinner" in the second part of the book. That is incontestable. I would nevertheless like to maintain my hypothesis that the covenant formulary was used in Jewish and early Christian texts, and that it can be used to elucidate various relationships (one might mention, for instance, the question of how the New Testament Epistles are structured). There is, for example, the striking fact that the liturgy of "entry into the covenant" (1QS i. 18–19) at Qumran preserves the covenant formulary so completely that the individual elements of the Old Testament texts can simply be inserted as they stand. On the other hand, the connection with early Christian church orders is unmistakable.

Critics have objected to my failure to cite certain texts that should be taken into account. During my research, the number of texts discussed and their quite different dates led to the opposite worry. If other texts are now to be cited, they will have to be examined carefully to determine their form-critical, substantial, and historical relationship to the present texts. The same is true of the "covenant" concept and its associated terminology. I may close with the request that scholars utilize the possibilities but also observe the limitations of each method.

I should like to thank the translator, David E. Green, for his careful work, help with the Bibliography, and preparation of the index.

Klaus Baltzer

University of Munich

March, 1970

Part One

THE COVENANT FORMULARY:
ITS ORIGIN AND USE IN
THE OLD TESTAMENT

A

THE PROBLEM

In the Old Testament, the word בְּרִית designates the basis of the relationship between the God of Israel and his people.[1] Clear as this fact is, it never ceases to raise new problems.

Wellhausen's opinion was decisive for the verdict of historical-critical study in its earlier period:[2]

> The idea of a *covenant* (berith) entered into between Yahweh and Israel, which our authorities in Biblical Theology think they can use as a key to an understanding of the entire Old Testament, does not occur in the earlier prophets at all. . . . In all cases the relationship is natural, not entered into conditionally. . . .
>
> The idea of a covenant between Yahweh and Israel did not gain general significance until shortly before the Exile, when the people had become quite familiar with the conditional nature of the relationship and the possibility of its dissolution. . . .
>
> Berith is frequently used for capitulation, whose conditions are imposed by the stronger upon the weaker. As a consequence, it comes to mean simply: injunction, requirement, law. . . .
>
> Not until the late period was the Berith of Yahweh interpreted according to the original meaning of Berith; as so often happens, the word gave birth to the idea. Even in late usage, however, the dominant idea is still very much that of God's *requirement*, the law; a *promise*, something performed by Yahweh, is not easily associated with בְּרִית.

This quotation raises the most important points that were to play a rôle in subsequent discussion.

1. The restriction placed on the meaning of the covenant with Yahweh in the Old Testament in contrast to the views of 'Biblical Theology.'[3]

2. The explanation of the relationship between 'covenant' and 'law' as a change of meaning. According to Wellhausen, '*berît*' is understood at the outset as a relationship guaranteed by a superior to his inferior. This leads secondarily to the meaning 'law.'[4] Others,

---

[1] See W. Eichrodt, *Theology of the Old Testament* (E.T. Philadelphia, 1961–67), vol. 1, pp. 36ff.

[2] This quotation comes from a note in his *Geschichte Israels* (Berlin, 1878), vol. 1, pp. 434–35, n. 1.

[3] See, for example, Quell's article in G. Kittel (ed.), *Theological Dictionary of the New Testament* (E.T. Grand Rapids, 1964–), vol. 2, p. 111, n. 27.

[4] This view is also espoused by Franz Delitzsch, Gesenius, Dillmann, H. Schultz, Öhler, Guthe, Bredenkamp, König, and Cremer. See the list in R. Kraetzschmar, *Die Bundesvorstellung im AT in ihrer geschichtlichen Entwicklung* (Marburg, 1896), pp. 3f.

however, can explain this change as taking precisely the opposite direction. The meaning 'ordinance,' 'law,' gives rise to the meaning 'covenant,' 'treaty.'[5]

3. The view that the entire matter is an historically late development.

4. The understanding of '*bᵉrît*' as an idea.[6]

In the case of Wellhausen, the points just mentioned combine to yield a distinctly negative assessment of '*bᵉrît*': the idea of the *bᵉrît* with Yahweh has, like every idea, undergone change. In this case, however, the end result is not progressive clarification, but legal petrification. This development is a mistake and a perversion. But the very application of the term '*bᵉrît*' to the relationship between Israel and God is, in Wellhausen's opinion, inadequate, because it measures faith by legal categories. In contrast to this approach, Wellhausen emphasizes the positive aspects of the 'natural relationship with God' that existed in the early period.

Kraetzschmar elaborated in detail on Wellhausen's thesis in his fundamental monograph, *Die Bundesvorstellung im Alten Testament in ihrer geschichtlichen Entwicklung*. In his assumption of a development that 'progresses in logical stages,'[7] as well as in his estimate of the 'covenant concept,' Kraetzschmar is in complete agreement with Wellhausen.[8] Kraetzschmar's methodology, however, remains important. He begins with an exegesis of the texts in which בְּרִית occurs. He has no intention, however, of limiting his study to the mere words of the text. As his organizing principle, as well as the basis of his dating, he takes the literary strata recovered by source analysis.[9] In

---

[5] This view is espoused by David Schulz, von Hofman, Buhl, Friedrich Delitzsch, von Orelli, Cheyne, Strack, Siegfried-Stade, and Nowack; see Kraetzschmar, *Die Bundesvorstellung*, p. 5.

[6] In subsequent discussion, this understanding can be noted even by observing the titles of books and articles: Kraetzschmar, *Die Bundesvorstellung im AT*; P. Karge, *Die Geschichte des Bundesgedankens im AT* (Münster, 1910); J. Begrich, 'Berit, Ein Beitrag zur Erfassung einer at-lichen *Denkform*,' *ZAW*, NF 19 (1944), 1–11.

[7] Kraetzschmar, *Die Bundesvorstellung*, p. 6.

[8] 'From the purely religious point of view, however, it [the covenant concept] is a falling away from the heights of the prophetical knowledge of God. Faith is the more precious, the less it has by way of concrete foundation. Therefore the faith of those prophets seems so high to us . . . , because it is not based on external support, but only on the living inward consciousness of God. . . .' 'It [the covenant concept] represents a compromise between the ideals of the prophets and the capacity of the general population' (ibid., p. 146).

[9] Besides some observations that remain valid today, there are instances of cavalier treatment of the text. For example, after literary criticism has excised a whole series of passages from the Sinai pericope, what remains is 'that the content of the Berith with God on Sinai, according to the earliest narrative, was probably the institution of that ancient shrine, the ark' (ibid., p. 96).

the following period, Kraetzschmar's 'single presupposition' proved fruitful. He assumed

> . . . that before בְּרִית was used in the religious sphere, i.e., to refer to the relationship between God and man, it was rooted in the soil of secular life, and was limited to relationships between ordinary men.[10]

For the secular sphere, Kraetzschmar arrives at the following conclusion:

> The Berith, then, is that cultic act whereby obligations or agreements of whatever sort were solemnly made absolutely binding and inviolable.[11] Its content and therefore its meaning derive solely from the nature of the obligations; depending on what these are, it can mean covenant, agreement, treaty, solemn assurance, obligation, oath.[12]

The important thing is the cultic act, the 'ritual.'[13] From this beginning, the concept was transferred to the 'religious sphere,' becoming increasingly abstract. In its most extreme development, in the Priestly Code, it becomes a religious *terminus technicus*,[14] signifying a unilateral declaration of God's will concerning man.[15]

Kraetzschmar's interpretation of '*berît*' has been criticised most vigorously by Pedersen.[16] He accuses Kraetzschmar in particular of 'being led astray by the European concept "treaty" or "contract," so that he interprets *berît* as the inauguration of a relationship, the agreement or decision upon which the relationship rests.'[17]

Pedersen introduces the viewpoint of comparative religion into the discussion. He extends the area of study from the secular use of the concept in the Old Testament to its use among the kindred Semitic peoples, especially the Arabs. He cites comparative material for both linguistic usage and the various concomitant ceremonies.

According to Pedersen, '*berît*,' like the Arabic '*ahd*,' means the 'mutual relationship of solidarity, with all the rights and obligations this relationship involves for the parties concerned.'[18] In other words, '*berît*' refers to the relationship itself.[19] A 'union of the spheres' of the parties involved makes the agreement inviolable.[20] Through

---

[10] Ibid., p. 6.

[11] The original is printed with emphasis to this point.

[12] Kraetzschmar, *Die Bundesvorstellung*, pp. 40–41.

[13] Ibid., p. 41.

[14] Ibid., p. 199.

[15] Ibid., pp. 200ff.

[16] J. Pedersen, *Der Eid bei den Semiten in seinem Verhältnis zu verwandten Erscheinungen, sowie die Stellung des Eides im Islam* (Straßburg, 1914), pp. 38–40.

[17] Ibid., p. 39.

[18] Ibid., pp. 33–34.

[19] Ibid., pp. 39, 33.

[20] Ibid., pp. 21ff., 27, and 31.

word and ritual, two originally separate spheres are joined.[21] The covenant produces a new community of life, which is like a blood relationship.[22] In contrast to Wellhausen, Pedersen rejects a late dating of the 'b^erît-concept,' finding its beginnings in the early period.

Pedersen's admonition against applying European categories too hastily is certainly not unjustified. It is an important observation that, 'to the Semitic mind, "b^erît" refers to the establishment of a "primary relationship".'[23] Problems arise, however, when Pedersen, using the phrase 'union of spheres,' applies directly to Israel concepts from the world of primitive and uncivilized peoples.[24] This approach raises the question of whether here, too, we are not dealing with the application of 'alien categories.' Pedersen's presupposition leads to certain consequences when applied to an understanding of the b^erît relationship between Yahweh and Israel. Even if individual ceremonies reflect more primitive notions, careful study must determine whether these ceremonies really still define Israel's understanding of the relationship.—For the Babylonian and Assyrian material, even Pedersen assumes a definition approaching the modern meaning 'treaty,' 'contract.'[25] He rejects, however, all attempts to use these texts as parallels, since they presuppose a completely different culture. It is interesting to note that here Pedersen takes a position similar to that of Wellhausen.

Our study must show whether it is not in fact too one-sided to limit extra-biblical parallels from the outset to Arabic sources.

Köhler's sketch marks the temporary limit of what a concept study alone can attain as an understanding of בְּרִית: 'The Covenant or the Agreement as the Form of the Relationship between Jahweh and Israel.'[26] In contrast to Pedersen, Köhler stresses once again that with בְּרִית, even in 'untheological contexts,' we are dealing with a

---

[21] Ibid., p. 27.

[22] Ibid., pp. 21–22.

[23] Ibid., p. 42.

[24] Here the influence of Grönbech's studies is probably at work.

[25] *Der Eid bei den Semiten*, p. 51.

[26] In L. Köhler, *Old Testament Theology* (E.T. London, 1957), pp. 60–75. The English translation was made from the third German edition of 1953, which repeated this section without change from the second edition of 1947, with the addition of a paragraph (p. 62) in which Köhler states his agreement with the theory of Begrich (see below). Köhler refers to the derivation of the word *b^erît* in his lexicon (Leiden: Brill, 1953, p. 152a): 'table-fellowship, which a healthy person offers to a sick person, one therefore who because of his sickness is socially and religiously suspect.' In the lexicon itself, however, we find only the definition 'table-fellowship.' The elaboration in *Old Testament Theology* is stated without grounds. Köhler stresses particularly his agreement with Begrich's statement that the concept becomes 'thought of more and more as being an agreement.'

legal transaction and a legal relationship between two partners concerning a definite matter.[27] The partners are Yahweh and the people
of Israel.[28] According to Köhler it is the nature of the covenant with
Yahweh to be bilateral. Both parties have rights and obligations.[29]
'Jahweh protects Israel as His people . . . and . . . Israel worships
Jahweh and obeys Him.' Both parties join in the agreement 'of their
own free will,'[30] although the initiative and resolution derive uni-
laterally from one of the two parties, in this case Yahweh.[31]

Köhler assumes that the covenant concept was familiar to Israel
even in the nomadic period. 'The whole covenant was contained in
the saying: "I will take you to me for a people and I will be to you
a God", Ex. 6:7.'[32] Here the covenant exists as yet without any
'historical perspective' or 'territorial perspective.'[33] The relationship
with Yahweh 'was primarily an attitude and disposition towards
Jahweh, a silent recognition of His lordship within the covenant.'[34]
The crucial 'alteration to the covenant idea'[35] is occasioned, according to Köhler, by the occupation of Canaan. What had once been
obedience now becomes worship and cult.[36] Nature is drawn into the
relationship with God. The extent to which the 'covenant idea' in
its new form continues to play an important rôle is not made quite
clear in Köhler's sketch.

In another passage,[37] Köhler states 'that the covenant or agreement form was more and more found *unsuited* to represent the relationship between Jahweh and Israel.' He draws this conclusion from
a change in linguistic usage. The formula (עִם) כָּרַת בְּרִית אֶת is
replaced by הֵקִים בְּרִית אֶת and finally by the formula (לוֹ) נָתַן (הִנְנִי)
אֶת־בְּרִיתִי.—But is it possible to say so much with any degree of
assurance? The foundation remains insecure so long as we do not
know for sure what the formula כָּרַת בְּרִית actually means. Why
should we say that in הֵקִים בְּרִית 'the authoritative, constraining,
initiating will of God receives still clearer expression'? The question
remains, for instance, whether the formula 'to give a covenant
(+suffix)' is not every bit as ancient as the other formulas.

---

[27] Ibid., p. 63.
[28] Köhler states, 'The idea of the people of Israel, as far as the covenant concept is
concerned, is taken out of the category of time altogether; it is supra-temporal, or
a-temporal' (ibid., p. 65). This seems to me to be an abstraction that is methodologically
not beyond question.
[29] Ibid., pp. 68–69.   [30] Ibid., p. 68.   [31] Ibid., p. 62.
[32] Ibid., p. 73.   [33] Ibid.   [34] Ibid., p. 72.
[35] Heading to §23, p. 71.   [36] Ibid., p. 72.   [37] Ibid., pp. 62–63.

This attempt, too, to trace a course of development is not really convincing.

But here we have probably reached the limit beyond which a mere concept study cannot go. Nor is anything really changed when Begrich,[38] attacking Köhler, goes on to say that at the outset we have an understanding of בְּרִית according to which the term designates a relationship 'toward a more powerful party into which the more powerful party places the less powerful,'[39] while the bilateral relationship, with mutual rights and obligations, represents a later degeneration. Originally, according to Begrich, there is no relationship between $b^e r \hat{\imath} t$ and law.[40] Later, $b^e r \hat{\imath} t$ is looked upon as a treaty or contract.[41] The development of $b^e r \hat{\imath} t$ in the direction of 'treaty' reaches its climax when the $b^e r \hat{\imath} t$ is given fixed form in a treaty document.[42]

It is striking how close this view is to that of Wellhausen sketched at the beginning. It is strange, too, how colorless and two-dimensional the concept of בְּרִית remains, despite all efforts to understand it. When all critical reservations are taken into account, the result is amazingly out of proportion to the importance of the concept בְּרִית in the Old Testament. Purely on the statistical level, according to Köhler's own figures,[43] it occurs 286 times in the Old Testament.

A new approach to the question has provided a possibility for breaking the scholarly impasse. Instead of restricting themselves narrowly to the concept בְּרִית, some scholars have inquired into the 'Old Testament institutions,' the corresponding literary types, and the 'accompanying linguistic formulas,'[44] in which the concept is rooted.

Mowinckel provided the initial impetus by pointing out the connection between the autumnal festival, the 'covenant renewal,' and the decalogue.[45]

Noth's study of the amphictyony of the twelve tribes of Israel[46] has indicated the institution in which the concept of the covenant with

[38] J. Begrich, 'Berit. Ein Beitrag zur Erfassung einer alttestamentlichen Denkform,' ZAW, NF 19 (1944), 1–11.

[39] Ibid., p. 4.   [40] Ibid., p. 7.   [41] Ibid., pp. 4ff.   [42] Ibid., pp. 9–10.

[43] L. Köhler, Lexicon in Veteris Testamenti Libros (Leiden, 1953), p. 150b.

[44] See M. Noth, 'Old Testament Covenant-Making in the Light of a Text from Mari,' in The Laws in The Pentateuch and Other Studies (London, 1966; Philadelphia, 1967), pp. 108–117.

[45] See especially S. Mowinckel, 'Le Décalogue,' Études d'histoire et de philosophie religieuses, 16 (1927).

[46] M. Noth, Das System der zwölf Stämme Israels (BWANT, 4. F., 1, Stuttgart, 1930).

Yahweh is rooted. At the same time, this represents a decision in favor of the great antiquity of the tradition of the covenant with Yahweh.—Alt has shown that apodictic law goes with the covenant.[47] In many individual studies, he has done much to increase our understanding of the early history of Israel, thus casting light on the background of the covenant idea.—By rigorous application of the form-critical approach, von Rad succeeded in sketching a much clearer picture of the covenant cult as well as the substance of the covenant.[48] The structure of major textual units like the Sinai tradition, Deuteronomy, and finally the Hexateuch as a whole was placed in a new light. The constituent elements of the covenant cult were recognized: proclamation of the law, ratification of the covenant, blessings and curses.

The present study seeks to go further in the direction marked out by these scholars.[49] Our analysis of the literary type will begin with non-biblical secular texts. As our point of departure, we shall take Eißfeldt's statement in the section 'Contracts' of his introduction to the Old Testament:[50]

> Related to the treaties concluded between tribes and peoples and their representatives, and certainly influenced by the style of these, is the agreement between God and a human community, which has, however, its own special characteristics. There were certainly prescribed for this not only specific ceremonies, but also specific forms.

We shall work out the characteristics of the literary type as precisely as possible in the non-biblical texts, so as then to be able to answer the question of the structure and employment of the formulary of that agreement between God and a human community with its own

[47] A. Alt, 'The Origins of Israelite Law,' in *Essays on Old Testament History and Religion* (E.T. New York, 1966), pp. 79–132.

[48] In 'The Form-Critical Problem of the Hexateuch,' in *The Problem of the Hexateuch and Other Essays* (E.T. New York, 1966), pp. 1–78; also *Studies in Deuteronomy* (SBT 9, E.T. Chicago, 1953).

[49] The basic conception of this work was completed before the publication of G. E. Mendenhall's article 'Law and Covenant in Israel and the Ancient Near East,' *BA*, 17 (1954), 26–76, reprinted by the Biblical Colloquium (Pittsburgh, 1955). It is gratifying to note that, despite our different presuppositions, it is possible to agree on many points in our results. Mendenhall also bases his work on Korosec's study of the Hittite treaties (see below, p. 9, note 2). He is more interested in historical questions, while the present work limits itself to the form-critical approach. No doubt further conclusions, not least in the historical sphere, can be drawn on the basis of this beginning; but I consider it methodologically dangerous to bring both sets of questions together prematurely. See also O. Eißfeldt's discussion in *JSS*, 1 (1956), 188–89.

[50] O. Eißfeldt, *The Old Testament: An Introduction* (E.T. New York, 1965), p. 20.

special characteristics. Comparison will make the individuality of the biblical texts easier to define. Our study of the literary type is intended to further our understanding of how the covenant was entered into, renewed, and ratified.[51] This will help us rethink the manner in which Israel was bound to Yahweh.

---

[51] In the following pages, we shall continue to translate ברית as 'covenant.' On the problem of the translation, see Quell's article διαθήκη in G. Kittel (ed.), *Theological Dictionary of the New Testament*, vol. 2, p. 109.

B. I

THE STRUCTURE
OF THE TREATY FORMULARY

Eißfeldt points out the 'relationship' between covenant and treaty. It is therefore logical to begin our study with an analysis of treaties. For texts, we have abundant material from the entire Near East at our disposal. One of the earliest treaties is preserved on the Vulture Stele of Eannatum of Lagash.[1] This treaty suggests the existence of a long legal tradition. In comparison to this treaty, the treaties of the Hittite Empire exhibit a much more highly developed form. Primarily for practical reasons—they have been excellently published by Weidner and Friedrich[2]—these treaties will form the basis of our study. Fifteen treaties in all have been preserved (nine in Akkadian, six in Hittite), which the Hittite kings from Šuppiluliumaš (*ca.* 1375–1335 B.C.) to Tutḫaliyaš IV (1250–1220) concluded with their vassals in Asia Minor and Syria.[3] They are preserved on clay tablets from the Boghazköy archives.

[1] In F. Thureau-Dangin, *Die sumerischen und akkadischen Königsinschriften* (Leipzig, 1907), pp. 11ff.

[2] E. F. Weidner, *Politische Dokumente aus Kleinasien, die Staatsverträge in akkadischer Sprache aus dem Archiv von Boghazkoi* (Leipzig, 1923); J. Friedrich, *Die Staatsverträge des Hatti-Reiches in hethitischer Sprache* ('Mitteilungen der Vorderasiatisch-Ägyptischen Gesellschaft,' Jg. 31 and Bd. 34, H. 1, Leipzig, 1926–30). For the abbreviations used in citing these treaties, see the key at page 181 below.

I have based the following discussion essentially on the excellent study by V. Korosec, *Hethitische Staatsverträge, ein Beitrag zu ihrer juristischen Wertung* ('Leipziger rechtswissenschaftliche Studien,' 60, Leipzig, 1931). The historical question of whether there is a direct or indirect connection cannot be gone into here. It will be difficult to discover more precise details, since the law and traditions of government offices are 'international.' I nevertheless find it striking that the developed form of the Hittite treaties as well as the details of their content come very close to the parallels in the Old Testament texts. On the question of what the relationship might be, see, for instance, A. E. Cowley, *The Hittites* ('The Schweich Lectures,' 1918, London, 1920); A. F. Puukko, *Die altassyrischen und hethitischen Gesetze und das AT* (Helsinki: Societas Orientalis Fennica, 1925); A. Jepsen, *Untersuchungen zum Bundesbuch* (BWANT, F. 3, H. 5, Stuttgart, 1927); M. R. Lehmann, 'Abraham's Purchase of Machpelah and Hittite Law,' *BASOR*, 129 (1953), 15–17; M. Noth, *The Old Testament World* (E.T. Philadelphia, 1966), see index under 'Hittites'; A. Malamat, 'Doctrines of Causality in Hittite and Biblical Historiography, a Parallel,' *VT*, 5 (1955), 1–12; A. Goetze, *Kleinasien* (München, 1957); Bittel and Güterbock, 'Hethiter,' in *Die Religion in Geschichte und Gegenwart* (3rd ed., Tübingen, 1956), cols. 299ff.

[3] Apart from certain details, the Ramses Treaty remains outside the scope of our study, since special circumstances obtain for it.

We shall also refer to some texts from the international treaties found in the archives of Ras Shamra (Ugarit).[4]

It will be found that these treaties are composed according to a definite schema. Examination reveals the following structure:

(1) Preamble
(2) Antecedent history
(3) Statement of substance concerning the future relationship
(4) Specific stipulations
(5) Invocation of the gods as witnesses
(6) Curses and blessings.[5]

This schema can be found, with minor variations, in all the treaties. It remains so constant that, if a treaty is preserved only in fragments, they can be arranged in order with a high degree of assurance.[6] One can also determine, for example, which parts are missing.[7] The structural regularity, however, does not go hand in hand with uniformity in detail. The treaties give the impression of having been reworked in each case to conform to the special situation for which they were framed.[8] Despite the formalism to be expected in a legal document, they exhibit striking variations in the use of literary and especially stylistic resources.[9] We may conclude that the technique of composing such treaties was already highly developed in the chancelleries of the Hittite court.

---

[4] J. Nougayrol, ed., *Le palais royal d'Ugarit IV* (Paris, 1956).
These texts are especially noteworthy because Ugaritic texts have already shed light on various aspects of the Old Testament.

[5] A. Goetze outlines the structure of the treaty between 'Muršiliš II and Dubbi-Tešup of Amurru' as follows: (1) Preamble, (2) Historical Introduction, (3) Future Relations of the Two Countries, (4) Military Clauses, (5) Dealings with Foreigners etc., (6) Invocation of the Gods, (7) Curses and Blessings; in J. B. Pritchard, ed., *Ancient Near Eastern Texts Relating to the Old Testament* (2nd ed.; Princeton, 1955), pp. 203–204. See also Korosec, *Hethitische Staatsverträge*, pp. 12–14.

[6] See Friedrich, *Staatsverträge*, part 2 (1930), pp. 45ff., on the treaty between Muwattališ and Alakšanduš of Wiluša.

[7] Cf. Weidner, *Politische Dokumente*, p. 110, n. 2.

[8] See G. R. Meyer, 'Zwei neue Kizzuwatna-Verträge,' *Mitteilungen des Instituts für Orientforschung*, 1 (1953), 120–21.

[9] For example, in the midst of the stipulations of Šuppiluliumaš' treaty with Ḫukkanaš and the people of Ḫayaša, we find the precept, 'And you shall be very much on guard against a woman of the palace' (F 6 §31, col. iii, 44ff.). By way of illustration, a story is told whose outcome makes it appear inadvisable to disobey the precept (ibid., 53–58). Direct speech is quoted repeatedly (see in the same treaty §28, 8–24, as well as W 2, ro. 23–24; cf. the interpolation of a letter in W 9, ro. 22–23). The treaty between Muwattališ(?) and Šunaššura, the king of Kizzuwatna, is considerably more conciliatory in tone than, for instance, the treaty between Muwattališ and Alakšanduš of Wiluša (W 7 and F 5). See especially F 5 §19, col. iii, 76: 'These agreements ("words"), however, are by no means based on reciprocity, [77] but rather come from the land of Ḫatti.' See M. Riemschneider, *Die Welt der Hethiter* (Stuttgart, 1954), p. 34.

A number of details in the content of the treaty texts are significant for our present study.

(1) *The Preamble*

'The preamble of the treaty comprises the name and title of the Ḥatti ruler issuing the document in question, followed by the name and title of his father, together with the names and titles of more distant ancestors, and finally the epithet "hero".'[10] The formula, which is found again and again, reads: 'Thus speaks A, the great king, king of the land of Ḥatti . . . , son of B, the great king . . . , the hero.'[11] Some treaties, after 'king of the land of Ḥatti,' insert 'the favorite of the god . . . .'[12]

(2) *Antecedent History*

This section comprises the 'description of the previous relationships between the Ḥatti ruler or the Ḥatti Empire and the vassal in question or the land assigned to him.'[13] The description must be considered as a form of historiography.[14] It goes beyond mere annalistic recitation of events. The course of the narrative is arranged according to the sequence of the generations of ancestors of the parties to the treaty. It may comprise from one to five generations.[15] It is oriented by the treaty relationship to the great king, which is evaluated positively or negatively.[16] His benefactions are duly emphasized.[17] The antecedent history often concludes with the bestowal

10 Korosec, *Hethitische Staatsverträge*, p. 12. Divergences from this structure are described here.

11 Ibid.

12 F 1 §1, A 1; F 5, B i, 1; W 1, ro. 1.

13 Korosec, *Hethitische Staatsverträge*, p. 13.

14 Cf. A. Malamat, 'Doctrines of Causality in Hittite and Biblical Historiography,' *VT*, 5 (1955), 1ff.

15 W 2, ro. 8: 'The king my great-grandfather' (in fact, we are dealing with the great-great-grandfather; see Weidner, *Politische Dokumente*, p. 38, n. 3); W 5, ro. 2; W 6 extends from Ḥattušiliš (*ca.* 1680 to 1650) to Muršiliš II (1334–1306) or Muwatalliš (1306–1282), i.e., about 350 years. W 7, ro. 5; W 9, ro. 4; F 1 §2, A 2; F 3 §2, D 5; F 5, §2, B 2: 'Ages ago, when Lab[arnaš] . . . the father of my fathers . . . .'

16 For example, positively: F 5 §2, B 6: '. . . Nev]er [7] did the land of Wiluša [re]volt against the land of Ḥa[tti], but . . . [8] they remained loyal to the kings of the land of Ḥatti. . . .' Cf. F 5 §3, B 15. Negatively: W 6, ro. 15: 'When Tutḫaliyaš, the great king, [as]cended the throne of the m[onarchy], [16] since [. . .] the king of the land of Ḥalap with him [. . .] had turned away from him. . . . [19] The king of the land of Ḥalap committed the si[n of the] king of the land of Han[ig]albat [20] but against Ḥattuš[iliš, the king of the land of] Ḥatti, he sinned [especially].'

17 W 3, ro. col. i, 9: 'And I, the Sun, sent soldiers and horses to assist him.' W 6, ro. 31; F 1 §7, col. i, 16; F 3 §8, C 23: 'But now I, the Sun, have done nothing to harm you, Kupanta-ᵈKAL [24] and I have not rejected you and I have not taken from you the house of your father, nor even your [25] land,'

of authority to the vassal and his enfeoffment. The nature and extent of the land entrusted to the vassal are stated precisely. Several treaties contain extended boundary descriptions.[18]

(3) Statement of Substance Concerning the Future Relationship of the Partners to the Treaty[19]

This section is most clearly developed in the treaties written in the Hittite language.[20] On the one hand, it is intimately connected with the antecedent history, for the facts recounted in it constitute the basis for the treaty relationship. On the other hand, the statement of substance summarizes the purpose of the following specific stipulations. These stipulations are the legal consequence of the treaty

[18] F 1 §7, col. i, 18: 'And I [. . .?] have invested you with responsibility for your brothers and the land of Amurru.' F 3 §8, C 26: 'And you I have appointed to exercise authority in the land, and have given you the land of Mirā [27] and the land of Kuwaliya; but as the boundaries were in the earlier time of Mašḫuiluwaš, [28] so shall they now be for you.' There follows a boundary description: §9, C 29, 'On this side, from the city of Maddunnaššaš, the fortified camp of Tutḫaliyaš [30] shall be your boundary; on this side [furthermore] the military outpost of the city of Wiyanawanda shall be your boundary; [31] and you shall not come over into the city of Aura. On this side [also] [32] your boundary shall be the river Aštarpa [and] the land of Kuwaliya. And that shall be your land, [33] protect it. . . .' See also F 4 §5, col. i, 63ff.; F 5 §4; W 9, v. 37 and *passim*.

Cf. also J. Nougayrol, *Palais royal d'Ugarit IV*, pp. 48ff., text no. 17.340. Cf. the reproduction of the text below, pp. 187–8.

We are dealing here with a treaty between Šuppiluliumaš and Niqmadu. This treaty exhibits the following structure:

(1) Preamble
(2) Antecedent history
(3) Description of the land
(4) Statement of substance
(5) Invocation of the gods as witnesses.

[19] The 'statement of substance' could also be called a 'general clause.'

[20] See, for example, F 1 §8, i, 23–3.

In Pritchard, *ANET*, p. 204, Goetze defines this section somewhat differently. In my opinion, however, i, 19–22 belongs with 11–18 and constitutes, with the granting of authority, the conclusion of the antecedent history.

i, 23: 'Now keep the oath of the king and the power [literally "hand"] of the king; but I, the Sun, shall protect you, [24] Dubbi-Tešup. And when you marry your wife [25] and beget a male heir, in the land of Amurru he shall later[?] [26] be king. . . . [32] And do not set your eyes upon another; [33] your fathers gave tri[but]e [34] to the land of Egypt; you [however, shall not give tribute].' W 1 contains an Akkadian example. The antecedent history is reported in the perfect tense from ro. 1, '[e-nu-]ma,' to ro. 58, 'at-ta-din-šu.' Ro. 59 continues with a nominal sentence: 'Mat-ti-ú-a-za . . . lu-ú ší-ú . . . ,' 'He is king!' In contrast, ro. 60–78 lays down the future relationship to the great king (see especially *i-na arkât ûmî^{mi}*, 63, 64, 65, 68).

Ro. 72: 'Just as he is the enemy of the land of Mitanni, so (also he is) the enemy [of the land of Ḫatti. . . . The friend] [73] [of th]e king of the land of Ḫatti (is also) the friend of the king of the land of M[itanni . . . .'

In this treaty, the basic stipulations clearly include also the definition of the position of the great king's daughter, who had been given in marriage to the vassal. See ro. 61.

relationship: if a party remains loyal to the treaty, he will comport himself in such and such a way. This connection is further emphasized by the fact that the statement of substance can be repeated before the specific stipulations.[21] The statement of substance itself comprises primarily general imperatives. Their basic requirement is loyalty on the part of the treaty signatory.

(4) Specific Stipulations of the Treaties

The specific stipulations of the treaties are usually in the form of conditional statements based on the following schema: 'If the following takes place, you shall comport yourself as follows' (Akkadian 'šum-ma . . . ù-šum-ma').[22] The relationship with the great king does not permit the signatory to continue relations with foreign powers. 'It means the loss of diplomatic rights, both active and passive.'[23] In some cases even trade is restricted.[24] 'Evil words,' i.e., defamatory rumors, whether from abroad or of conspiracies at

---

For another Akkadian treaty, cf. W 7, ro. i, 49–59. The nature of the statement of substance is especially clear in the treaties found at Ugarit. See treaty 17.340 already cited (Nougayrol, *Palais royal d'Ugarit IV*, pp. 48ff.): 'Niqmadu est ainsi avec mon ennemi, ennemi, et avec mon ami, ami. Au Soleil Grandroi son maître il est tout dévoué et il garde l'accord d'amitié du Hatti. Ainsi le Soleil Grandroi a connu la loyauté de Niqmadu.'
Akkadian:
11 '*ni-iq-ma-an-du* [12] *it-ti* amil*nakri-ia na-ki-ir ù it-ti ša-la-mì-ia ša-lim*
13 *ù a-na* ilŠamši5i *šarri rabî be-li-šu i-ta-na-ah dan-niš*
14 *ù ri-kil-ta ša-la-ma ša* mat*ha-at-ti na-și-ir*
15 *anumma*ma ilŠamšu5u *šarru rabû ki-it-ta-ša* '*niq-ma-an-di i-ta-mar*.'
Here '*rikilta šalama*' is strikingly similar to the OT בְּרִית שָׁלוֹם (cf. Num. 25:12; Isa. 54:10; Ezek. 34:25; 37:26).

---

[21] For example, F 1 §10, col. ii, 13–14; 'Just as I, [the S]un, protect you, Duppi-T[ešup], so shall you furnish auxiliary troops for the Sun and the land [of Hatti]. . . .' This is followed immediately by a series of specific stipulations beginning 'Now if . . . .'
Cf. also F 3 §11, D 33–41 and §13 and 14 as far as C ii, 12; F 5 §6–9, Z 47 (text partially damaged); F 6 §2, col. i, 8–16. In 16–30, a curse is immediately appended. §5, 31–38 continues the statement of substance. Within the specific stipulations, there occurs another basic statement of substance: §13, col. ii, 22–25.
In a series of treaties the statement of substance is broken up as a literary unit. We find instead a basic appeal to loyalty preceding specific stipulations. This does not change the legal construction: the specific requirement derives from the basic relationship of loyalty to the great king.
[22] Cf., for example, the series in W 7, ro. i, 60ff.; W 9, ro. 5ff., and *passim*. On conditional sentences with '*šumma*,' see W. von Soden, *Grundriß der akkadischen Grammatik*, (Rome, 1952), §161.
[23] Korosec, *Hethitische Staatsverträge*, p. 46. See W 7, ro. iv, 28–31.
[24] Ibid., pp. 75ff., following Forrer, *MDOG*, 1924, p. 17, no. 63. KUB xxiii, 1, iv, 14ff.: 'Your merchant shall not enter into the land of Aššur, nor shall you let his merchant into your land.'

home, are to be reported without delay.[25] In the nature of things, various military stipulations occupy considerable space. They prescribe the way the signatories are to provide mutual protection and assistance.[26] Characteristic are the detailed stipulations concerning repatriation of fugitives, prisoners of war, etc.[27] The nature and amount of tribute is fixed precisely.[28] The vassals are obligated, among their other duties, to visit the court regularly.[29] Their relationship to each other is that of 'confederates.'[30] They are obliged to call upon the great king as mediator. 'One shall not undertake to slay the other in secret.'[31] Among the rights of the vassal are protection by the great king against foreign and domestic enemies, as well as a guarantee of the right of succession for his descendants.[32]

(5) *Invocation of the Gods as Witnesses*

It is an ancient legal tradition that, when a treaty is concluded, witnesses are necessary. In the international treaties, the gods perform this function. They must, however, be expressly called upon to act as witnesses.[33] Typical of the Hittite treaties are the very detailed lists of gods,[34] which follow the invocation formula. These comprise, for instance, the gods of the land of Ḫatti, the gods of the vassals, and finally—probably considered as gods—mountains, rivers, springs, the great sea, heaven and earth, winds and clouds.[35]

(6) *Blessings and Curses*

The gods, however, are not merely 'witnesses' in the hackneyed sense that they vouch for the correctness of the agreement; they act as guarantors that the stipulations of the treaty will be carried out,

---

[25] Korosec, *Hethitische Staatsverträge*, pp. 77–78.

[26] Ibid., pp. 78ff.

[27] Ibid., pp. 80ff.

[28] Ibid., pp. 82ff.

[29] Ibid., p. 85; cf. W 3, ii, 3ff., '. . . and Tette shall come each year to the land of Ḫatti, to the Su[n] his lord.' See also W 4, ro. 3ff.; W 7, ro. i, 40ff.

[30] W 3, ro. ii, 6ff.; F 2 §11, v. 17ff.

[31] F 2 §10, v. 13.

[32] Korosec, *Hethitische Staatsverträge*, pp. 89ff.

[33] A typical summons (W 1, v. 38ff.) reads as follows: 'On the basis of this treaty we desire to summon the gods [39] of the secret and the gods that [are] lords of the oath. May they approach, may they give ear, and may they [be] witnesses.' See also F 5 §19, iii, 80–83; F 6 §6, i, 39ff.

[34] W 1, vo. 40–58; W 2, vo. 12–24 and 40–43; W 3, iv, 9–44; W 4, vo. 1–10; F 1 §18f., iv, 1–19; F 4 §12ff., vo. iv; F 5 §20, iv, 1–29; F 6 §7f., i, 41–59. For more details, see Korosec, *Hethitische Staatsverträge*, pp. 94ff.

[35] W 3, vo. iv, 44–45; F 1 §19, iv, 18f.

as 'lords of the oaths.'[36] They are to 'pursue relentlessly'[37] all who break their oath, but reward those that adhere to the terms of the treaty. And so together with the list of gods goes the list of blessings and curses.

In the curses, death and destruction in every possible form are threatened.[38] Sometimes a series of similes emphasizes the horror of the curse.[39] The curse is inexorable.[40]

In later texts of the Babylonian and Assyrian period,[41] the curse formulas clearly exhibit a further expansion in comparison to the Hittite treaties. Peculiar to them is the connection of the lists of gods with the series of curses in such a way that specific gods are to bring about specific plagues.[42] In addition, these treaties mention a whole series of symbolic actions intended to demonstrate what will happen to any vassal who breaks the treaty.[43]

The promised blessings are: 'The protection of the gods, prosperity of the land, eternal reign';[44] or: 'Abundant harvests, joy of heart, and peace of mind for ever.'[45]

We find thus a clear picture of the treaty formulary as a whole and of its individual components. A kind of 'normal form' can be determined, upon which, adapted to each specific situation, the

[36] Akkadian '*bêlê ma-mi-ti*'; W 1, vo. 61 and 63.

[37] E.g., F 3 §10, D 25; §15, C 25; §17, C 21.

[38] See, for example, F 1 §20, iv, 21–26; F 5 §21, iv, 31ff.; F 6 §45, iv, 50ff. The curse falls not only on the signatories to the treaty, but also on their family and property. In the Akkadian versions, more emphasis falls on the list of consequences of the curse; see, for example, W 1, vo. 59ff.

[39] 'Like a reed may they [these gods] break you,' W 1, vo. 65. 'Like a cedar when it is cut down . . . ,' W 2, vo. 46. See also W 2.

[40] F 6 §10, ii, 7ff.: 'And oaths shall not pardon this in you, and neither shall they make it legitimate for you . . . .'

[41] The following treaties are referred to: (1) Marduk-Zâkir-šumi I of Babylonia and Šamši-Adad V of Assyria (*ca.* 823–810); (2) Aššurnirâri VI of Assyria and Mati'ilu of Bît-Agusi (754); (3) an Aramaic treaty of the eighth century; (4) Esarhaddon of Assyria and Baal of Tyre (677). The treaties are published in *AfO*, 8 (1932/33). Only fragments of them are preserved, and so little can be said with assurance about their structure as a whole.

[42] The same correlation is especially well developed in the Babylonian *kudurru* inscriptions, which record the bestowal of land. See W. J. Hinke, *A New Boundary Stone of Nebuchadrezzar I from Nippur* (Philadelphia, 1907), pp. 58ff.

[43] See the treaty of Aššurnirâri VI, published by E. F. Weidner in *AfO*, 8 (1932/33), pp. 18–19, vo. i, 15ff.; 'In case Mati'ilu [transgresses] against the stipulations of the treaty, his oath in the presence of the gods, just as this ram brought [up] from his fold will not return to his fold . . . , so may Mati'ilu together with his sons . . . and the people of his land [be brought up] out of his land, and he shall not return to his land. . . .'

[44] W 1, vo. 72ff.

[45] W 2, vo. 56ff. Cf. also F 1 §21, iv, 27ff.; F 5 §21, iv, 45–46: 'And in the hand of the Sun see good prosperity and in the hand of the Sun grow old.'

Hittite treaties are based. The present texts make it possible to define the treaty formulary as a fixed literary type.

But what is the relationship between the 'treaty document' and the 'conclusion of the treaty'? According to Korosec, 'In line with the view prevalent everywhere in the ancient Near East, execution in writing is essential to the conclusion of a treaty. The treaty document is not merely evidence of a treaty that exists, say, by virtue of a mutual agreement. The treaty in fact comes into being only when the document is written (Akk. *ṭuppa šaṭāru* = "write a document," *epēšu* = "make"; = *hiyawar* = "make"). The treaty document therefore belongs to the class of dispositive documents.[46] The relationship between the document and the conclusion of the treaty is therefore extremely intimate. The document, like the actual conclusion of the treaty, exhibits a two-part structure. The treaty formulary can be analysed into conditions and sanctions. The conditions comprise the antecedent history, the statement of substance, and the individual stipulations; the sanctions comprise the invocation of the gods as witnesses, together with the curses and blessings. This division is even expressed in the Akkadian term for a treaty document. It is called 'tablet of binding (*riksu* or *rikiltu*) and incantation (*mamītu*).'[47]

As we may conclude from the texts, the process of concluding a treaty consisted essentially of two corresponding actions.[48] The treaty conditions were recited to the vassal by the great king,[49] and the vassal had to confirm them by oath.[50]

On the basis of the demonstrated parallel structure, one might term the treaty document the record of the conclusion of the treaty. The significance of the document, however, goes beyond the 'merely

---

[46] Korosec, *Hethitische Staatsverträge*, pp. 15–16. In note 6, Korosec quotes the Code of Hammurabi §128: 'If a seignior acquired a wife, but did not draw up the contracts for her, that woman is no wife' (quoted from Pritchard, *ANET*, p. 171).

[47] W 2, vo. 63: '*ṭuppu . . . šá ri-ik-si-šú ù šá ma-mi-ti-šú*' (see Weidner, *Politische Dokumente*, p. 57, n. 7). W 9, vo. 24: '*ṭup-pu šá ri-kil-ti ù šá ma-mi-ti.*' On the translation of these phrases, see Korosec, *Hethitische Staatsverträge*, pp. 23ff. and W. Muss-Arnolt, *Englisch-deutsch-assyrisches Handwörterbuch* (Berlin, 1905), vol. 1, pp. 965–66, vol. 2, p. 553.

[48] See Korosec, *Hethitische Staatsverträge*, pp. 26–27, 34–35.

[49] Cf. the formulation of the historical introduction in the 'first person style': F 1; F 3; F 4; W 1; W 3; *et al.*

[50] See F 4 §4, i, 60ff.; W 2, vo. 44–45: 'If *I*, Mattiuaza, the son of the king, and (we) people of Ḫarri do not keep the words of this treaty and the oath, [45] then shall *I*, Mattiuaza, together with the other wives and *we* people of Ḫarri together with our women . . . [47] . . . have no seed.'

On the peculiar double execution of the treaty between Šuppiluliumaš and Mattiuaza, see Korosec, *Hethitische Staatsverträge*, pp. 7ff.

evidential.'[51] The treaty 'comes into being'[52] when the great king exhibits the treaty, seals it, and gives it to the vassal.[53] These actions are constituents of the actual conclusion of the treaty. The significance of the 'written form'[54] is further evidenced by the fact that 'writing the tablet of the treaty' can be used as a synonym for 'guaranteeing the treaty relationship.'[55] Conversely, 'erasing' the tablet means the end of the treaty relationship.[56]

Publication of the stipulations of the treaty, invocation of the gods, and written execution are the most important acts in the conclusion of a treaty. It is safe to assume that a series of other ceremonies grew up around this nucleus. As we mentioned above, for example, the tablets of curses suggest a series of 'substitutionary actions'[57] during the invocation of the gods. It is impossible to pursue these questions further in this context.

The parties to the treaties are the great king and his vassal.[58] The latter can have the rank of a 'king'[59] or merely of a 'lord.'[60] Ḫukkanas may be a man of lower birth.[61] Under certain circumstances a collective entity like the 'people of the land'[62] can be party to a treaty; the phrase probably refers to the important men. Finally, one of the parties may be an entire nation.[63]—In each case, the party with whom the great king concludes the treaty agrees thereby to adapt to the political and social structure of the land in question.

---

[51] Ibid., p. 16.   [52] Ibid.

[53] W 6, ro. 4–5; cf. W 9, ro. 6–7, 29–30.

[54] Korosec, *Hethitische Staatsverträge*, p. 15.

[55] W 9, ro. 24–25: '*ṭuppu šá ri-kìl-ti ù šá ma-mi-ti* [. . .] *li-el-du-r*[*u* . . . .]' Cf. ro. 10: '[*ṭ*]*up-pa šá a-ba a-bi-ia ú-ga-a-al-lu*.'

[56] W 7, vo. iv, 25–26.

[57] See, for instance, E. F. Weidner, 'Der Staatsvertrag Aššurnirâris von Assyrien mit Matti'ilu von Bît-Agusi,' *AfO*, 8 (1932/33), p. 19, n. 12, on the 'idea of representation of a man by an animal,' with a bibliography on comparison with the OT 'scapegoat.' It seems to me an especially important point that we are not dealing with a sacrifice in the strict sense. This can be seen expressly in the treaty of Aššurniräri VI; cf. Weidner, ibid., ro. i, 10–14.

See also J. Pedersen, *Der Eid bei den Semiten* (Straßburg, 1914), pp. 111ff.; M. Riemschneider, *Die Welt der Hethiter*, p. 111.

[58] See Korosec, *Hethitische Staatsverträge*, §4, 'treaty signatories,' pp. 36ff.

[59] '*Šarru*,' in contrast to the great king, who is 'šarru rabû.' W 1, ro. 59; W 7, col. i, 39; W 9, ro. 25; see Korosec, *Hethitische Staatsverträge*, p. 6.

[60] F 2 §8, v. 1; F 3 §4, D 27.

[61] F 6 §1, col. i, 2ff.; see Friedrich, *Staatsverträge*, part 2, p. 137 *ad loc.*

[62] Akk. '*mârê* [pl]*Ḫarri* . . .' W 1, vo. 70; W 2, vo. 25, 35ff., 44ff., 53ff., *et al.*; cf. W 1, vo. 59.

[63] F 6, col. iv; see Korosec, *Hethitische Staatsverträge*, p. 57.

C

We may assume from the concluding notice of the treaty between Muršiliš II (Muwatalliš) and Rimi-šar-ma[64] that the highest dignitaries and officials of the Ḫatti Empire were in attendance at the official exhibition of the treaty document. Among others, the 'great(est) of the scribes'[65] is mentioned. The text probably concluded with the name of the scribe who wrote the document.

This points expressly once more to the locus of the tradition on which the composition of such treaties is based. This is the *chancellery of the great king*. The texts indicate that the officials were well educated. They are jurists interested in precise formulation, diplomats who understand how to express the finest nuances in defining a treaty relationship, and, last but not least, 'historians' familiar with the archives.

The treaties are preserved in the form of copies made on clay tablets. The original documents are described as having been written on iron, silver, and even (possibly) gold.[66]

The document and, if appropriate, a duplicate was laid 'before' (or 'at the feet of') the major deities of the lands in question.[67] The Aramaic treaty mentioned above was inscribed on a basalt stele. In this case, the original place where the treaty was deposited in a sanctuary can still be determined.[68]

It was not intended, however, that the treaty should merely be preserved in some archive. Knowledge of the content of the treaty is frequently enjoined upon the vassals in the treaties. To this end the text of the treaty was to be *recited regularly* in the presence of the vassal.[69]

---

[64] W 6, v. 17ff.

[65] Ibid., l. 21: *rabî ṭupšarre*[pl].

[66] Korosec, *Hethitische Staatsverträge*, p. 3, n. 6 and 7.

[67] W 1, vo. 35–36; W 2, vo. 7; for other passages, see Korosec, *Hethitische Staatsverträge*, p. 100.

[68] 'It belongs to a group of steles, all of which were set up at a place named Sujin, 1300 meters northwest of Sefire, which must once have been an open-air sanctuary,' H. Bauer, 'Ein aramäischer Staatsvertrag aus dem 8. Jahrhundert v. Chr.,' *AfO*, 8 (1932/33), pp. 1–16.

[69] See F 5 §19, col. iii, 73–75; W 1, vo. 36–37.

COMPARISON BETWEEN THE TREATY FORMULARY AND THE OLD TESTAMENT COVENANT FORMULARY

The following discussion will examine the extent to which Israel employed the treaty formulary that we have traced in 'secular' texts.[1] Our point of departure will be an analysis of Joshua 24.[2]

Joshua's speech (vv. 2–15) can be analysed as follows:

(1) The *preamble* reads (v. 2): כֹּה־אָמַר יהוה אֱלֹהֵי יִשְׂרָאֵל.[3] This means that the following section is to be understood as spoken by God. As in the treaties, we have the self-designation of the one that grants the covenant. 'The God of Israel' is here a formal title.

(2) The *antecedent history* (vv. 2–13) presents a brief historical retrospect of the relationships that have existed hitherto between Yahweh and his people.[4] Its purpose is to document Yahweh's saving acts from generation to generation, down to the present generation of those under Joshua's command who now stand before

---

[1] From here on the term 'covenant' will be used in place of 'treaty.' Although our study is primarily concerned with external form, this distinction will suggest the uniqueness of the biblical situation.

[2] For a literary analysis of Joshua 24, see C. Steuernagel, *Das Buch Josua* (HKAT, 2nd ed., Göttingen, 1923), pp. 297–98; M. Noth, *Das Buch Josua* (HAT, 2nd ed., Tübingen, 1953), pp. 135–36. Our discussion can take account of details of literary analysis only when they affect the argument. A complete fragmentation and rearrangement of the chapter like that undertaken by C. A. Simpson on the basis of source analysis does not appear appropriate (see his *The Early Tradition of Israel* [Oxford, 1948], pp. 316ff., 646). Cf. also H. Greßmann, *Die Anfänge Israels*, 2nd ed. (Göttingen, 1922), pp. 156ff. The similarities of the parallels cited are, in my opinion, similarities in form; there need not originally have been in each case a direct historical or literary connection.

[3] 𝔊 translates with present meaning, as do Steuernagel *et al.*; Noth translates as a perfect. The present emphasizes Yahweh's presence more strongly (cf. v. 1: 'They presented themselves before God.'). Joshua speaks as the representative of God. Most striking is the prophetical stylization of Joshua's speech by means of the introductory 'כֹּה־אָמַר יהוה...'.' The question remains whether in this case the formula must not be explained on the basis of the form used for the proclamation of a treaty rather than as a prophetical messenger formula. Cf. treaty preambles such as W 3, col. i, 1: 'Thus (says) [Akk. *um-ma*] the Sun Šuppiluliumaš, the great king, the king of the land of Ḫatti, the hero.'

[4] On the various discrepancies in this section, see Noth, *Josua*, p. 137. These do not, however, alter the total picture. On the change in subject from the first to the third person, see also F 1, col. i, 23; W 1, ro. 57ff.: 'The great king has . . . I have . . . .'

Yahweh. It therefore concludes appropriately with a mention and description of that unique gift of God's bounty, the land.

A detail of this conclusion shows with particular clarity that the 'antecedent history' is intended to provide a legal basis for the covenant. In the first place, there is the position accorded the 'land' as an element in the general context. As was mentioned above, enfeoffment with a land frequently concludes the 'antecedent history.' Furthermore, the nature and compass of the land is described precisely, after the manner of a land-register. Noth[5] points out that Josh. 24:13a,b agrees almost word for word with Deut. 6:10, 11. This agreement, however, scarcely admits the conclusion that Josh. 14:13 is secondary and deuteronomistic. The enumeration is based on earlier prototypes in lists of 'real estate.' For purposes of comparison, we shall juxtapose the texts in question:

Josh. 24:13	Deut. 6:10–11	Neh. 9:24–25
land	land	land
cities	cities	cities
		farmland
	houses	houses
	cisterns	cisterns
vineyard	vineyards	vineyards
oliveyards	olive trees	olive orchards
		trees

Ugarit:[6]			
No. 16138	No. 16204	No. 17340[7]	No. 1762[7]
	maison	frontières	frontières
terre	terre	villes	
'castel'	'castel'		terres
oliveraie	oliveraie		champs
vigne	vigne	montagnes	montagnes
verger	verger		
avec tout	avec tout		
(autre) chose	(autre) chose		

[5] Noth, *Josua*, pp. 135–36.

[6] The lists occur in 'deeds of gift' of the kings of Ugarit. See Nougayrol, *Le palais royal d'Ugarit. Textes accadiens et hourrites des archives est, ouest et centrales* (Paris, 1955). Cf. also texts 16269, 16160, 16353, 15122, and many others.

[7] Nougayrol, *Le palais royal d'Ugarit IV. Textes accadiens des archives sud* (*Archives internationales*) (Paris, 1956), pp. 48, 65.

The texts show that such lists are based on precise regulations of the law governing real property. Josh. 24:13 contains a list expanded by the inclusion of additional material. These additions stress once more what is in fact already implicit in the context, namely, that the land is the free gift of Yahweh.

(3) The *statement of substance* (v. 14) begins with וְעַתָּה, which draws the conclusion of the antecedent history.[8] The conduct of Yahweh's people is to correspond to Yahweh's own actions. This relationship is defined both positively and negatively in a series of imperatives:

וְעַתָּה יִרְאוּ אֶת־ יהוה

וְעִבְדוּ אֹתוֹ בְּתָמִים וּבֶאֱמֶת

וְהָסִירוּ אֶת־ אֱלֹהִים[9] אֲשֶׁר עָבְדוּ אֲבוֹתֵיכֶם

וְעִבְדוּ אֶת־ יהוה

The point is absolute loyalty toward Yahweh. This loyalty presupposes rejection of the service (i.e., the cult) of 'foreign gods.'[10]

The chapter does not continue as direct speech of Yahweh. This

---

[8] On this connection between the treaty stipulations and the antecedent history, cf. F 1 §8, col. i, 23; F 6 §2, col. i, 8: 'Now, Ḫukkanaš, you shall recognize only the Sun with respect to sovereignty. . . .' Formally, it is not this transition (as Noth argues, *Josua*, p. 140) that is abrupt, but rather the transition to v. 15.

[9] ⵎ reads: τοὺς θεοὺς τοὺς ἀλλοτρίους.

[10] Cf. F 1 §8, i, 32: 'And do not set your eyes upon another'; F 3 §11, D, 40–41: 'No foreign sovereignty however [41] shall you desire, hencef[orth] hold to the Sun with respect to sovereignty'; F 6 §3, i, 14–15: 'Henceforth however recognize . . . no other lord.' Here in the political realm, then, we find the parallel of a strict exclusiveness of association such as is not found in the religious sphere outside of Israel. Cf. M. Noth, *Die Gesetze im Pentateuch* ('Schriften der Königsberger Gelehrten Gesellschaft,' Geisteswissenschaftliche Klasse, Jg. 18, H. 2 [Halle, 1940]), p. 42, English version in *The Laws in the Pentateuch and other Studies* (E.T. Edinburgh, 1966), p. 51. See also W 6, ro. 15: 'When Tudḫaliyaš, the great king, as[cen]ded the throne of the k[ingdom], [16] since [. . .] the king of the land of Ḫalap together with him [. . .] turned a[way from him] . . . . [19] The king of the land of Ḫalap committed the si[n of the] king of the land of Ḫan[ig]albat, [20] but against Ḫattuš[iliš, the king of the land of] Ḫatti, he sinned [especially].'

Akk.: '[19] šar mât ᵃˡḪa-la-ap ḫi-i-t[a šá] šar mât ᵃˡḪa-n[i-g]al-bat iḫ-ti [20] ú it-ti ᵐḪa-at-tu-š [i-li šar mât ᵃ]ˡḪa-at-ti [ma-gal] iḫ-ti-ma.' 'ḫi-i-t[a . . .] iḫ-ti' corresponds to the Old Testament 'חָטָא חַטָּאת.' In Joshua 24, the requirement of not serving foreign gods clearly does not constitute one of the stipulations, but is a part of the statement of substance. Perhaps this helps provide an explanation for Noth's observation that 'a basic general prohibition of cultic worship of "other gods" is never of common occurrence in the law-codes of the Old Testament' (ibid., p. 43; Eng. p. 52). Reasons of form alone make the occurrence of such a prohibition in the legal codes themselves most improbable. Noth goes on to show how the individual laws are natural consequences of the presupposed covenant relationship.

is peculiar, since v. 27 refers to 'the words of Yahweh,' with the probable intention of including the covenant stipulations.[11]

Further *individual stipulations* detailing what it means to serve Yahweh are lacking.[12]

This first section announces the *conditions of the covenant*.[13] 'Conditions' here refers not only to legal stipulations, but also in equal measure to the saving acts described in the antecedent history. These are the pre-requisites for the loyalty demanded of Israel. The three points just mentioned correspond formally to the section called '*riksu*' or '*rikiltu*' in the Hittite treaties.

The second act[14] in the conclusion of a treaty, which can be reconstructed for the Hittite treaties only inferentially from various hints,[15] is described in detail in Joshua 24: the *confirmation of the covenant by oath*.

This second portion begins with verse 15. Here Joshua changes rôles: he no longer speaks as the authorized representative of Yahweh, but of the people. As is appropriate to his prominent position, he is the first to confirm the covenant: 'As for me and my house, we will serve Yahweh.'[16]

In vv. 17–18*a*, the people respond to the *antecedent history*, which they have heard and experienced.[17] The main points of this history are cited once more. The people thus confess that they have ex-

---

[11] The change from the personal form of the historical introduction to the impersonal form in the stipulations occurs, for example, in W 7. The impersonal form is more common within the treaty stipulations.

[12] Note, however, the summary expression in v. 25: חֹק וּמִשְׁפָּט. Steuernagel suggests (*Josua*, p. 298) that portions of the Covenant Code belong here, but this goes too far. His observation is correct, however: the lack of individual stipulations, which the form would lead one to expect, is peculiar. Noting that the form is put together out of various elements does not mean that we can say with assurance which corpus belongs in this particular framework. See on this point Noth, *Gesetze*, pp. 31ff. (Eng. pp. 38ff.), where he points out the tendency of Old Testament tradition to take 'what in reality came into being during the course of a long history of successive law and law-books' and assign it to Moses, and especially to the Sinai tradition. This could be a reason why the individual stipulations were suppressed in this passage.

[13] The summons to make a choice and Joshua's own commitment in verse 15 belong to the further course of the covenant ceremony and must be examined in that context.

[14] On the bipartite structure of the treaty ceremony, see Korosec, *Hethitische Staatsverträge*, p. 26: 'The ruler of Ḫatti announces the "*riksu*," the treaty stipulations, while the vassal expresses his consent to the treaty by oath, the "*mamītu*." This gives the vassal treaty its binding force. The vassal retains the option of refusing his "*mamītu*" ' (see above, p. 16).

[15] Ibid., with references.

[16] Cf. W 2, vo. 53ff.: 'Thus (says) Mattiuaza, the king's son, thus (say) also the people of Ḫarri.' See especially the treaty between Šuppiluliumaš and Ḫukkanaš and the people of Ḫayaša, F 6.

perienced the gracious acts of their God in their history down to
the present time. They acknowledge that they have received the
land, not conquered it (v. 18). They bear witness that the actions
of their God always precede what they do themselves.

Verses 16 and 18*b* are counterparts to the *statement of substance* in
v. 14. They contain—and v. 15 has made it clear that this is 'free
consent'[18]—the people's promise of absolute loyalty toward 'their
God.'[19] The express repetition of 'we will serve' three times in
vv. 18, 21, and 24 points up the liturgical, or, better (with reference
to the treaty aspect), juridical nature of the text.

In the treaty pattern found in the Hittite texts, there follows here
an *invocation* of the gods as witnesses, together with *curses* and *blessings*.

The ceremonial takes precise account of the rank and station of those taking part.
(Cf. also Neh. 10:1ff. and 1QS ii. 20–24). According to Noth ('Das alttestamentliche
Bundschließen im Lichte eines Mari-Textes,' *Annuaire de l'Institut de philologie et d'histoire
orientales et slaves*, 13 [Brussels, 1955], p. 442 [Eng. *Laws*, p. 116]), 'Joshua as "third
party" here (Josh. 24:25) mediates a covenant between God and people.' Verse 15,
however, shows that Joshua is also a partner to the covenant! The use of the first person
plural in v. 27 may also refer to this circumstance.

[17] On the response of the people, cf. Ps. 106:48; 136. This response is the 'Credo'
proper.

---

[18] See especially: '*Choose* this day whom you will serve' (... בַּחֲרוּ לָכֶם).

[19] This detail is important for an understanding of the covenant as a treaty. The fact
that one party to a covenant is superior does not necessarily mean that the covenant
ceases to have the nature of a treaty.—It is interesting that in legal discussion it has also
been disputed whether the Hittite vassal treaties have in fact the nature of treaties (an
argument advanced by von Schachermeyr, 'Zur staatsrechtlichen Wertung der hethitischen Staatsverträge,' in *Festschrift Meissner* [Leipzig, 1929], p. 182, where he refers to
them as 'decrees,' ... since they are in essence unilateral actions on the part of the Ḥatti
kings'; for further discussion of this point, see Korosec, *Hethitische Staatsverträge*, p. 18).
Korosec, however, states: The essence of a treaty does not consist in both parties' having
collaborated equally in determining its stipulations. ... In such a case we may speak of
parity treaties. On the contrary, all that is necessary for a treaty is that the parties have
assented to the legal action of their own free will' (p. 20).—See also ibid., pp. 26 and 29.

Korosec cites as parallels the modern collective tariff treaties, which individual parties
can only accept without modification or reject (p. 20, n. 3).—For a discussion of treaty
law, see also Karl Engisch, *Einführung in das juristische Denken* (Stuttgart, 1956), p. 32.

J. Begrich ('Berit, ein Beitrag zur Erfassung einer alttestamentlichen Denkform'
ZAW, N. F. 19 [1944], pp. 1–11, especially p. 4) does not distinguish sufficiently between
parity and bipartite treaties. This point is an additional objection to Begrich's alternatives:
'A treaty between two equal parties or the concession of a special relationship on the part
of a superior' (see M. Noth, 'Bundschließen,' pp. 443–44; *Laws*, pp. 116–17).

I also consider it impossible to determine a temporal arrangement in which 'the
concept of covenant mediation is traditio-historically earlier than that of covenant
concession, and naturally much earlier than that of a covenant treaty' (H. W. Wolff,
'Jahwe als Bundesvermittler,' *VT*, 6 [1956], p. 319). The nature of the treaty as well as
the nature of the relationship the treaty represents cannot be determined from formal
criteria alone; questions of content must be considered as well. In the case of the 'covenant,'
this means that it cannot be understood without its theological presuppositions,

As has been indicated, the gods in these treaties are not only witnesses to the words or actions in the sense that they 'are present at
a ceremony and can vouch for it in case of doubt';[20] they are also
guarantors of the treaty, i.e., in case of default, for example, they
become 'avengers,' carrying out the curse.[21]

In Israel, Yahweh is invoked as a 'witness' in this sense in the case
of a secular treaty.[22] But what happens when, in the case of a covenant
between God and people, Yahweh is both party to and guarantor of
the covenant? That there is a difficulty here is shown by Deut. 4:26;
30:19; 31:28,[23] where precisely at this point in the structure of the
covenant ceremony, i.e., before the curse, 'heaven and earth' are
invoked as 'witnesses against you.'[24]

[20] L. Koehler, *Lexicon in Veteris Testamenti Libros* (Leiden, 1953), p. 681, *s.v.*

[21] See W 1, vo. 39; W 2, vo. 11, 25; F 5 §9, ii, 57; §13, iii, 2; §16, iii, 30; §17, iii, 56.
For curses that go so far as to threaten complete destruction, see W 1, vo. 61; W 2,
vo. 27; W 4, vo. 16; F 1 §20, iv, 26; F 4 §19, vo. iv, 39, and passim.

[22] Gen. 31:50; I Sam. 20:12.

[23] After the invocation of heaven and earth as witnesses, Deut. 4:27 continues: 'And
Yahweh will scatter you among the peoples.'

[24] A text like Enoch 100:10–13 is instructive in this context. The passage stands at
the end of a long series of 'woes.' It clearly goes far beyond the invocation of 'heaven and
earth.' One gains the impression that with the 'angels' the old list of 'a thousand gods'
has been restored. A kind of metamorphosis seems to have taken place. In contrast, the
treaty formulary in Joshua 24 has been revised much more critically on the basis of
Yahwism. There is clearly also a process of 'mythologization.'

(The text translated is that of G. Beer in E. Kautzsch, ed., *Die Apokryphen und Pseudepigraphen des Alten Testaments* (Tübingen, 1900 [reprinted 1921]), vol. 2, p. 305, with a
few omissions.)

'Know now that the angels in	heaven
from the	sun
the	moon
and the	stars
search out your deeds with	
respect to your sin because	
upon	earth
you exercise judgment	
upon the righteous.	
Therefore ( )	cloud(s)
	mist
	dew
and	rains
will be made *witnesses*	
against you. . . .	
In those days, when the	frost
and	snow
with their	cold
and all the	snow-winds
with all their	plagues
fall upon you, you will not	
be able to withstand them,'	

Yahweh can also act as witness in his own behalf against human beings, in both senses of 'witness': as one who can vouch for something,[25] and a guarantor of the treaty, who can put the curse into effect, as he originally could do with the blessing.[26]

In Josh. 24:19–22,[27] Yahweh is not expressly named as a 'witness.' He is, however, considered to be present throughout the entire ceremony (see v. 1). I would suggest that the solemn statement (v. 19): ... אֱלֹהִים קְדֹשִׁים הוּא אֵל־קַנּוֹא הוּא לֹא־יִשָּׂא has taken the place of an invocation.[28] It is followed immediately by the *curse*, which here Yahweh himself puts into effect in case the obligation is broken: 'He will turn and do you harm, and consume you.'[29] There is no explicit formula of blessing. The *blessing* is implied in the statement: 'After having done you good.'[30] The threatened curse lies as a possibility in the future; the present is felt and acknowledged to be a blessing.

The summons to the people to be answerable as 'witnesses against [them]selves' is peculiar.[31] In the present context, however, it probably means nothing more than acceptance of the curse in the

---

[25] Jer. 29:23: 'I am witness, says Yahweh.' See W. Rudolph, *Jeremia* (HAT, Tübingen, 1958), p. 156, ad loc.; also *BH*.

[26] Mic. 1:2ff.; Mal. 3:5; Jer. 42:5–6.

[27] Noth (*Josua*, p. 136 ad loc.) considers the entire section vv. 19–24 Deuteronomistic. The verses contain the announcement of blessings and curses as well as the invocation of witnesses. These parts are essential components of the ratification of the covenant, corresponding to the *mamītu* in the Hittite treaties. They are therefore meaningful in the present context, and can hardly be dispensed with. In the section vv. 14–28 (cf. 2b–3a) service to Yahweh is demanded, i.e., in the sense of a statement of substance: unconditional loyalty toward him who grants the covenant. Here this loyalty means concretely a decision between Yahweh and the foreign gods.

If one considers the section to be a single original unit without redactional additions, the beginning of v. 19 presents a difficulty. V. 19a states expressly, 'You cannot serve Yahweh.' Here I would agree with Noth, that the words as they now stand 'were added *ex eventu* during the Exile, on the basis of the insight that apostasy after a decision once made in favor of Yahweh implies a fundamentally different responsibility that does remaining heathen' (Noth, ibid.).—It is a striking fact, however, that in the following section there is no further mention of the impossibility of serving Yahweh. I think it is possible that a later redactor made his special point by eliminating the phrase 'and [at the same time] foreign gods' after 'Yahweh' in v. 19. Cf. II Kings 17:33: 'So they feared Yahweh but also served their own gods'; see also I Sam. 7:3; I Kings 18:21.—Steuernagel (*Josua*, p. 301) expressly rejects this possibility. He attempts to explain v. 19 psychologically, and assumes: 'For him [Joshua] to say, You will not be able to, is of course only rhetorical hyperbole.' I do not consider this latter interpretation to be likely.

[28] On this formula, cf. Exod. 34:6; Num. 14:18; Joel 2:13; Jon. 4:2; Nah. 1:2ff.; Pss. 86:15; 103:8; 145:8; Neh. 9:17; Ecclus. 2:13. The formula remains remarkably constant through the various strata of the Old Testament. See below, p. 113, n. 69.

[29] Cf. the short curse formula in F 1 §20, col. iv, 21ff.

[30] Ibid., §21, lines 27–28.

[31] For a different formulation, see Jer. 42:5.

sense of a 'conditional curse' in case the treaty is broken.[32] Within the ceremony of covenant-making, with its repeated alternation between Joshua's speaking and the people's response, the answer '(We are) witnesses' in v. 22 makes sense; in place of the actual oath, it is even necessary.[33]

In v. 23, Joshua explicitly obligates the people to 'put away the foreign gods.'[34] With the people's assurance once more that they wish to serve Yahweh, the ratification of the covenant by oath is concluded (v. 24).

In 24:25–26, we read that a *written copy of the covenant* was drawn up.[35] Several commentators suggest that this feature of the report reflects a definitely late conception of covenant-making.[36] This assumption can hardly be maintained. Our examination of the

---

[32] J. M. Price, 'The Oath in Court Procedure in Early Babylonia and the O.T.,' p. 23, cited in Korosec, *Hethitische Staatsverträge*, p. 97: 'Indeed, mamîtu was a conditional curse, wherein the oath-taker invoked upon himself the punishment of gods if he failed to keep his promise.'

[33] The omission of this statement by 𝕲 can be explained as a misreading. On this oath ceremony as a whole, cf. Test. Levi 19:1ff. Note especially 19:3 'The Lord is witness, and his angels are witnesses'; see above, p. 24, n. 24 on Enoch 100:10ff. (The text is cited according to R. H. Charles, *The Greek Versions of the Testaments of the XII Patriarchs* (Oxford, 1908).

1. Καὶ νῦν, τέκνα μου, πάντα ἠκούσατε.
   Ἐκλέξασθε ἑαυτοῖς ἢ τὸ φῶς ἢ τὸ σκότος
   ἢ τὸν νόμον κυρίου ἢ τὰ ἔργα τοῦ Βελίαρ.
2. Καὶ ἀπεκρίθησαν αὐτῷ οἱ υἱοὶ αὐτοῦ λέγοντες.
   Ἐνώπιον κυρίου πορευσόμεθα καὶ κατὰ τὸν νόμον αὐτοῦ.
3. Καὶ εἶπεν αὐτοῖς ὁ πατὴρ αὐτῶν.
           Μάρτυς   ἐστι κύριος
   καὶ μάρτυρες οἱ   ἄγγελοι αὐτοῦ
   καὶ μάρτυρες   ὑμεῖς
   καὶ μάρτυς   ἐγὼ
                περὶ τοῦ λόγου τοῦ στόματος ὑμῶν.
   Καὶ εἶπον αὐτῷ οἱ υἱοὶ αὐτοῦ·
           Μάρτυρες.

[34] On this expression, see A. Alt, 'Die Wallfahrt von Sichem nach Bethel,' in his *Kleine Schriften zur Geschichte des Volkes Israel* (München, 1953–64), vol. 1, pp. 81ff.
On the way in which this command was 'now' carried out, the text tells nothing. This also shows the schematic way the covenant ceremony is reported. Only the most important elements are described; further details of the action are taken for granted because they are familiar.

[35] Josh. 24:25: וַיִּכְרֹת יְהוֹשֻׁעַ בְּרִית לָעָם וַיָּשֶׂם לוֹ חֹק וּמִשְׁפָּט בִּשְׁכֶם

Neh. 10:1 (Eng. 9:38): וּבְכָל־זֹאת אֲנַחְנוּ כֹּרְתִים אֲמָנָה

Josh. 24:26: ....וַיִּכְתֹּב יְהוֹשֻׁעַ אֶת־הַדְּבָרִים הָאֵלֶּה בְּסֵפֶר תּוֹרַת אֱלֹהִים

Neh. 10:1: ....וְכֹתְבִים וְעַל הֶחָתוּם

[36] See Greßmann, *Anfänge*, p. 162: '(In the earlier stratum) . . . there is no mention of a written document.—Only according to the later stratum does Joshua write "these words" in a law-book.'—H. W. Hertzberg, *Die Bücher Josua* . . . (ATD, Göttingen, 1953), pp. 137–38; Begrich, 'Berit,' p. 10.

Hittite texts has shown the significance of written documents for the conclusion of a treaty.[37] The treaty document is an inseparable part of the treaty.[38] What held for the announcement of the covenant conditions and for the oath holds true also for the making of a written copy. In this respect, too, Joshua 24 follows a legal schema very precisely.

The setting up of a large stone in the sanctuary serves as public documentation of the covenant.[39] It seems worth suggesting that the stone that 'heard all the words of Yahweh' (v. 27) was conceived of as a written stela.[40]

In a legal act the external circumstances are also fixed by protocol.[41] The place and participants are named in v. 1.

The date remains indefinite. In the present text, vv. 29ff. furnish a secondary connection with the death of Joshua. The covenant is made to appear as his last official act. The significance of this particular emphasis can be observed better in other texts, however, and so we shall now only note it in passing.

The Covenant Formulary in the Sinai Pericope (Exodus 19–34)

A further textual group that illustrates the use of the treaty form in Israel is the Sinai pericope in Exodus 19–34.[42] The reason we did not take this 'classical' covenant ceremony as the point of departure

[37] W 6, v. 3ff.; W 9, ro. 5–6: My [gr]andfather granted him [grace]. He wrote a tablet of the treaty. . . .'

[38] Cf. B. Meissner, *Babylonien und Assyrien* (Heidelberg, 1920–25), vol. 1, p. 154. The concept of the 'divine covenant' as a mere 'undertaking of a formal obligation' (Hertz-berg, *Josua*, p. 138) is too much an accommodation to modern ways of thinking. It is impossible to exaggerate the concreteness of the way the 'divine covenant' was concluded.

[39] According to 𝔐, this stone stood at Shechem. But cf. the remarkable variants in 𝔊, which locate the action at Shiloh! These variants are not recorded in Kittel's *Biblia hebraica* (4th printing, 1949).—On the location, see also von Rad, *Das formgeschichtliche Problem des Hexateuchs*, BWANT (Stuttgart, 1928), pp. 41–42.—For an etiological inter-pretation of the text on the basis of the mention of the stone, see A. Alt, *Kleine Schriften*, vol. 1, p. 191; for a different view, see Noth, *Josua*, p. 139.

[40] Cf. the Aramaic treaty discussed above, published by Bauer.—See also Deut. 27:2–3.

[41] Cf. the framework of the treaty between Ḫattušiliš and Ramses II in its Egyptian version (Pritchard, *ANET*, pp. 199ff.) and its Hittite version (ibid., p. 201); cf. also W 6, vo. 17ff.

[42] On the passage as a whole, see S. Mowinckel, *Le Décalogue* (Paris, 1927). The relationship between the Decalogue and the covenant formulary demands a special study. Here we can only point out the importance attaching to the phrase '. . . who brought you out of the land of Egypt, out of the house of bondage' if it can be understood as an 'antecedent history.' In the same way, the first commandment can be equated with a statement of substance. Zimmerli has pointed out the dominating position of this com-mandment ('Ich bin Jahwe,' in *Geschichte und Altes Testament* [Festschrift A. Alt] (Tübingen 1953), pp. 179ff., especially pp. 204ff.).—Now see also W. Beyerlin, *Die Kulttraditionen Israels in der Verkündigung des Propheten Micha*, (FRLANT, Göttingen, 1959), pp. 29ff., 42ff.

for our study is only that the text itself presents so many difficulties, which must complicate any results.[43] Our analysis will show once again that in this section we are dealing literarily with a series of independent texts deriving from different sources, which have been brought together in the present recension under the rubric 'revelation at Sinai.'[44] Some literary units, however, can still be distinguished.

Exodus 19:3–8

Exod. 19:3–8[45] comprises in summary form the following elements of a covenant formulary:

(1) *Antecedent history* (v. 4). This extends from Egypt to the assumed present at Sinai. It is formulated once more as direct speech from the mouth of God.

> 'You have seen what I did to the Egyptians,
> and how I bore you on eagles' wings
> and brought you to myself.'

(2) *Statement of substance* (vv. 5–6a). This section is introduced by וְעַתָּה. It contains two general conditions: 'obey my voice and keep my covenant.' It describes the status accorded Israel by its God (v. 6a):[46]

> 'Now therefore, if you will obey my voice and keep my covenant,
>   you shall be my own possession among all peoples;
>   for all the earth is mine,
>   and you shall be to me a kingdom of priests and a holy nation.'

Verses 7–8 presuppose an assembly[47] in which the content of the

---

[43] W. Rudolph, *Der Aufbau von Exodus 19–34* (Gießen, 1936), pp. 41–48.—M. Noth, *Überlieferungsgeschichte des Pentateuch* (Stuttgart, 1948), p. 157.

[44] Noth, *Überlieferungsgeschichte*, pp. 155ff.

[45] According to Greßmann, *Anfänge*, this text belongs to J; according to Eißfeldt, *Hexateuch-Synopse* (Leipzig, 1922), it belongs to E; according to Noth, *Überlieferungsgeschichte*, p. 33, n. 112, Exod. 19:3b–9a(b) is 'an addition in Deuteronomistic style' to J. The differences of opinion show how hard it is to decide with assurance on the source of the text.

[46] Von Rad, *Hexateuch*, p. 35 (*Gesammelte Studien*, p. 47) assumes that vv. 4–6 were 'a parenetic introduction to the proclamation of the law.' According to the covenant formulary we should expect individual stipulations at this point. This is also suggested by the parallels to Exod. 19:7b in Exod. 24:3a and 24:7a.

Mowinckel, *Le Décalogue*, p. 128, emphasizes the rhythmical structure of this passage. He calls it an '*imitation des prophéties cultuelles*.' It is probably better understood, however, as a legal declaration.

[47] Whether this assembly comprises only the זִקְנֵי הָעָם (v. 7) or 'all the people' (v. 8; cf. v. 3) is not completely clear. Cf. Exod. 34:31–32.

covenant was recited by an authorized party—in this case Moses. The assembly responds 'as one' (יַחְדָּו v. 8)[48] with the assurance 'All that Yahweh has spoken we will do.' This gives the consent of the party to whom the covenant is granted. The response of the people is then brought—by Moses—to Yahweh.

Further details (the taking of the oath, the framing of a written document) are lacking. In this respect the passage is somewhat like Josh. 24:2–18.[49] *In nuce*, however, it is already a complete covenant ceremony.

Exodus 24

Exodus 24 also exhibits the two corresponding actions: the declaration of 'all the words of Yahweh' and the affirmative response of the people. For the sake of comparison we place the three relevant texts in parallel:[50]

(I = Exod. 19:7–8; II = Exod. 24:3–4*a*; III = Exod. 24:7)

```
I     So Moses came and called the elders of the people
II         Moses came
III   — — —                                    Then he took
I     and all these words which Yahweh had commanded him
II    and all the    words of      Yahweh and all the ordinances
III              the   book of the covenant
I     he set before them.
II    he told the people.
III   and read it in the hearing of the people;
I     And all the people answered together        and said,
II    And all the people answered with one voice and said,
III   — — —                                     and they said,
I     'All that          Yahweh has spoken we will do.'
II    'All the words that Yahweh has spoken we will do.'
III   'All that          Yahweh has spoken we will do, and
                                             we will be obedient.'
```

[48] Or does this mean 'at once'? See Isa. 46:2; 48:13; Jer. 6:11; Ps. 4:9 (Eng. 4:8). It would then correspond to the 'amen' to be spoken by all the people (Ps. 106:48; cf. 1QS i. 20, 24; ii. 10, 18).

[49] In v. 9*a* there follows the announcement that Yahweh himself confirms Moses' office in the presence of all the people, 'that the people . . . may also believe [him] for ever.'

[50] Cf. also Exod. 34:29ff., esp. 34:32: 'And afterward all the people of Israel came near, and he gave them in commandment all that Yahweh had spoken with him in Mount Sinai.'

I   And Moses reported the words of the people to Yahweh.

II   And Moses wrote all the words of Yahweh.

III   — — —

It is therefore probable that these two actions constituted an essential portion of the covenant ceremony between Yahweh and Israel.

Our survey also shows that form-critical analysis raises new questions for literary criticism. When Eißfeldt, for example, assigns the three texts just quoted to E, it is peculiar that one source reports the same process three times. The juxtaposition in 24:3–8 is especially awkward. In v. 4, 'early in the [next] morning' marks a new beginning. A sacrifice and blood ritual are described. Literary analysis makes it probable that v. 7 (III in the text above) has been interpolated secondarily into the context of the blood ritual.[51] As Holzinger correctly notes,[52] the conclusion of v. 8, 'in accordance with all these words,' is associated with v. 7. This means, according to Holzinger, that these verses 'drop out.'—The conclusion that a passage is literarily secondary, however, does not absolve us from the duty of inquiring into the views of the redactor who assembled the entire section in a particular way. He obviously placed great value on associating the proclamation of the covenant with the obligation of the people and the blood ritual. The blood ritual may therefore be compared with the ceremonies mentioned in our examination of the Hittite treaties.[53] There a series of ceremonies is employed primarily for the 'ratification by oath' (*mamītu*) of the treaty.[54]

[51] This is the view espoused, for example, by H. Holzinger, *Das Buch Exodus*, KHAT, (Tübingen, 1900), pp. 103–104 ad loc.

[52] Ibid., p. 104.

[53] See above, p. 17.

[54] In the same connection, I would look upon the theophany described in vv. 9–10, in what is surely a very ancient form, together with the meal shared by the elders, as an act confirming the conclusion of a covenant. (This view is espoused by Holzinger ad loc.; cf. Gen. 31:53–54 [Eng. 31:54–55], the meal on the occasion of the treaty between Laban and Jacob.) Here, too, the source involved is a matter of dispute. Beer's view (*Exodus*, HAT [Tübingen, 1939], p. 127), according to which v. 10 reflects 'warm delight in nature,' is most unlikely. Zimmerli (*Ezechiel*, BKAT [Neukirchen, 1956–], p. 56) inquires whether 'Yahweh was thought of as sitting down, with, in the fashion of the Jerusalem conception, a "stool for his feet".'—This view may find support in a passage from the account of Sargon of Akkad's march to Asia Minor (E. F. Weidner, 'Boghazkoi-Studien,' H. 6 [Leipzig, 1922], p. 69):

Vo. 13: '. . . [an enclosure] on the upper side of which is a foot-stand of lapis lazuli, at the lower side of which (are located) some fifty-five chiefs. [14] [Zabab]a sits before him, who, like him, sits upon a golden throne: there sits the king like the deity!'

Weidner (ibid., p. 74) suggests that we are dealing with a 'block of lapis lazuli which apparently serves Sargon (?) as a footstool. . . .' 'giš GIR-Du = ḳirṣappu, "foot-stand".'—If so, Exodus 24 depicts a kind of audience in the presence of the 'God of Israel' upon his throne.

Noth doubts whether Exod. 24:3–8 belongs to any of the sources, considering it possibly a 'secondary appendix to, say, the Covenant Code.'[55] In this fashion he escapes a further difficulty that the text raises. There is no statement concerning the content of the covenant, such as the form would lead us to expect, at least not in brief form like that found in Exod. 19:3–8.[56] The redactional 'in accordance with all these words' in v. 8 also appears to presuppose some additional detailed statements. The question of what may once have come at this point must probably remain unanswered.

The Covenant Formulary in Deuteronomy

Deuteronomy provides a good illustration of the literary form we have been studying. However complex its structure may be in detail, in its present form it represents a unified whole.[57] Elements of the structure of the whole recur again and again in the various parts.[58] This uniformity remains remarkably constant even in the Deuteronomistic additions and revisions. We shall attempt to study the framework passages surrounding the actual legal code of Deuteronomy (chapters 12–26) from the same point of view we have been using all along.[59]

Deuteronomy 1–4:40

The first major unit in Deuteronomy is 1–4:40 (41–43).[60] The unit[61] can be structured as follows: Deut. 1:1–5 indicates the situa-

---

[55] Noth, *Überlieferungsgeschichte*, p. 33, n. 115.

[56] Cf. also Beer, *Exodus*, p. 126: 'It is a striking fact that in 24:3 the expected outline of the covenant is missing,' and p. 127: 'In Exodus 24 the covenant is completed through Israel's acceptance of the obligation to obey the law proposed by Yahweh, the text of which is unfortunately not preserved in the present text of chapter 24.'

[57] See von Rad, *Hexateuch*, p. 24 (*Gesammelte Studien*, p. 34). He characterizes the structure of Deuteronomy as follows:
'1. Historical description of events at Sinai and parenesis: Deuteronomy 1–11.
2. Reading of the law: Deuteronomy 12–26:15.
3. Acceptance of the covenant obligation: Deuteronomy 26:16–19.
4. Blessings and curses: Deuteronomy 27ff.'

[58] Von Rad in particular has pointed this out (ibid., p. 30 [*Gesammelte Studien*, p. 41]). Cf. also his *Studies in Deuteronomy* (E.T. SBT 9, Chicago, 1953), pp. 12–13.

[59] It is impossible in this context to take into account the enormous body of literature that surrounds Deuteronomy. The difficulties involved in delimiting the individual units are shown by a synopsis of the results of various analyses. See the survey in Steuernagel, *Deuteronomium*, pp. 8–9; also S. R. Driver, *Critical and Exegetical Commentary on Deuteronomy* (3rd ed., Edinburgh, 1902), p. lxxvi; J. Hempel, *Die Schichten des Deuteronomiums* (Leipzig, 1914); G. Hölscher, 'Komposition und Ursprung des Deuteronomiums,' *ZAW*, 40 (1922), p. 225.

[60] Deut. 4:41–43, the setting apart of the cities of refuge, will not be considered here.

[61] There is general agreement that this unit, in its present form, is Deuteronomistic.

tion. The section 1:6–3:17 (18–29) contains the *antecedent history*. It begins in 1:6 with the departure from Horeb. The time with which this section begins is in striking contrast to the other historical introductions. The next section, 2:26–3:17, reports the occupation of the land east of the Jordan and describes the extent of the territory. The 'description of territory' is found once more in the expected place. Even if we must think in terms of some additions from an earlier recension in 3:8–17, the text is again reminiscent of the lists usually found in treaties.[62]

According to the pattern observed up to now, this would bring us to the conclusion. In contrast, 3:18–29 gives the appearance of being an addition, presupposing the assumed situation in which all of Deuteronomy was spoken before the advance into territory west of the Jordan.[63]

The presentation of events in 1:6–3:17 is not quite a unified whole. It is composed of various elements.[64] This is not the place for more detailed analysis. The character of the section as an historical introduction remains constant in all the strata.

Deut. 4:1 serves as an introductory formula for a legal section:[65] וְעַתָּה יִשְׂרָאֵל שְׁמַע אֶל־הַחֻקִּים וְאֶל־הַמִּשְׁפָּטִים. The laws that were announced are lacking. Probably they once came between vv. 4 and 5.[66]

A few basic stipulations are preserved. They refer to:
(1) The integrity of 'the word which I command you' (v. 2).

---

[62] Cf., for example, Deut. 3:15–17: 'To Machir I gave Gilead, and to the Reubenites and the Gadites I gave the territory from Gilead as far as the valley of the Arnon, with the middle of the valley as a boundary, as far over as the river Jabbok, the boundary of the Ammonites; the Arabah also, with the Jordan as the boundary, from Chinnereth as far as the sea of the Arabah, the Salt Sea, under the slopes of Pisgah on the east.'—See text no. 17340 in Nougayrol, *Palais royal IV*, pp. 48ff.: 'Pugul'i [Šet]a, Ya'aniya [jusqu'au Mont-] Champ-au-Cerf, avec le Mont-Ḫadamgi, 5' [. . .]tkitiya, Paništa'i, Nakḫati, [Ḫal]pi, le Mont-Nana, Šalma, Gulbata, [Z]amirti, Sulada, Mara'ili, Ḫimul[l]i.

'Ainsi, Šuppiluliuma Grand-roi, roi du Ḫatti, le héros, ces [frontières], villes, montagnes, à Niqmadu, 10' [roi de] l'Ugarit, les a attribuées par sceau, ainsi qu'à ses fils et fils de ses fils, à jamais[6]'

In this text the 'antecedent history' precedes, the 'statement of substance' follows (see above p. 12, n. 18 and 20; cf. the text below, p. 187).—In this context a study of Joshua 13–22 would probably be worthwhile.

[63] See also Deut. 4:21–22.

[64] The peculiar 'we'-style of this section, which holds it together as a unit despite a series of irregularities in its present form, is reminiscent of the second historical retrospect in Josh. 24:17–18, the actual 'credo' of the people.

On the structure of the section, see S. R. Driver, *Deuteronomy*, pp. xivff.

[65] Cf. Deut. 10:12; Josh. 24:14.

[66] See Steuernagel, *Deuteronomium*, p. 65: 'After the announcement in v. 1, we expect a reading of the laws to follow immediately; the perfect לִמַּדְתִּי in v. 5 and the reference to the laws in 8 . . . prove that such a recitation actually took place.'

In other respects, too, the present context does not admit facile restoration.

(2) The obligation to know and pass on 'the things which your eyes have seen' (v. 9).[67]

(3) The prohibition against making a 'פֶסֶל' (vv. 15–18).

(4) The prohibition of the astral cult (vv. 19–20).

One new feature was not found in Joshua 24: more or less detailed motivations are given for the commandments.[68] This is in line with the parenetic character of the framework sections of Deuteronomy. With respect to the making of a פֶסֶל, for instance, this motivation takes the form of an 'antecedent history.' It recounts the events at Horeb. It is more detailed, however, than the context necessarily requires. The effect is that of a lengthy quotation. The catchword for the passage is found in v. 12: וּתְמוּנָה אֵינְכֶם רֹאִים. It is taken up again in v. 15: כָּל־תְּמוּנָה כִּי לֹא רְאִיתֶם. Now, however, 'פֶסֶל' is no longer understood as an idol (see v. 16: תְּמוּנַת כָּל־סֶמֶל תַּבְנִית זָכָר... אוֹ נְקֵבָה׃ תַּבְנִית כָּל־...), but as a concrete image of God; in other words only the latter is probably a real possibility for the text in its present form.

V. 23 summarizes the commandment sections: הִשָּׁמְרוּ לָכֶם פֶּן־תִּשְׁכְּחוּ אֶת־בְּרִית יהוה. Deut. 4:24–31 contains the sanction of a covenant. V. 24 corresponds formally to Josh. 24:19aβ,b. Once again an invocation of Yahweh is replaced by a statement concerning Yahweh.[69] This verse leads into a curse. In v. 26, heaven and earth are called upon to be witnesses.

The curse formula in v. 26 corresponds to the short Hittite form that threatens primarily death without offspring.—'From the land which you are going over the Jordan to possess' once more presupposes the situation of Israel before crossing the Jordan, and can therefore be left out of account.[70]

The blessing formula in v. 40 is parallel in content to the curse formula.[71] In contrast to v. 24, the predication of Yahweh before the blessing is here greatly expanded by the addition of vv. 32–39. What is developed here is a kind of 'theology.' In its structure, it once again

---

[67] See Steuernagel, ibid.

[68] Vv. 3–4, 6–8, 10–14, 19b–20.

[69] כִּי יהוה אֱלֹהֶיךָ אֵשׁ אֹכְלָה הוּא אֵל קַנָּא׃.

[70] As in v. 40, אֲדָמָה may originally have stood here. Cf. Josh. 23:13.

[71] The curse (vv. 26–27) is the second person plural, the blessing (v. 40) in the second person singular (as in Deut. 11:13–17). From the standpoint of the literary form, it would be undesirable to separate blessing and curse.—It is a striking fact that the alternation occurs in Hittite treaties that are addressed both to an individual and to a group (see W 2, vo. 25–39!; F 4 §20, vo. 40–41).

D

follows the course of an antecedent history. This extends from 'the day that God created man upon the earth' (v. 32) to the gift of the land (v. 38).[72]

In this short form the curse and blessing by no means must presuppose the Exile. Vv. 27–30, however, give them quite a different character. In 27–28, the curse is transformed into a prophecy of disaster, and is now clearly understood to refer to an exile. The curse and blessing are linked temporally: first the time of the curse is awaited, then the time of the blessing.[73] A completely new element now intervenes between curse and blessing: 'conversion' (vv. 29–30).[74]

Deuteronomy 28:69–30:20 (Eng. 29–30)

Deut. 28:69–30:20 (Eng. 29–30) exhibits a similar picture. The 'special superscription and introductory formula (28:69; 29:1a [Eng. 29:1–2a]) distinguish it clearly from its environment as an independent passage.'[75] A new section begins with 31:1.[76] Probably no one doubts that the section from 28:69 (Eng. 29:1) through 30:20 is for the most part of late (i.e., at least exilic) date,[77] even if individual passages are earlier. Within the larger unit there are a whole series of inconsistencies, for example, a frequent change of number[78] and tense, and above all various additions.[79] Nevertheless the unit in its present form exhibits a simple, rational structure.

---

[72] 38. כַּיּוֹם הַזֶּה ;32 יָמִים רִאשֹׁנִים אֲשֶׁר־הָיוּ לְפָנֶיךָ

[73] The statement בְּאַחֲרִית הַיָּמִים (v. 30) is striking.

[74] Analysis shows that Deuteronomy 1–4 is a self-contained unit. This tells against the assumption that we have here the beginning of the Deuteronomistic History (see Noth, *Überlieferungsgeschichtliche Studien*, p. 14). Neither does the section have to be an 'introductory speech leading up to the Deuteronomic law.'

[75] See Steuernagel, *Deuteronomium*, p. 155. Steuernagel, however, treats chapter 30 separately. According to Bertholet, Östreicher, Hempel, König, et al., 28:69 (Eng. 29:1) is the superscription to what follows; according to Holzinger, Smend, Eißfeldt, et al., it concludes the preceding section.

[76] For a discussion of whether chapters 29 and 30 belong together, see Holzinger, *Einleitung in den Hexateuch* (1893), pp. 263ff.; Eißfeldt, *Introduction*, 230–31.

[77] According to Cornhill, D[p]; according to Kuenen, D[2] and later (see Holzinger, ibid.); according to Smend, a later supplement to the second recension of Deuteronomy; according to Bertholet, 28:69–30:14 (Eng. 29:1–30:14) is an exilic exhortation and comfort discourse, while 30:15–20 belongs to 'D' (*Deuteronomium*, pp. 88ff.; 91). Steuernagel includes chapter 29 in a 'fourth special redaction of the Deuteronomic law' (ibid., p. 155).

[78] Cf. also 𝔊.

[79] Staerk calls 30:15–20 a 'heap of rubble' (quoted by Bertholet, *Deuteronomium*, p. 91); Steuernagel speaks of its 'mosaic character' (p. 159).

Deut. 29:1–7 (Eng. 29:2–8) is an *antecedent history*.[80] It extends
from the events in Egypt to the occupation of the land east of the
Jordan. Special emphasis is placed on Yahweh's miraculous inter-
vention, which is meant to bring men to the realization that Yahweh
is the God of Israel (v. 5 [Eng. v. 6]). Formally, the antecedent
history is not homogeneous. It alternates between address ('You
have seen all . . .') with mention of Yahweh in the third person and
direct first-person speech on the part of Yahweh (at least from v. 5
[Eng. v. 6] on).[81] V. 6 (Eng. v. 7) continues in the first person
plural.

The *statement of substance*[82] begins in v. 8 (Eng. v. 9) with:
וּשְׁמַרְתֶּם אֶת־דִּבְרֵי הַבְּרִית הַזֹּאת. In content, vv. 9 ff. (Eng. vv. 10ff.) fit
into the context well, since they define the relationship between
Yahweh and his people: לְמַעַן הָקִים־אֹתְךָ הַיּוֹם לוֹ לְעָם וְהוּא יִהְיֶה־לְּךָ לֵאלֹהִים
(v. 12 [Eng. v. 13]). Unconditional loyalty renders it impossible to
worship foreign gods (v. 17 [Eng. v. 18]).

In what follows, the text is considerably expanded vis-à-vis
chapters 1–4. Vv. 17b–20 (Eng. vv. 18b–21) interpret serving the
gods of the nations as 'walking in stubbornness of heart.'[83]

We do not come to a simple formula of *blessing and cursing* until
30:16–18. In a series of infinitives, the commandments requiring
loyalty are summed up once more before the blessing:

לְאַהֲבָה אֶת־יהוה אֱלֹהֶיךָ

לָלֶכֶת בִּדְרָכָיו

וְלִשְׁמֹר מִצְוֹתָיו וְחֻקֹּתָיו וּמִשְׁפָּטָיו

If, however, 'your heart turns away, and you will not hear, but are
drawn away to worship other gods,' the curse is threatened.

In 30:19, heaven and earth are called upon as *witnesses*.

---

[80] From the standpoint of the literary form at hand, it is hardly possible to follow
Steuernagel in eliminating vv. 6–7 (Eng. 7–8) as an 'historical element interrupting the
connection between 8 and 3, quite unrelated to the parenthesis' (*Deuteronomium*, p. 155).

[81] On the alternation between the third and first person, see also above p. 19, n. 4.

[82] I should like to direct attention to the way the covenant is referred to in v. 13
(Eng. v. 14; cf. v. 11 [Eng. v. 12]):

אָנֹכִי כֹּרֵת אֶת־הַבְּרִית הַזֹּאת

וְאֶת־הָאָלָה הַזֹּאת

In my opinion, this terminology is exactly parallel to the practice of referring to a
Hittite treaty as '*riksu u mamītu*.'

[83] On this view, cf. the expanded quotation in 1QS ii. 11–17, especially line 17. See
also 1QH, hymn 4 (cited by G. Molin, *Die Söhne des Lichts*, [Wien, 1954]), p. 37).

The intermediate passage 29:21–30:10 (Eng. 29:22–30:10), which we have so far omitted from our analysis, contains an additional group of blessings and curses, corresponding to 4:27–30. It develops the themes that first appear there. It is now quite clear that the curse is recognized as being operative in the present (29:27 [Eng. 29:28]: כַּיּוֹם הַזֶּה). The consequences of the curse are described in detail. The statements belonging to the original curse series become a means of depicting present distress.

In 30:1–10, the idea of 'conversion' is developed at much greater length than in chapter 4.[84] The return of Israel to its obligations of loyalty, 'obeying Yahweh's voice' (vv. 2, 10), will be followed by 'restoration' through Yahweh. The passage is clearly concerned, however, to see that this restoration is not reduced to a mere automatic consequence. Therefore what is elsewhere presented as a fundamental requirement,[85] לְאַהֲבָה אֶת־יהוה אֱלֹהֶיךָ, is here understood as a possibility granted by Yahweh:

> 'And Yahweh your God will circumcise your heart and the heart of your offspring, so that you will love Yahweh your God with all your heart and with all your soul, that you may live' (v. 6).

The promised blessing comes only through Yahweh's mercy.[86]

Isolated Elements

In chapters 5–11, 26–28, and 31, the form is not preserved in its entirety.[87] Individual elements can probably be recognized in many cases. It is impossible to say with any assurance, however, how these should be put together.

Antecedent histories occur as follows:

	Content:	Continuation:
6:21–23	From Egypt to the occupation ...	6:24 וַיְצַוֵּנוּ יהוה לַעֲשׂוֹת
8:2–4	Wandering in the desert	8:5 וְיָדַעְתָּ עִם־לְבָבֶךָ ...
		8:6 וְשָׁמַרְתָּ אֶת־מִצְוֺת יהוה ...
9:7–10:11	From the exodus to the occupation(?)[88] (especially the events at Horeb)	10:12 וְעַתָּה יִשְׂרָאֵל ...

[84] Note the many plays on the word שׁוּב in this section.

[85] See 6:5; 10:12; 11:1, 13, 22.

[86] On the content of the promise, cf. the series of blessings in 7:13; 28:4.

[87] See von Rad, *Studies in Deuteronomy*, p. 53, on chapters 6–11: 'It can be taken as certain that this section is not to be claimed as a homogeneous structure either from the form-critical or the literary point of view, but it represents a compilation of several liturgical "formularies" for the festival of the reading of the law.'

[88] The section contains material of very different sorts; see Steuernagel, *Deuteronomium*, p. 83.

11:2–7	Egypt, march through the desert 'to this place' (11:5)

11:8 וּשְׁמַרְתֶּם אֶת־כָּל־הַמִּצְוָה

	Description of the land[89]	Continuation:
6:10–11		6:12 הִשָּׁמֶר לְךָ פֶּן־ ...
8:7–10		8:11 הִשָּׁמֶר לְךָ פֶּן־ ...

The *statement of substance* has undergone the most marked changes.
In most cases it can no longer be delimited with certainty. In the
passages cited above, in which it follows the antecedent history
directly, it is at least possible to see where it begins. There are, however, a whole series of passages whose content is identical with the
material usually found in this section. Deut. 6:4–5, the beginning of
the *š^ema'*, deserves special mention in this regard. The clearest
definition of the relationship between Yahweh and his people is
found in Deut. 26:16–19. This relationship can be described by the
formula 'I will be your God, and you shall be my people.'[90]

The statement of substance is further elaborated by means of
specific statements, which occur again and again in similar groupings.
We are dealing here for the most part with a series of verbs that are
either briefly listed or elucidated in greater detail by means of various
additions. Two forms can be distinguished: series comprising jussives
and series comprising infinitives with 'לְ'. What these statements
have in common is that, in various ways, they describe a relationship
of obedience and fidelity. These are the formulas that later, for
instance, characterize the Deuteronomistic History.[91]

6:2	תִּירָא אֶת־יהוה אֱלֹהֶיךָ לִשְׁמֹר אֶת־כָּל־חֻקֹּתָיו
6:3	וְשָׁמַעְתָּ יִשְׂרָאֵל
	וְשָׁמַרְתָּ לַעֲשׂוֹת ...
6:12	הִשָּׁמֶר לְךָ פֶּן־תִּשְׁכַּח אֶת־יהוה ...
6:13	אֶת־יהוה ... תִּירָא
	וְאֹתוֹ תַעֲבֹד
	וּבִשְׁמוֹ תִּשָּׁבֵעַ:

---

[89] On the description of the land as part of the formulary, see above pp. 12, 20.

[90] On this formula, cf. Exod. 6:7; Lev. 26:12; Deut. 27:9; 29:12 (Eng. 29:13);
Jer. 7:23; 11:4; 13:11; 24:7; 30:22; 31:33; 32:38; Ezek. 11:20; 14:11; 36:28; 37:23
and 27; Zech. 8:8.

[91] We might ask to what extent the term 'Deuteronomistic,' in the context of the
'covenant,' may not also indicate a specific *Sitz im Leben.*

6:14		לֹא תֵלְכוּן אַחֲרֵי אֱלֹהִים אֲחֵרִים
8:2		וְזָכַרְתָּ אֶת־כָּל־הַדֶּרֶךְ...
8:5		וְיָדַעְתָּ עִם־לְבָבֶךָ ...
8:6		וְשָׁמַרְתָּ אֶת־מִצְוֹת יהוה אֱלֹהֶיךָ לָלֶכֶת בִּדְרָכָיו...

10:20	אֶת־יהוה אֱלֹהֶיךָ תִּירָא	
	אֹתוֹ	תַעֲבֹד
	וּבוֹ	תִדְבָּק
	וּבִשְׁמוֹ	תִּשָּׁבֵעַ:...

31:12	לְמַעַן יִשְׁמְעוּ	
	וּלְמַעַן יִלְמְדוּ	
	וְיָרְאוּ אֶת־יהוה אֱלֹהֵיכֶם	
	וְשָׁמְרוּ לַעֲשׂוֹת אֶת־כָּל־דִּבְרֵי הַתּוֹרָה הַזֹּאת	

10:12	וְעַתָּה יִשְׂרָאֵל מָה יהוה אֱלֹהֶיךָ שֹׁאֵל מֵעִמָּךְ כִּי אִם־	
	לְיִרְאָה אֶת־יהוה אֱלֹהֶיךָ	
	לָלֶכֶת בְּכָל־דְּרָכָיו	
	וּלְאַהֲבָה אֹתוֹ	
	וְלַעֲבֹד אֶת־יהוה...	
10:13	לִשְׁמֹר אֶת־מִצְוֹת יהוה...	

11:22	כִּי אִם־שָׁמֹר תִּשְׁמְרוּן אֶת־כָּל־הַמִּצְוָה הַזֹּאת...	
	לַעֲשֹׂתָהּ	
	לְאַהֲבָה אֶת־יהוה אֱלֹהֵיכֶם	
	לָלֶכֶת בְּכָל־דְּרָכָיו	
	וּלְדָבְקָה־בוֹ:	

Examination of the additional *blessing* and *cursing* passages in Deuteronomy is not necessary in the present context.

On the basis of the texts that have been studies, I think it is possible to say that the covenant formulary, as a literary type, was familiar in Israel. In what follows it will be our task to show the ways in which this formulary was employed and transformed.

III

THE COVENANT FORMULARY
AT THE RENEWAL OF THE COVENANT

Exodus 34

The nucleus of Exodus 34 (vv. 10–27, '28')[1] reproduces the first half of the formulary used in making a covenant, i.e., all but the oath ceremony. Now, however, we must take into account alterations based on the position of the chapter in the context of the Sinai pericope; these alterations were probably undertaken during the final redaction of the text.[2]

These alterations appear at once in the 'antecedent history' (vv. 10 + 11b). The items listed here, in Joshua 24, for example, such as the driving out of the foreign nations and the occupation of their territory, are still in the future from the standpoint of the assumed situation at Sinai. But the only alteration undertaken in the ante-cendent history in this passage consists in the transposition from the perfect to the future. Instead of 'I have done marvels,'[3] we read here 'I will do marvels' (v. 10). Similarly, we do not find the statement 'I gave you a land';[4] instead, v. 12 speaks of 'the land whither you go.' As in Joshua 24, the 'antecendent history' is composed as first-person speech from the mouth of Yahweh.

The *statement of substance* can no longer be delimited with assurance in the present state of the text. In my opinion, its beginning is found in v. 11a:[5] שְׁמָר־לְךָ אֵת אֲשֶׁר אָנֹכִי מְצַוְּךָ הַיּוֹם. V. 14, 'You shall worship no other god,' with its explanation, 'for Yahweh, whose name is Jealous, is a jealous God,' is best thought of as a basic commandment. The prohibition against cultic worship of another god implies the

---

[1] According to Eißfeldt (*Hexateuchsynopse*, pp. 158ff.), the text, v. 28 included, belongs to J, followed by P. According to Noth (*Überlieferungsgeschichte*, p. 33, n. 118), however, the basic stratum of vv. 29–35 also belongs to J. For additional bibliographical references on this point, see Alt, *Kleine Schriften*, vol. 1, p. 317, n. 1. Alt terms Exod. 34:10(14)–26 a 'secondary composition.' But the structure of the chapter in its present form is itself of interest, since this structure is clearly still subject to formal constraints.

[2] Our study will show that these alterations are in complete harmony with the material present in the sources. They are limited, in my opinion, to merely superficial changes, e.g., the addition of '. . . like the first [tables]' in vv. 1 and 4.

[3] Cf. Ps. 78:4; 105:5; also Deut. 29:2 (Eng. 29:3); Ps. 135:9; and elsewhere.

[4] See Josh. 24:13.

[5] See the tables above, pp. 36–38.

rejection of a covenant with those who dwell in the land. This commandment, most remarkably, is inculcated twice (in v. 12a and in v. 15a) in the same words.[6]—In vv. 15–16, the form of strict prohibition is abandoned in favor of a more parenetic form, which not only prohibits but also admonishes and parades the consequences before the eyes of the listener.

Vv. 11a, 12–16 set forth the relationship with Yahweh that will obtain in the future.

Further *individual commandments* follow in vv. 17–26.[7] In all the biblical texts we have examined so far, these have been missing. Here we may see for the first time that our assumption, based on the Hittite texts, of where the individual stipulations would be found in the structure of the formulary was correct. They follow from the statement of substance, of which they are the consequence.

The change in person—first Yahweh speaking in the first person, then use of the neutral third person with reference to Yahweh as 'God of Israel'—can also be a stylistic feature typical of treaties.[8] It can therefore not be used without restriction as a means for literary criticism to distinguish various strata within the commandments.

The antecedent history, statement of substance, and individual stipulations therefore perserve the content of the covenant to the extent that it proceeds from Yahweh. Verse 27 is therefore correct in stating that Yahweh has concluded a covenant.[9]

Though other texts state only in general terms that Yahweh is present at the conclusion of the covenant, here a theophany is explicitly presumed.[10]

When the parties to the covenant are mentioned, a distinction

[6]
הִשָּׁמֶר לְךָ פֶּן־תִּכְרֹת בְּרִית לְיוֹשֵׁב הָאָרֶץ   12

פֶּן־תִּכְרֹת בְּרִית לְיוֹשֵׁב הָאָרֶץ   15

[7] For details, see Alt, *Kleine Schriften*, vol. 1, pp. 317ff. Alt points out that 'stipulations formulated for priests predominate over the cultic obligations of the laity' (p. 317, n. 1).

The stipulation 'Three times in the year shall all your males appear before lord Yahweh, the God of Israel' (v. 23) is reminiscent of the obligation to appear at court in W 3, ii, 3ff.; W 4, ro. 3–4. Cf. W 7, ro. i, 40ff.: 'Šunaššura shall appear before the Sun, the "countenance" of the Sun he shall behold. . . .'

[8] Cf., for example, F 1. In the stipulations, the subject changes frequently from 'I, the Sun' to 'the king of the land of Ḫatti.'

[9] The perfect should probably be taken as a declarative: 'I hereby conclude . . .'; see W. Gesenius, *Hebrew Grammar*, (E.T. 2nd ed.; Oxford, 1910), §106 m.

[10] Vv. 5–8. There are some inconsistencies in these verses (see the commentaries). The 'invocation of the name' is somehow linked with the theophany. But who is the speaker in vv. 6–7? See also W. Beyerlin, *Kulttraditionen*, pp. 30ff., 39.

is made between Moses and Israel (vs. 27)—between him who leads Israel and the people.[11]

In Exodus 34 we find once more a close connection between the conclusion of the covenant and the written record of its content.[12] In contrast to 34:1, where Yahweh himself writes upon the tablets, the commission given to Moses (vs. 27) represents a distinct weakening.

In vv. 29ff. the etiology of the 'veil' has been worked in. This interrupts the continuity of the text somewhat. But the recitation of 'all that Yahweh had spoken with him in Mount Sinai' is still found in v. 32.[13] There is no mention of the people's solemn assent or of a lengthy oath ceremony.

To this point the covenant in Exodus 34 does not differ essentially from others. The passage forms such a unified whole that it can well have existed as an independent entity. The introduction in vv. 1–9, however, as found in the present text, gives it a special accent.

It is probably safe to say that the phrase 'two tables of stone like the first' (vv. 1 and 4) is a secondary addition, connecting this section with what has been narrated in the preceding chapters.[14] The connection, however, is not really quite so superficial as it may seem at first. One must recognize clearly the importance that attaches to the 'breaking of the tablets' (32:19). It is not just a violent image; the

---

[11] Cf. F 6; W 10; see also Weidner, *Politische Dokumente*, p. 139, n. 4: 'And so Lab'u . . . was probably mayor of Tunip and the president of the college of elders.'

[12] 27 כְּתָב־לְךָ אֶת־הַדְּבָרִים הָאֵלֶּה

כִּי עַל־פִּי הַדְּבָרִים הָאֵלֶּה כָּרַתִּי אִתְּךָ בְּרִית וְאֶת־יִשְׂרָאֵל:

The covenant document is here referred to as לֻחֹת הָעֵדֻת (v. 29). Cf. Exod. 31:18; 32:15 and לֻחוֹת הַבְּרִית in Deut. 9:9, 11, and 15.

If v. 27*b* in fact picks up 10*a* once more, we may assume that 'these words' (v. 27) also include the 'antecedent history' in v. 10. I consider it therefore all the more unlikely that 'the ten commandments [Heb.: "words"]' (v. 28) are original. Scholars have hitherto been unsuccessful in defining the 'ten commandments' in the legal section with precision. On the discussion, see Holzinger, *Exodus*, p. 119; Rudolph, *Aufbau*, p. 47.

[13] Cf. above, pp. 29–30, the parallels Exod. 19:7–8; 24:3–4 and 7–8.

31 וַיִּקְרָא אֲלֵהֶם מֹשֶׁה (וַיָּשֻׁבוּ אֵלָיו אַהֲרֹן וְכָל־הַנְּשִׂאִים בָּעֵדָה) וַיְדַבֵּר

Did vv. 31 and 32 originally distinguish a recitation first in the presence of Aaron and the 'leaders of the congregation,' then (אַחֲרֵי־כֵן) in the presence of the entire people? If so, distinction in rank would be maintained here, too, during the acceptance of obligation.—On נָשִׂי see M. Noth, *Das System der zwölf Stämme Israels*, BWANT (2nd ed., Darmstadt, 1957), Excursus 3, pp. 151ff., 154.

[14] Noth, *Überlieferungsgeschichte*, p. 33, n. 116.

loss of the 'tablets of the treaty' in any form spells the end of the treaty relationship.[15] If this takes place, the covenant must be renewed. Verse 9 states the internal reason for invalidating a covenant: 'iniquity and sin,' i.e., apostasy on the part of the one to whom the covenant has been granted.[16] Such apostasy puts an end to שָׁלוֹם, and the curse threatened when the covenant was made comes into play at once. The only deliverance from the curse is unconditional submission to the one that granted the covenant. This is the significance of Moses' bowing to the earth before Yahweh (v. 8).[17] He thereby acknowledges the sin as sin. Yahweh alone can decide whether to "forgive"[18] and grant the covenant once more. Moses can only make the request.[19]

Here the response to the prayer of penitence is:[20] 'Behold, I make a covenant' (v. 10). Yahweh has accepted the repentance.[21]

Von Rad has shown[22] that the Sinai pericope in Exodus 19–24 reflects essentially the making of a covenant in the form of a cultic ceremony. Our study of Exodus 34 raises the question whether the association of repentance and covenant renewal within this chapter does not also represent something 'typical.' We can answer this question only if a similar structure, involving such a covenant renewal, can be verified in other texts.

We shall begin with some late texts from the Chronicler's History,

---

[15] Cf. W 7, vo. iv. 25ff.: 'The tablet with the oath in the presence of the gods, which has been made, we wish [26] to erase; the word of Ḫarri we truly wish to cast aside. [27] Šunaššura is by no means (any longer) Ḫarr[i's servant]. [28] We wish to make another tablet. . . .' W 6, ro. 3–8 (speaking of the theft of the tablet of the treaty): '[4] I, the Great King, wro[te for him] a second tablet . . . [5] . . . (for all the future) no one shall change the wor[d]ing (lit.: "the word of the mouth") of this [tablet]. The word of the edict of the Great King (is a word) not to be cast aside and not to be broken' (see Weidner ad loc., p. 81, n. 8).

[16] W 6, ro. 19–20: 'The king of the land of Ḫalap committed the si[n of the] king of the land of Ḫan[ig]albat. But against Ḫattuš[iliš] . . . he sinned [especially].' Akk.: 'ḫi-i-ta . . . iḫ-ti.'

[17] Cf. F 4 §3–4, col. i, which records how Manapa-Dattaš broke a treaty and then fell at the feet of his lord: '[41] [And] you sent [as fol]lows [to me], "My lord, spare my life . . . [42] [do not de]stroy me, and take me into your service, and [protect] my person. . . .'

[18] On סלח as a technical term, see J. J. Stamm, Erlösen und Vergeben im AT (Bern, 1940), esp. pp. 105ff.

[19] 'O lord, go in the midst of us' and 'take us for they inheritance' correspond to the formula 'I will be your God, and you shall be my people,' which essentially determines the relationship between Yahweh and his people. Cf. Exod. 29:45; Lev. 26:12; Deut. 7:6ff.; Ezek. 37:26–27; Zech. 2:15–16 (Eng. 2:11–12).

[20] For the contrary possibility, see Isa. 22:14; Jer. 5:6–7.

[21] The parallel text in Deut. 9:18–19, 25–29; 10:10–11 shows plainly an expansion of the penitential element. For example, the forty days and nights in Yahweh's presence are now understood as a period of intercession on the part of Moses (Deut. 9:18–19, 25–26). Cf. the synopsis in Driver, Deuteronomy, pp. 112–13, also p. 115.

[22] Hexateuch, pp. 18ff. (Gesammelte Studien, pp. 28ff.).

because in them we can still recognize to a considerable extent the form, its content, and the cultic ceremony in which it was employed.

Nehemiah 9–10

Though not undisputed,[23] the literary unity of Nehemiah 9 and 10 remains probable.[24] On the basis of the texts studied so far, we can state only that the association is appropriate. Nehemiah 9 stands as an *antecedent history* to Nehemiah 10. We may assume that this is what the beginning of chapter 10, וּבְכָל־זֹאת...., refers to.[25]

The historical retrospect in chapter 9 extends from the recollection of Abraham (vv. 7–8) to the present: עַד הַיּוֹם הַזֶּה...וְעַתָּה....[26]

Following the superscription in 10:1 (Eng. 9:38), chapter 10 reproduces the document recording the 'firm covenant.'[27] Verses 30b–40 (Eng. 29b–39) list the conditions of the agreement. Here we can observe clearly the distinction between basic stipulations and individual commandments.

The portion containing the basic stipulations consists of a series of infinitives:[28]

30 לָלֶכֶת   בְּתוֹרַת הָאֱלֹהִים אֲשֶׁר נִתְּנָה בְּיַד מֹשֶׁה עֶבֶד־הָאֱלֹהִים
וְלִשְׁמוֹר
וְלַעֲשׂוֹת   אֶת־כָּל־מִצְוֹת יהוה אֲדֹנֵינוּ
וּמִשְׁפָּטָיו
וְחֻקָּיו:

When compared to the expressions 'serve Yahweh,' 'obey his voice,' and 'incline your heart to him' found in Josh. 24:23–24, it is striking how much more formal the basic relationship is as defined here.

[23] On the difficult questions of literary criticism posed by Nehemiah 8–10, see L. W. Batten, *A Critical and Exegetical Commentary on the Books of Ezra and Nehemia*, ICC (Edinburgh, 1913), pp. 4ff., 352ff.; H. H. Schaeder, *Esra der Schreiber* (Tübingen, 1930), esp. pp. 7–8, 12, 15, 24; W. Rudolph, *Esra und Nehemia samt 3. Esra*, HAT (Tübingen, 1949), pp. 153ff.; K. Galling, *Die Bücher der Chronik, Esra, Nehemia*, ATD (Göttingen, 1954), p. 232; Noth, *Gesetze*, pp. 67f. (*Laws*, pp. 81–82); idem, *Überlieferungsgeschichtliche Studien*, pp. 128ff., 149.

[24] Noth, *Überlieferungsgeschichtliche Studien*, p. 149; for the contrary view, see Rudolph, *Esra*, pp. 172–73, 162–63.

[25] This view is espoused by Rudolph, ibid., p. 172; for a different view, see Galling, *Chronik*, p. 242.

[26] For details, see Noth, *Gesetze*, pp. 67–68 (*Laws*, pp. 81–82); von Rad, *Hexateuch*, p. 11 (*Gesammelte Studien*, pp. 19–20).

[27] אֲמָנָה is synonymous with בְּרִית; see Rudolph, *Esra*, p. 172, on 10:1a (Eng. 9:38a). Cf. Josh. 24:25–26.

[28] Cf. the series on pp. 37–38 above. See Rudolph, *Esra*, p. 173, and especially p. 174 on 30c (Eng. 29c): 'But 1b, as well as 29 and 30aα, are circumstantial clauses dependent on 1a, so that the infinitives of 30 go back beyond 29/30 and 1b, depending directly on 1a.'

The individual stipulations begin in v. 31 (Eng. 30) with וַאֲשֶׁר[29] and comprise:

(1) a prohibition of mixed marriages (v. 31 [Eng. 30]);
(2) a regulation dealing with commerce with the 'peoples of the land' on Jewish festivals (v. 32a [Eng. 31a]);
(3) an obligation to observe the year of release, letting the fields lie fallow and remitting debts (v. 32b [Eng. 31b]);[30]
(4) payment of tribute for the support of the Temple (vv. 33ff. [Eng. 32ff.].

Points one through three are concerned with setting Israelites apart from non-Israelites; point four is summarized in 40b (Eng. 39b) with the solemn vow 'We will not neglect the house of our God.'

The sanctions involved in the covenant are not specified in more detail, but are mentioned in v. 30 (Eng. 29).[31]

For a document to be legally valid, it must be sealed. This idea, found throughout the Near East, differs little from the modern view. Neh. 10:1ff. [Eng. 9:38ff.] confirms the sealing of the present agreement.[32] This is an additional detail showing how precise was the legal practice we must imagine at the making of a 'covenant.'[33]

The schema we have been studying can therefore be recognized in its essentials in Nehemiah 9–10; we may nevertheless note some differences between this section and the texts previously studied. For

---

[29] According to Rudolph (ibid., p. 174), v. 31a (Eng. 30a) begins with an emphatic 'ו'; cf. Gesenius, *Hebrew Grammar*, §154, n. 1b.

On the transition from general infinitives to individual stipulations in the jussive, cf. 1QS i. 10–11; see also v; ix. 12ff.

[30] 'Here, too, the concern is to distinguish between Jews and foreigners (cf. Deut. 15:3),' according to Galling, *Chronik*, p. 242.

[31] Neh. 10:30: וּבָאִים בְּאָלָה וּבִשְׁבוּעָה. Koehler, *Lexikon*, p. 940, ad voc. שְׁבוּעָה, translates the passage: 'to place oneself under a curse with an oath.' אָלָה emphasizes the curse (Deut. 29:19 [Eng. 29:20]; Isa. 24:6 [cf. 24:5!)], שְׁבוּעָה the oath by which the threatened curse is accepted. See Korosec, *Hethitische Staatsverträge*, pp. 21ff., on *mamītu*; p. 92, on the treaty sanctions.

[32] On v. 2 (Eng. v. 1), see Rudolph, *Esra*, p. 172. The sealing of a treaty document is mentioned in W 6 (25). In contrast to Nehemiah 10, the Great King who grants the treaty affixes his seal (W 6, 4–5). Cf. also the description of the seal in the Egyptian version of the treaty of Ramses II (Pritchard, *ANET*, p. 201. On the list in Neh. 10:2–28 (Eng. 10:1–27), see Rudolph, *Esra*, pp. 173–74. To be sure this list interrupts the continuity; but it would be good to know what the original of such a document looked like and how a later copyist would go about his work. In the treaty between Šuppliluliumaš and Niqmadu (Nougayrol, *Palais royal IV*, pp. 48ff.), for example, the seal of Šupiluliumaš is impressed in the middle of the text (see plate XLVIII, rs. 17.340); cf. also the other illustrations in this volume. The unique position of the list could mean that the text is somehow based on ancient documents.

example, in Josh. 24:16 the people promise not to forsake 'Yahweh';
Neh. 10:40 (Eng. 10:39) refers to 'the house of our God.' Now the
phrase 'to serve God' refers primarily to the 'cult' v. 33 (Eng. 32).[34]
This change in accent reflects the passage of time. It cannot be
understood apart from its theological background.

But even the covenant formulary itself has undergone changes in
form. The characteristic content of the legal section of the document
in Nehemiah 10 is not the repetition, as in Exodus 34, of commandments given by God, who grants his people a covenant,[35] but the
acceptance of obligations by the entire people.[36] Therefore the
stipulations are formulated, not as imperatives or jussives in the
second person, as they are elsewhere, but as voluntatives in the first
person.

The reason for this change may be that there is no longer anyone
authorized to pronounce commandments in the name of God, like
'Moses the servant of God' (10:30 [Eng. 10:29]). The 'law, commandments, ordinances, and statutes' of God have been unambiguously laid down; now it is only possible to promulgate 'regulations
for their observance.' I think it is possible, however, that even this
form of document, in which the people state their obligations, goes
back to earlier prototypes. Some Hittite treaties exhibit duplicate
documents.[37] An example is the treaty between Šuppiluliumaš and
Matiuaza. The Hittite Great King is clearly the superior party.[38]
Two versions of the treaty have been preserved, one having Šuppiluliumaš as its author, the other, Mattiuaza. In the latter version, the
antecedent history is written more from the point of view of
Mattiuaza. In particular, the oath, in the form of a self-curse, is

---

[33] For similar reasons I do not find it necessary to take offense at the 'statements, in
part irrelevant or going into extreme detail,' (Galling, *Chronik*, p. 243) that come within
the individual commandments. They are in line with a kind of legal propensity for detail.
Cf. the minute precision of the treaty stipulations in the Hittite treaties, e.g., W 3, col. ii
(pp. 61ff.), or the stipulations concerning the 'evil word'; for the relevant passages, see
Korosec, *Hethitische Staatsverträge*, p. 78.

[34] .לַעֲבֹדַת בֵּית אֱלֹהֵינוּ

[35] The framework in Neh. 9:3 presupposes reading from the סֵפֶר תּוֹרַת יהוה.

[36] Once again order of precedence is observed precisely; cf. 10:29–30 (Eng. 10:28–29).

[37] W 1; W 2; see Korosec, *Hethitische Staatsverträge*, pp. 7–8.

[38] W 2, ro. 27ff.: 'I Mattiuaza . . . have spoken to the Great King, my lord: "I[f] you,
my lord, bring me to life . . ., but I will place myself under the command of his (i.e., the
Great King's; see Weidner, *Politische Dokumente*, p. 42, n. 4) 'bondage' and rule the land
of Mitanni. Šuttarna has acted in evil fashion against the lands, but I will do no additional wrong".'

recorded in detail.[39] Formally, Nehemiah 9–10 could correspond to such a second version from the point of view of the party to whom the covenant has been granted. This could explain the change in style in the formulary.

Like Exodus 34, Nehemiah 9–10 reports a *renewal* of the covenant. It is presupposed that Yahweh 'keeps the covenant and steadfast love' (9:32); Sinai is mentioned explicitly (9:13–14); the law was given law ago (9:13–14; 10:30 [Eng. 10:29]). But Israel has broken the covenant repeatedly.[40] Therefore the threatened curse has taken effect.[41] Only thanks to the gracious mercy of Israel's God has the curse not achieved its full effect, so that Israel is not yet completely extirpated (9:31). The only possibility for deliverance consists in turning back to Yahweh (9:26). He alone, the guarantor of the covenant, can lift the curse and re-institute the covenant. Thus what Exod. 34:9 only mentions briefly in passing is here depicted in detail. Seen from this perspective, the antecedent history in Nehemiah 9 becomes a list of Yahweh's saving acts, in which he has shown himself to be צַדִּיק (9:8; cf. 9:33), i.e., in this case, faithful to the covenant. The antecedent history is at the same time a confession of Israel's sins.[42] This confession also acknowledges the justice of the curse.[43]

[39] The curse formulas pronounced by the Great King are recorded in their entirety; see W 2, vo. 25ff. Cf. W 2, vo. 44ff.: 'If you, Mattiuaza, and (you) the people of Ḫarri . . . , then. . . .'
44: "If I, Mattiuaza, and (we) the people of Ḫarri do not keep the words of this treaty and the oath, [45] then I, Mattiuaza, together with the other consort, and we the people of Ḫarri, together with . . . .'

[40] See 'forgetting God's saving acts' (9:9, 17). Also involved are contempt for God's gift of the land (9:25, 35), refusal of service (9:35) and of loyalty (9:16–17, 26, 28, 29), and transgression of the commandments (9:29, 34).

[41] Israel has been defeated by the enemy (9:30; cf. Lev. 26:17, 25), subjected to foreign rule (9:37; cf. Lev. 26:25; Deut. 28:47–48), deprived of the yield of its own land (9:36–37; cf. Deut. 28:51). Cf. the list of curses in Weidner, 'Staatsvertrag,' p. 33.

[42] The nature of this section is best described by the instructions in 1QS i. 21–24 (see below, p. 190). In i. 24–ii. 1 there follows the formal confession of sins on the part of all 'who enter into the covenant.'

[43] Neh. 9:33, 37; cf. 1QS i. 26 (following the conjecture of Brownlee, *The Dead Sea Manual of Discipline* [New Haven, 1951], p. 9, n. 42).—The confession thus becomes what has been called a 'judgment doxology' (see F. Horst, 'Die Doxologien im Amosbuch,' *ZAW*, 49 [1927], pp. 45ff.).—'The guilty party did more than merely acknowledge the justice of his punishment by means of the judgment doxology; his confession also had a very real significance in the realm of sacral law, because it brought the proceedings to a close' (G. von Rad, 'Der Lobpreis Israels,' in *Antwort, Karl Barth zum 70. Geburtstag* [Zürich, 1956], p. 677).—The same holds true for Ezra 9:6–15; 10:10–11 (see below, p. 48) and Josh. 7:19–20 (see below, p. 58).—This emphasizes even more strongly the legal nature of the actions described.—Von Rad describes the tone of this confession as being 'remarkably ambivalent': 'In recognition of a judgment that has been justly pronounced, the person concerned confesses his transgression; and he clothes this statement in the guise of a confession glorifying God' (ibid., pp. 677ff.). Cf. also F 4 §4, 34–46, the submission of Manapa-datta after he has broken his treaty.

The prayer therefore concludes as a plea for help.[44]

Ezra 9–10

Ezra 9–10 gives us a similar picture of a covenant-renewal cere-mony.[45] The framework presupposes an assembly 'before the house of God.'[46] It is not quite clear whether this assembly comprises at first only the leaders (9:1; 10:5)[47] or includes a larger group from the outset (10:1).

[44] According to Noth, Nehemiah 9–10 is 'a composition written by the Chronicler' (*Überlieferungsgeschichtliche Studien*, p. 148; see also p. 160). This would make the section a purely literary production; but it would still be interesting to note that it presupposes acquaintance with the schema of a covenant renewal.—Galling (*Chronik*, pp. 293ff.), however, has put forward several arguments against this section's being a free com-position of the Chronicler (Galling's 'Chr.**'). In the penitential prayer 'the Mosaic period is central . . ., although elsewhere the Chronicler's History passes over this period in silence.' The penitential prayer 'makes no mention of mixed marriages.' The same holds true of Nehemiah 10, where 'the prohibition of future (*sic*!) mixed marriages appears *together with other* ordinances.' There is 'no complete correspondence between the document and the measures taken by Nehemiah as described in Nehemiah 13.'—Study of the literary type shows, in my opinion, that the formal and stylistic similarity to Ezra 9–10, together with Deuteronomy and the Deuteronomistic literature (see Rudolph, *Ezra*, p. 163), as well as other texts (Psalms, etc.), does not necessarily indicate direct literary dependence. The common element can be the original *Sitz im Leben*. I think it is possible that the Chronicler had before him the document of a covenant renewal. Our study has shown that account must be taken of the existence of such documents, since a written document formed a part of the covenant and therefore of the covenant renewal. The Chronicler, then, undoubtedly reworked such a document for his own purposes. At one point he expanded it (see Galling, *Chronik*, p. 243), but he also abbreviated it. Between chapters 9 and 10, the literary form leads us to expect some statement concerning the acceptance of penance, the mediation of assurance of forgiveness, and the restoration of the covenant by Yahweh (see below).

The Chronicler is also probably responsible for the placing of the section in its context. Originally there need have been no such connection. That the passage was taken from some 'memoirs of Ezra' (Noth, *Überlieferungsgeschichtliche Studien*, p. 148) seems improbable to me.—It is worth asking whether 'the twenty-fourth day of this month' (9:1) did not originally refer to the dates in chapter 8. This dating is somewhat difficult to understand (see Galling, *Chronik*, p. 235). There may also be a secondary point of connection in the statement: 'And the Israelites separated themselves from all foreigners' (9:2*a*). This sentence interrupts the continuity: '. . . the people of Israel were assembled with fasting and in sackcloth, and with earth upon their heads (. . .), and they stood and confessed their sins. . . .' (with parentheses indicating the position of the omission). This would be in line with Galling's observation that the question of mixed marriages does not occupy the foreground either in the penitential prayer Nehemiah 9 or in the acceptance of obligation.

[45] The order in which we have discussed the Nehemiah–Ezra texts is based only on practical considerations; it does not represent an opinion on the problem of their historical relationship, which we cannot examine here. On this question, see Galling, *Chronik*, Introduction; M. Noth, *History of Israel* (E.T., 2nd ed.; London, 1960), pp. 316ff., esp. pp. 318.

The unity of Ezra 9–10 is also disputed. Galling (*Chronik*, p. 212) thinks only 9:1–2; 10:2–6 represent an original report.—Rudolph (*Ezra*, p. 93 ad loc.) emphasizes that the connection is 'seamless,' but then proceeds with an interpretation that is too psychological.

[46] On לִפְנֵי בֵית הָאֱלֹהִים (10:1, 6), cf. לִפְנֵי הָאֱלֹהִים Josh. 24:1.

[47] Galling (*Chronik*, p. 211, n. 5) conjectures instead '*sarê jisrael*.' L. W. Batten (*Ezra*, p. 341) suggests: 'the leaders of the priests, Levites and of all Israel.'

The prayer in Nehemiah 9 has as its counterpart Ezra 9:6–15. The antecedent history, which was expanded greatly in Nehemiah 9, is here summarized: 'From the days of our fathers to this day we have been in great guilt' (v. 7). Only God's gracious action in the present is depicted in more detail.[48] As in Nehemiah 9, the antecedent history is seen from the viewpoint of the party to whom the covenant is granted. Here, however, the 'antecedent history' becomes even more clearly a 'confession of sins.' The present review of history shows that God's saving acts were called forth by Israel's guilt. The literary type is clearly still sufficiently vital that a new situation can lead to such a fundamental but meaningful transformation of the form. The prohibition of marriage with non-Israelites, which is crucial for the context, is expressly cited, together with the blessing promised if the command is obeyed (v. 12*b*). The connection between breaking of the covenant by transgression of the commandments on the one hand and curse and misfortune on the other is emphasized (vv. 7 and 13). God's judgment is acknowledged to be just (v. 15).[49] From Israel's perspective there is no longer any hope.

This penitential prayer of Ezra is followed by the confession of Israel in response, here spoken by Shechaniah, the son of Jehiel,[50] as Israel's representative: 'We have broken faith with our God and have married foreign women from the peoples of the lands . . .' (10:2). There is no similar response between Nehemiah 9 and 10. Ezra 10:3 corresponds to Neh. 10:1 (Eng. 9:38).[51] The content of the covenant is reproduced in a single sentence, whereas Nehemiah 10 cites detailed stipulations (v. 3). The people agree to put away their 'foreign' wives. Ezra 10:5 mentions an oath of obligation undertaken by the leaders. Ezra 10:7ff. records the assumption of this obligation by the entire community.

Daniel 9:4*b*–19

Dan. 9:4*b*–19 is a penitential prayer that gives clear indications of its association with the 'covenant.'[52] Its structure is less regular

---

[48] In vv. 8–9. For the important Greek variants, see Batten, *Ezra*, pp. 338–39.

[49] יהוה... צַדִּיק אַתָּה כִּי־נִשְׁאַרְנוּ פְלֵיטָה כְּהַיּוֹם הַזֶּה

[50] It is hard to define his position. Since he is authorized to speak for Israel, he must have had high status.

[51] וְעַתָּה   נִכְרָת־ בְּרִית לֵאלֹהֵינוּ   Ezra 10:3

וּבְכָל־זֹאת אֲנַחְנוּ כֹּרְתִים אֲמָנָה   Neh. 10:1

[52] In its present context, it represents a secondary addition; see A. Bentzen, *Daniel*, HAT (2nd ed., Tübingen, 1952), p. 75. Cf. also the similar penitential prayer in Neh. 1:4–11.

than that of Nehemiah 9, nor does it refer so concretely to a specific case as Ezra 9 does to the question of mixed marriages. A great variety of expressions, especially from among those found in the statements of substance, are used to describe the breach in the loyalty demanded by the covenant.[53]

Dan. 9:11 is especially illuminating. The text presupposes familiarity with the linking of 'law' and 'curse' in a covenant.[54] In the תּוֹרַת מֹשֶׁה the curse is written down (vv. 11 and 13).[55] Here we can see especially clearly that תּוֹרָה does not always mean merely 'laws.'[56]

It is difficult to describe the over-all course of a covenant renewal as well as the nature of the individual elements composing it. The reasons is that the texts we have been examining in their present context seek to record a unique, specific act.[57] It is difficult to determine in each case how much is universal, how much peculiar to the particular text. We would give much to know what the 'normal liturgy' of a covenant renewal looked like.

1QS i. 18–ii. 18 (The 'Manual of Discipline')

In this context is it appropriate to cite the liturgy for a covenant renewal that is contained in 1QS i. 18–ii. 18.[58] In its present form, the text is very late; but it may well go back to earlier prototypes.[59] It is remarkable how well the elements worked out so far in our study can be fit into the framework of this liturgy.[60]

---

[53] Dan. 9:5: 'We have sinned and done wrong and acted wickedly and rebelled, "turning aside" [see Bentzen ad loc.] from thy commandments and ordinances; [6] we have not listened to thy servants the prophets . . .' (cf. v. 9b).

[54]
וְכָל־יִשְׂרָאֵל עָבְרוּ אֶת־תּוֹרָתֶךָ   11
וְסוֹר לְבִלְתִּי שְׁמוֹעַ בְּקֹלֶךָ
וַתִּתַּךְ עָלֵינוּ הָאָלָה וְהַשְּׁבֻעָה
אֲשֶׁר כְּתוּבָה בְּתוֹרַת מֹשֶׁה עֶבֶד־הָאֱלֹהִים
כִּי חָטָאנוּ לוֹ׃ (לָךְ׃)

[55] כַּאֲשֶׁר כָּתוּב בְּתוֹרַת מֹשֶׁה אֵת כָּל־הָרָעָה הַזֹּאת בָּאָה עָלֵינוּ 13. Cf. the formula in W 3, vo. iv. 46–47: 'All the words of the treaty and of the oath which are written upon this tablet, [i]f Tette does not keep the words of the treaty and of the oath and trans[gr]esses the oa[th] . . .' (there follows a curse!).

[56] It is worth investigating to what extent תּוֹרָה can be synonymous with בְּרִית. See also von Rad, Gesammelte Studien, pp. 210–11.

[57] It is likewise impossible to discuss in each case the difficult question of the extent to which we are dealing with historical documents rather than stylized descriptions of the covenant renewal revised by later redactor to harmonize with their own conceptions.

[58] See also the translation of the entire text in part two, below, pp. 168–69.

[59] See also F. Baumgärtel, 'Zur Liturgie in der "Sektenrolle" vom Toten Meer,' ZAW, 65 (1953), pp. 263ff.

[60] See pp. 181ff., supplement to part one.

E

Our survey shows that the most important new element, which does not appear in the simple covenant formulary, is the interpolation of a confession of sins. Its nucleus is the statement 'God is צַדִּיק.'[61] This statement recognizes that Yahweh has acted in accordance with the covenant and is therefore justified in taking action as plaintiff against the other party, who has broken the covenant.[62] At this point we see the effect of the peculiar legal situation, in which Yahweh is both a party to the covenant and its guarantor. He is therefore also the only one that can delay the consequences of the curse brought on by the breaking of the oath.

The confession of sins turns into a prayer for forgiveness.[63] But what follows next? The texts do not furnish a unanimous and clear answer, and so we must resort to conjecture.

In Exod. 34:10, God speaks directly: 'I make a covenant.' This restores the state of שָׁלוֹם. We can see from Nehemiah 10 that the obligations of the covenant were once more accepted. According to Ezra 10, Israel states its willingness to accept the obligations in the hope that Yahweh will grant their request and put an end to the curse.[64] Yahweh's 'response' is therefore perceived in this case as the effective cessation of the disaster brought about by the curse.[65] It is therefore striking to observe that 1QS presents blessings and curses immediately after the confession of sins, without saying a word about forgiveness and renewal of the covenant. I am unable to explain this fact.

There is one final question to bring up: to what extent, at the renewal of the covenant, was assurance of forgiveness mediated in the form of specific cultic acts?[66] To pursue this question further would take us beyond the limits of this study.

[61] See Ezra 9:15; Neh. 9:33 (cf. vv. 8 and 32); Dan. 9:14 (cf. vv. 4 and 7); Deut. 32:4 (see also v. 5); 1QS i. 26 (see Brownlee, *Manual*, ad loc.).

[62] See K. Koch, *Sdq im Alten Testament*, Dissertation, Heidelberg, 1953.

[63] Hebrew סְלִיחָה; see Neh. 9:17; Dan. 9:9; cf. Exod. 34:9; Dan. 9:19; 1QS ii. 8.

[64] Ezra 10:2, 14.

[65] See Stamm, *Erlösen*, p. 127, with reference to Solomon's prayer at the dedication of the Temple: 'Forgiveness takes effect . . . in the suspension of hardship and punishment.'

[66] In Jer. 31:34, this assurance is given directly by Yahweh in the context of the new covenant: 'I will forgive their iniquity, and I will remember their sin no more.' According to Ezek. 36:25, at the renewal of the covenant (see vv. 27–28) Israel will be sprinkled with clean water to be made clean. This probably refers to a purification ceremony (see Stamm, *Erlösen*, p. 120). A similar association is probably presupposed in 1QS iii. 6–12, albeit here with reference to the individual that 'enters into the covenant.' Sacrifice provides another form in which assurance of forgiveness can take place. See Stamm, *Erlösen*, pp. 54–55, 128, and especially 129: even when the priest acts as mediator, Yahweh is the source of forgiveness!

The Occasions of the Covenant Renewal

Following our study of the form, we shall attempt to define more precisely the occasions on which such a covenant renewal might take place.

II Chronicles 29:5–11

According to II Chron. 29:5–11, Hezekiah declares his reasons for renewing the covenant in a programmatic address to the assembled Levites.[67]

> Hear me, you Levites! Now sanctify yourselves and sanctify the Temple of Yahweh, the God of your fathers, and remove the filth from the sanctuary.
> 6 For: our fathers have been unfaithful
> and have done what was evil in the eyes of Yahweh, our God,
> and have forsaken him.
> They turned away their faces from the habitation of Yahweh,
> and turned their backs to it.
> 7 Also: they have shut the doors of the vestibule,
> and have put out the lamps 'in the sanctuary,'
> and have not burned incense,
> and have not offered burnt offerings to the God of Israel.
> 8 Therefore the wrath of Yahweh came on Judah and Jerusalem, and he surrendered them   'to horror,'
>   'to astonishment,'
>   and 'to hissing,'
> as you can see with your eyes.
> 9 And behold: Our fathers have fallen by the sword,
> and our sons and our daughters and our wives
> are in captivity for this.
> 10 Now, however, I have decided *to make a covenant* with Yahweh, the God of Israel,
> *that the heat of his wrath may turn away from us!*

Verses 6–9 constitute a kind of antecedent history down to the present.[68] In v. 6, violation of the loyalty demanded by the covenant is stated in general terms.[69] This violation shows itself concretely in refusal to keep up the worship of the Temple (v. 7). In consequence, the curse became operative (vv. 8–9). Here, therefore, the occasion for the making of a covenant is the disaster brought about by the efficacy of the curse; its purpose[70] is to avert the complete destruction that is the ultimate goal of the curse.

---

[67] The translation follows that of Galling, *Chronik*, p. 154; the arrangement is the author's own.

[68] See עָתָּה (v. 10).

[69] 'Turning from Yahweh' means here 'turning from the habitation of Yahweh,' i.e., the Temple.

[70] See v. 10.

Now, however, we encounter a difficulty in our study: the Chronicler, 'in order to give his narrative vitality in its own right, supplemented the picture offered by his sources on the basis of the life and institutions of his own day.'[71]

Such an idealized view of the course of events has also no doubt put its stamp on the Chronicler's report of the covenant concluded by King Asa (II Chron. 14:8–15:15).[72] The occasion given here is the attack of Zerah the Ethiopian. The covenant ceremony takes place after the enemy has been defeated in a 'Holy War.' Since 'they had sworn with all their heart,' 'Yahweh gave them rest round about' (15:15).

II Kings 22–23

There are also texts, however, in which we are on historically secure ground and which also illustrate the same association between disaster and covenant ceremony.

This is true, first of all, of the covenant concluded under Josiah (II Kings 22–23). It appears certain that we must distinguish on literary grounds the report of the discovery of the סֵפֶר הַתּוֹרָה[73] from the covenant ceremony that follows[74] and the report of Josiah's 'politico-cultic measures.'[75]

The description of the actual covenant ceremony (23:1–3) exhibits scarcely any peculiarities. The list of participants is clearly interested in mentioning representatives of as much of the people as possible. The king acts as 'membrum praecipuum of the קְהַל יהוה.'[76] After the public recitation of כָּל־דִּבְרֵי סֵפֶר הַבְּרִית, i.e., both the stipulations and the curses,[77] the king concludes the covenant in the presence of Yahweh.[78] The rest of the people give their assent to the covenant.

The context shows, however, that this act was preceded by penance on the part of the king and a response from Yahweh.[79] Here, too, therefore, we can make out the sequence of a covenant renewal:

[71] Noth, Überlieferungsgeschichtliche Studien, p. 159.

[72] On II Chron. 15:2–7 as a typical Levitical sermon of a particular sort, see von Rad, 'Die levitische Predigt in den Büchern der Chronik,' in Festschrift O. Procksch zum 60. Geburtstag (Leipzig, 1934), pp. 116–17, now also in his Gesammelte Studien, pp. 251–52.

[73] The terms סֵפֶר הַתּוֹרָה (22:8, 11) and סֵפֶר הַבְּרִית (23:2) are used here as alternatives!

[74] II Kings 22:3–23:3, 21–23 + 9, 24, and 25(?); see Alt, Kleine Schriften, Vol. 2, p. 253, n. 1.

[75] II Kings 23:4–8, 10–15, 19–20; ibid., p. 256, n. 1.

[76] Noth, Gesetze, p. 38; now in Laws, p. 46.

assurance that Yahweh will accept the repentance of Israel is followed by the making of a new covenant, or, more precisely, by the reaffirmation of the covenant.[80] The סֵפֶר הַבְּרִית (23:2) that has just been discovered provides the basis for the covenant.

If, however, we are dealing with a covenant renewal, we may inquire what the basis for this action was. At first glance, according to the Deuteronomistic History, the occasion seems to have been the chance discovery of the סֵפֶר הַבְּרִית while the Temple was being renovated. But the text before us suggests an even deeper reason. It is not made quite clear whether the 'wrath of God' has already flared up or is only threatened. II Kings 22:13 uses the perfect, suggesting that God's wrath is already kindled and the curse has become operative. Verse 17 is usually translated as a future: 'Therefore my wrath will be kindled against this place . . .'[81] or as a jussive: 'My wrath . . . shall be kindled.'[82] The tense used will also determine the translation of the particle מֵבִיא רָעָה in v. 16. But the sentence can also be translated as a perfect: 'Behold, I am in the process of bringing evil upon this place . . ., my wrath is kindled and it will not

---

[77] See 22:16–17 (cf. v. 19)   הִנְנִי מֵב י א רָעָה אֶל־הַמָּקוֹם הַזֶּה ... 16

וְעַל־יֹשְׁבָיו אֵת כָּל־דִּבְרֵי הַסֵּפֶר אֲשֶׁר קָרָא מֶלֶךְ יְהוּדָה:

Cf. II Chron. 34:24   הִנְנִי מֵבִיא רָעָה עַל־הַמָּקוֹם הַזֶּה ... 24

וְעַל־יוֹשְׁבָיו אֵת כָּל־הָאָלוֹת הַכְּתוּבוֹת עַל־הַסֵּפֶר

אֲשֶׁר קָראוּ לִפְנֵי מֶלֶךְ יְהוּדָה:

[78] The basic relationship to Yahweh is defined by infinitives:

לָלֶכֶת אַחַר יהוה   23:3

וְלִשְׁמֹר מִצְוֹתָיו וְאֶת־עֵדְוֹתָיו וְאֶת־חֻקֹּתָיו

בְּכָל־לֵב וּבְכָל־נֶפֶשׁ

לְהָקִים אֶת־דִּבְרֵי הַבְּרִית הַזֹּאת הַכְּתֻבִים עַל־הַסֵּפֶר הַזֶּה

The stipulations show that we are dealing with a covenant with Yahweh, although it is concluded 'before Yahweh' (23:3; cf. Josh. 24:1; Deut. 29:9–11 [Eng. 29:10–12]).
[79] Cf. 22:18–20. On the king's weeping in the presence of Yahweh, cf. Ezra 10:1; Dan. 9:20.

---

[80] Here 'הֵקִים' has the meaning 'confirm'; cf. Lev. 26:9; Deut. 8:18; Ezek. 16:60, 62 (Jer. 34:18, cf. 34:13?). See W 9, ro. 9–10: '[ṭ]up-pa . . . ú-ga-al-lu.' Weidner, *Politische Dokumente*, p. 126, n. 1, derives this word from *kâlu*, 'preserve, maintain' ('. . . . they preserved the [t]ablet of my grandfather').

[81] See, for example, A. Šanda, *Die Bücher der Könige* (Münster, 1911–12), v. 2, p. 327; Luther; *Die Zürcher Bibel*. If so, then וְנִצְּתָה is to be taken as a *perf. cons.*

[82] R. Kittel, *Die Bücher der Könige*, HAT (Göttingen, 1900); O. Eißfeldt in E. Kautzsch, *Die Heilige Schrift des Alten Testaments* (4th ed., Tübingen, 1922–23).

be quenched.' This translation would not present an unusual sequence of tenses.[83]

If our assumption is correct, the point is basically that the newly-discovered 'book of the covenant,' with the curses it threatens in case the covenant is broken, provides the explanation for what would otherwise be inexplicable disaster.[84]

Jeremiah 34:8–22

The historical occasion of Zedekiah's covenant can also be determined from Jer. 34:8–22.[85] According to this text, Jerusalem was being besieged by the army of Nebuchadnezzar. In this situation, King Zedekiah decided 'to make a covenant' (34:8). The narrator is concerned in his presentation to reinstitute a disregarded stipulation of the covenant made by Yahweh at the Exodus from Egypt (vv. 13–14).

Duhm,[86] Rudolph,[87] and Weiser[88] stress the civil nature of this covenant. According to vv. 13–14, however, the individual stipulations concerning the release of slaves form a part of the covenant with Yahweh. The same holds true for the stipulations in Deut. 15:1ff.

---

[83] Cf. Gesenius, *Grammar*, §116x; but see Montgomery, *The Book of Kings*, ed. H. S. Gehmann (Edinburgh, 1951), p. 527 on וְנִצְּתָה, which he calls 'irregular consecution'.

ᴳ translates (4 Kingdoms 22:17): Καὶ ἐκκαυθήσεται ὁ θυμός μου . . . καὶ οὐ σβεσθήσεται.' In the parallel passage, Kittel's BH reads חָתַּ֣ךְ וְתִתַּ֣ךְ. In the apparatus, Begrich suggests reading וְנִצְּתָה, following ᴳ and II Kings 22:17. But in II Paralip. 34:25, ᴳ has 'καὶ ἐξεκαύθη ὁ θυμός μου . . . καὶ οὐ σβεσθήσεται,' i.e., an aorist!

W. Nowack, *Die Bücher der Chronik und Esra, Nehemia und Esther*, HAT (Göttingen, 1902), p. 174, says with regard to v. 25: '"Has poured forth and shall not be quenched" is not a contradiction. Read thus therefore instead of וַתִּתַּךְ, following v. 17 in Kings. . . .' Roth-stein's translation in Kautzsch, *Heilige Schrift*, v. 2, also presupposes וַתִּתַּךְ. See also the Jewish Bible published by Meir Halevi Letteris, Vienna, 1885.

The text is therefore obviously ambiguous and admits of both translations.

[84] Cf. also the concluding statement in 23:26.

On the connection between disaster and the discovery of the סֵפֶר, cf. the prayers offered by Muršiliš during a plague (Pritchard, *ANET*, pp. 394–95): '[3] . . . Matters again got too much for me. So I made the anger of the gods the subject of an oracle. I learnt of two ancient tablets. The first tablet dealt with the offerings to the river Mala.' (The offerings were no longer being presented.)

'[4] The second tablet concerned Kurustama. . . .' (This refers to a treaty with Egypt, which had been broken by Muršiliš' father (!). Muršiliš is afraid the plague may be a consequence of the breaking of this treaty. He therefore ordered that search be made for the treaty document:)

'[5] Now, when I found that tablet dealing with the country of Egypt, I made the matter the subject of an oracle of the god (and asked): ". . . that the Hattians promptly broke their word—has this perhaps become the cause of the anger of the Hattian Storm-god, my lord?" And so it was established. . . .' (See also the continuation, especially 8–9.)

—'[11] See! I am praying to thee Hattian Storm-god, my lord. So save my life! If indeed

and Exod. 21:2ff., though in the latter passage only if it was already in its present framework.[89] בְּרִיתִי, 'my covenant' (v. 18), suggests also that we are dealing with a Yahweh covenant. According to Duhm, 'the "covenant" was presumably a covenant "before Yahweh" and with Yahweh (18).'[90] Duhm considers this observation proof that 'the midrashist was engaging in theological fantasy.'[91] I think it is worth considering whether the king is not here acting as *membrum praecipuum* in making the covenant. If so, the אֶת־ in v. 8 would mean 'together with. . . .'[92] The following לְהֶם would then also make sense.[93]—Does the king have no slaves whom he must release? On the basis of his presuppositions, Rudolph finds the guilt of the king and his officials in 'the disgraceful breach of faith, which, if they did not promote, they also did nothing to prevent.'[94]

The ceremony described in vv. 18–19 corresponds to the sanctions contained in the covenant.[95] Here the people swear to keep the דִּבְרֵי הַבְּרִית (v. 18). The context shows that the 'words to be enforced (again)'[96] are the stipulations of v. 14. The making of the covenant

it is for those reasons which I have mentioned that people are dying—as soon as I set them right, let those that are still able to give sacrificial loaves and libations die no longer! If, on the other hand, people are dying for some other reason, either let me see it in a dream, or let it be found out by an oracle, or let a prophet declare it, or let all the priests find out by incubation whatever I suggest to them. . . .'

[85] Rudolph, *Jeremia*, 'Einleitung,' p. xvi; pp. 203–204 places this section among the 'discourses of Jeremiah in Deuteronomic redaction (Mowinckel's source C).' According to Eißfeldt, *The Old Testament, an Introduction* (E.T., New York, 1965), p. 354, it forms a part of Baruch's narrative, which coincides with Mowinckel's source B (p. 355). The historicity of Zedekiah's covenant is undisputed.

[86] B. Duhm, *Das Buch Jeremia*, KHAT (Tübingen, 1901), p. 280.

[87] *Jeremia*, p. 205.

[88] A. Weiser, *Das Buch des Propheten Jeremia. Kap. 25, 15–52, 34* ATD (Göttingen, 1955), p. 320.

[89] For evidence that these legal stipulations are referred to, see Weiser, *Jeremia*, p. 321, n. 2, following Rowley, *Studies in Old Testament Prophecy* (Edinburgh, 1950), pp. 169–70. The argument to the contrary may be found in Rudolph.

[90] B. Duhm, *Jeremia*, p. 282.

[91] Ibid., p. 283. On the 'Yahweh covenant before Yahweh,' cf. Josh. 24:1; Deut. 29:9–11 (Eng. 29:10–12); II King 23:3.

[92] Ibid., on v. 20: 'Zedekiah and his people had no need to form a compact once more.'

[93] Duhm omits the word, following 𝔊; Volz interprets it as referring to the 'plural implied in הָעָם'; Weiser does not translate it; Rudolph's translation admits both possibilities for interpretation. Vv. 19–20 show that elsewhere, too, this text holds to the structure of rank.

[94] Rudolph, *Jeremia*, p. 206.

[95] For a discussion of the significance of this ceremony, see Quell, 'διαθήκη,' p. 118.

[96] See above, p. 53, n. 80 on הֵקִים. The large-scale excisions suggested by Volz,

ad loc., I consider unnecessary.

involves here both the conditions of the covenant and its ratification by oath.

The purpose of the entire action becomes clear the moment its occasion is removed. When the siege is lifted, the release of the slaves is revoked. Was the siege looked upon as the curse following the breaking of the covenant, and did the people have an especially guilty conscience with the regard to the commandment to release the slaves? In any event, the prophetical saying in vv. 17–18[97] draws this conclusion: disregard for the renewed obligation is followed by the curse of 'sword, pestilence, and famine. . . .' We are surely dealing with the making of a covenant in a desperate situation.

The futility of such a covenant ceremony when used as a means of 'psychological warfare' is shown by the prophet's message.

We must not assume, however, that a covenant renewal took place *every* time the situation became desperate. The following discussion will attempt to explain when a covenant renewal was necessary.

It was common practice to hold a 'fast' in Israel in cases of general disaster, such as war, captivity, pestilence, drought, famine, scanty harvest,[98] or a plague of locusts.[99] Prayers form the nucleus of this 'observance'; the 'communal laments' in the Psalter give us an idea what they were like.[100] Most of these laments, however, are far from presupposing that the covenant has ceased to be in force, and must therefore be renewed. Ps. 44:18–19 (Eng. 44:17–18) states expressly: 'We have not forgotten thee, or been false to thy covenant. . . .' Yahweh will help because Israel is his people (Pss. 74, 83, 115, *et al.*).—This declaration is completely out of place at a covenant renewal,[101] which presupposes the confession 'We have sinned' and the admission 'Yahweh is righteous.'[102]

In contrast to these laments, there is a group of texts that Gunkel describes as 'communal laments' or elements of communal laments which do contain a confession of sin.[103] It is striking that we find here for the most part texts that, as we have already seen, stand in the context of a covenant renewal.

---

[97] Cf. v. 21: הָעָלִים מֵעֲלֵיכֶם (see Rudolph, *Jeremia*, ad loc.); cf. also v. 22: וַהֲשִׁבֹתִים.

[98] See Hos. 7:14.

[99] See Joel 1 and 2.

[100] See H. Gunkel, *Einleitung in die Psalmen*, HKAT (Göttingen, 1933), pp. 117ff.

[101] 'It is all the more striking that most of the communal laments preserved in the Psalter contain no hint of sorrow and penitence' (ibid., p. 132).

The actual troubles that are lamented, however, do not differ from those in the other laments. In my opinion, though, the cause of the trouble is seen differently in the two groups of texts. In the first case, the trouble is a disaster that has overtaken Yahweh's people, against which he is called upon to help them. In other words, the covenant is intact.

In the second case, the trouble is the curse that falls upon Israel because Israel has broken the covenant with Yahweh. A disaster passes; during it hope remains. The curse achieves its purpose only in complete destruction, should Israel not repent and Yahweh renew his covenant.[104]

That such a distinction was in fact drawn is shown, for example, by the differing estimations of a similar situation.

According to II Kings 18–19,[105] the army of Sennacherib stands before Jerusalem. Hezekiah enters the Temple with all the signs of mourning (19:1). At the same time, he sends for Isaiah, who gives an oracle promising Yahweh's aid (19:6–7). At the repeated demand for surrender, Hezekiah goes into the Temple once more, describes the emergency—spreading Sennacherib's letter before Yahweh (v. 14)—, and prays for deliverance. Isaiah once more promises that the city will be saved (vv. 21–34). Sennacherib's successes are signs of his arrogance; they have come about as a kind of concession from Yahweh.[106] In the end, however, Sennacherib will not prevail, because Yahweh stands ready to help Jerusalem.—Of sin on the part of Hezekiah and of a curse there is no mention in this context!

In contrast, Jeremiah is forced again and again to proclaim the complete effectiveness of the curse, as a consequence of the breach of the covenant.[107] When Zedekiah makes inquiry during the threat

---

[102] Ps. 89:39–52 (Eng. 89:38–51) represents the contrary extreme.

[103] Pss. 79 (see v. 8; the consequences of the curse are depicted in vv. 1–4); 90:13–16 (cf. v. 8); 106 (see v. 6); Isa. 59:9–15b; 63:11–64:11; (Jer. 14:2–6, 7–9, 19–22); Hos. 14:2–3; Mic. 7:7–10, 14–17; Lam. 1:8, 5, 18; 4:6; 5:7; see also Josh. 7:7–9; Exod. 32:11–13; Deut. 9:25–29; 32:17–25; Ezra 9:6–15; Neh. 1:5–11; 9:6–37; Dan. 9:4–19.

[104] See H. W. Wolff, 'Das Thema "Umkehr" in der atl. Prophetie,' *ZThK*, 48 (1951), pp. 129–30: 'Now the first appearance of our theme in the prophetical literature shows in fact that its interest does not lie in establishing a contrast to the previous point of view, nor in emphasis on the new point of view, but in the restoration of an original status' (p. 134).

[105] For parallels, see Isa. 36–39, II Chron. 32. On the text and the historical problems, see Montgomery, *Kings*, pp. 513ff.

[106] See 19:25–26.

[107] For example, Jer. 3:4–5; 5:12–13, 19, 25; 9:12ff.; 11:11; 16:10–11; 22:8–9; 30:15.

from Nebuchadnezzar, Jeremiah can promise no miracle[108] (Jer. 21:1–7).

The differing interpretations of disaster are based on more than the divergent attitudes of the two great prophets. The true situation is shown by a text that comprises both possibilities.

According to Josh. 7:2–5,[109] Israel suffers an inexplicable defeat in the battle against Ai. Joshua and the elders thereupon assume all the tokens of mourning and prostrate themselves before the ark. Joshua pronounces a prayer, which, although in prose, is equivalent in content to a communal lament.[110] The prayer invokes Yahweh (v. 7), describes the trouble (v. 8), and recounts the 'reasons why God should intervene' (v. 9).[111]

The disaster is looked upon as a consequence of the enemies' power; their arrogance now threatens to dishonor the very name of Yahweh himself. This prayer would belong to the first, more extensive group of laments, viz., those that do not contain any confession of sin.—Yahweh's response represents a completely different point of view (vss. 10–11): "Israel has sinned!" The defeat is a consequence of transgressing the covenant—more concretely, of refusing to devote everything captured to Yahweh.[112] Joshua's prayer of lament was therefore misplaced.

In this case, the ultimate reason for the disaster that overtook all Israel was the sin of an individual. The only possibility for deliverance was for Israel to remove the guilty party from its midst.[113] After this had taken place, 'Yahweh turned from his burning anger.'[114] Then the Israelites succeed in taking Ai.

It is interesting to note that in the present textual context, which is the product of redaction, there follows in 8:30–35[115] a new ratification of the covenant.[116]

The three examples cited have this in common: Yahweh himself

----

[108] Jer. 21:1–7; cf. in chapter 28 the saying of the 'false prophet,' who announces the breaking of the yoke of the King of Babylon within two years. If so, the trouble would not have been a curse! Cf. 6:10; 14:13. See von Rad, 'Die falschen Propheten,' *ZAW*, 55 (1933), pp. 109ff.: 'It would probably not be difficult to demonstrate that the optimistic doctrine of those false prophets was intimately connected with a markedly positive covenant theology. . . .' (p. 117).

[109] The superscription in v. 1 anticipates the result. According to Noth, *Josua*, pp. 43 and 45, Josh, 7:1–8:29 is a single literary unit and definitely an early text.

[110] See Gunkel, *Psalmen*, p. 117.

[111] Ibid., p. 130.

[112] See also v. 15.

[113] In this case, Achan must pronounce the תּוֹדָה (vv. 19–20); see Horst, 'Doxologien,' pp. 45ff.; cf. above p. 46.

[114] V. 26: וַיָּשָׁב יהוה מֵחֲרוֹן אַפּוֹ.

gives the decision whether trouble is merely transitory or a curse has taken effect, i.e., whether the covenant has been broken. In the passage from Joshua this takes place directly; in the other two cases the decision is given through the mouth of the prophets.[117]

This allows us to give a preliminary answer to the question of when the covenant was renewed in Israel: the covenant had to be renewed whenever it was broken. Israel learned that the covenant had been broken when the שָׁלוֹם associated with the covenant ceased, but also definitively through Yahweh's statement.

When Israel's sin put an end to the state of שָׁלוֹם, there were certain consequences for Israel. These are best illustrated by the list in I Kings 8:33–40, part of Solomon's prayer at the dedication of the Temple:

Defeat before the enemy

Drought

Famine

Pestilence

Blight (on the grain, when the east wind comes too early)[118]

---

[115] There is general agreement that the text has been subjected to Deuteronomistic revision (Greßmann, Steuernagel, Noth, Alt). Since we are dealing here with the building of an altar outside of Jerusalem, Noth suggests (*Josua*, pp. 51–52) that the content represents fragments of a pre-Deuteronomistic historical tradition. There is no need to assume, with Greßmann and Steuernagel, that there has been borrowing from Joshua 24. The similarities are due to the nature of the covenant. On v. 34, הַבְּרָכָה וַהַקְּלָלָה, Steuernagel writes: 'Hardly appropriate to describe the content of the תּוֹרָה, because it refers only to the conclusion of the law; probably an addition, the more so because v. 35 emphasizes that the entire law was recited. This means that v. 33 must also be eliminated.' But stipulations, blessings, and curses together constitute the entire 'covenant,' so that סֵפֶר הַתּוֹרָה here also stand as a synonym of סֵפֶר הַבְּרִית (cf. II Kings 22:8, 11; 32:2) (see above, p. 49, n. 56). Cf. the invariable concluding formula of the Hittite treaties: 'All the words of the treaty and of the oath which are written upon this tablet. . . .' (W 3, vo. iv. 53–54; W 4, vo. 12–13; F 1 §20, iv. 21–22; and elsewhere.)

[116] Cf. also the train of events in II Chron. 14:8–15:15 (Eng. 14:9–15:15).

---

[117] On this point see also E. Würthwein, 'Der Ursprung der prophetischen Gerichtsrede,' *ZThK*, 49 (1952), pp. 1ff. Cf. the reply of F. Hesse, 'Wurzelt die prophetische Gerichtsrede im israelitischen Kult?' *ZAW*, 65 (1953), pp. 45–53. Hesse asks, 'And now are we to assume that the indictment of Israel was also rooted in the cult, in other words, formed a regular part of the Israelite "liturgy"?' (p. 52). To speak of a 'regular part' seems to me erroneous. The prophet speaks in answer to a pressing need. The listing of various possibilities for discovering the cause of a disaster in the prayer of Muršiliš during pestilence should warn us not to make our inquiry too narrow in this context. (See Pritchard, *ANET*, p. 396 a 11: '. . . either let me see it in a dream, or let it be found out by an oracle, or let a prophet declare it, or let all the priests find out by incubation whatever I suggest to them. . . .' See also ibid., text b, 16ff. Cf. I Sam. 28:6: 'And when Saul inquired of Yahweh, Yahweh did not answer him, either by dreams, or by Urim, or by prophets.')

[118] See Koehler, *Lexicon*, p. 950, on שְׁדֵפָה.

Mildew
Locusts
Caterpillars
Siege
Plague
Sickness

But since these plagues are traced back to sins,[119] they are recognized to be consequences of the curse. It is therefore not surprising that we find in this context a number of terms that we have already discovered to be associated with the covenant renewal.[120] The termination of the curse makes it possible to live in the land that Yahweh has given to his people as an inheritance,[121] i.e., restoration of the covenant.[122]

The plagues mentioned are all more or less sudden events. A disaster of long duration, which was probably not yet past at the time its description was appended, is mentioned in vv. 46–50: exile. Even the Exile is not a mere blow of fate, but the consequence of sin (v. 46)! Even in exile, however, there is still a chance for Israel to confess its sins (v. 47) and turn to Yahweh. It is moving to see, in the place where normally the prayer that Israel may dwell in its own promised land would stand, the prayer—here, too, first for forgiveness, and then—that they may find 'compassion in the sight of those who carried them captive.'

The Date of the Covenant Renewal

The text I Kings 8:33ff. takes us further in our inquiry into when a covenant renewal in the form described took place in Israel. On the one hand, the Exile is placed on a level with the other plagues; on the other hand, it is set apart by its duration. The continuation of the Exile means that the curse has not yet been completely lifted, even though the people have prayed. This suggests that, with the Exile, a transformation took place in the conception of when a covenant renewal should take place. Sudden 'plagues' had always been the occasions for covenant renewal. We should therefore not assume

---

[119] V. 33: ... אֲשֶׁר; 35: ... כִּי.

[120] שׁוּב vv. 33, 35; ידה 33, 35; סחל לְחַטָּאה 36, 34, 39.

[121] Vv. 34, 36b, 40.

[122] Cf. also v. 40: לְמַעַן יְרָאוּךְ.

that, before the Exile, renewal of the broken covenant formed an essential part of one of the regular festivals.

In Nehemiah 9–10, according to the present superscription (9:1), the covenant was concluded on the twenty-fourth day of the seventh month, in other words, in the general context of the Feast of Booths, but nevertheless distinctly separate. The measures taken by Ezra (Ezra 9–10) occupy a considerable period of time. The beginning comes $1 + 3$ days before the twentieth day of the ninth month[123] (10:9); in addition, the description mentions the twentieth day of the ninth month for the assembly of the people, the first day of the tenth month (10:16), and the next first day of the first month (10:17) as the conclusion.

King Asa makes a covenant in the third month of the fifteenth year of his reign (II Chron. 15:10). According to E. Kutsch, 'this can only refer to the Feast of Weeks.'[124] Kutsch shows clearly that the Feast of Weeks cannot be dated precisely, and that this explains the rather vague dating 'in the third month.' But the alternatives are not those Kutsch proposes (Feast of Booths or Feast of Weeks), but rather festival or a date freely chosen.

The measures taken by Hezekiah (according to II Chronicles 29) in the context of the covenant renewal (see v. 10) take place in the first month of his first regnal year. On account of his action, the Feast of Passover must be transferred, taking place exceptionally on the fourteenth day of the second month (30:15).

According to II Kings 23, the 'discovery of the law' and the making of the covenant take place before Passover (see vv. 21ff.), but both in the eighteenth year of Josiah.[125]

The recorded dates likewise argue against a specific time for the covenant renewal.

It is impossible in this context to trace the evidence from the Exile on. In my opinion, the inquiry concerning fasting in Zech. 7:1ff.; 8:18–19 furnishes the first key, for we read there of regular 'mourning and fasting' that has taken place for many years (7:3). This takes place, according to Zech. 8:19, in the fourth month (on the ninth day of the month, in memory of the capture of Jerusalem; see

---

[123] See Rudolph, *Esra*, ad loc., pp. 84, 94–95.

[124] E. Kutsch, *Das Herbstfest in Israel*, Dissertation, Mainz, 1955, p. 153, n. 53.

[125] According to Alt, *Kleine Schriften*, vol. 2, p. 256, n. 1, the two events and the two dates belong together.

$\mathfrak{G}^{B1'}$ adds to the eighteenth year the more precise statement 'in the eighth month.' According to $\mathfrak{G}^A$, it is the seventh month. See *BH* on 22:3; cf. 23:23.

Jer. 39:2), in the fifth month (on the seventh day of the month, the day the Temple was destroyed; see II Kings 25:8ff.), in the seventh month (—?,[126] in memory of the murder of Gedaliah and the end of the remainder of the people in the land; see Jer. 41:1), and in the tenth month (—?, in memory of the beginning of the siege of Jerusalem; see Jer. 39:1).[127] We may note once more the association with specific historical dates.

The content of the 'fasting sermon' in 7:4–14; 8:1–17, whether it derives from Zechariah himself or is a secondary composition, is a clear exposition of the meaning of covenant renewal. We find the antecedent history, typified by Israel's sin (7:7–14). In contrast to 'I gave you the land,' we here find at the conclusion 'the pleasant land was made desolate' (7:14), i.e., Israel brought the curse upon the land. Series of commandments are contained in 7:8–10; 8:16–17, 19b. Finally, blessings are promised in various forms (8:3–15, 20–23).

The crucial statement, however, occurs in 8:8: 'They shall (once again!)[128] be my people and I will be their God, in faithfulness and in righteousness.'—The fasting will be turned to feasting (8:19), but for Zechariah this still lies in the future.

This point of view, it seems to me, also helps understand 1QS i–ii, with its stipulation that the covenant shall be renewed with repentance each year 'as long as the time of Belial's dominion lasts.'[129]

This is the hope that looks to the future of the new covenant, of which Jeremiah says that iniquity will be forgiven and sin will no more be remembered' (31:34)! This covenant does not need to be renewed.

---

[126] If the Samaritan pilgrims really made a pilgrimage to Jerusalem for the Autumn Festival (Jer. 41:4ff.), the date of Gedaliah's death fell before the festival. This is the opinion of Duhm, Rudolph, and Weiser; Volz thinks otherwise. According to Volz (*Der Prophet Jeremia*, KAT, Leipzig, 1922, p. 350), the Autumn Festival was not yet precisely fixed and began at the beginning of the month. According to the Jewish calendar, Gedaliah was killed on 4 Tishri.

[127] On the dates, see F. Horst, *Die 12 Kleinen Propheten, Nahum bis Maleachi*, HAT (2nd ed., Tübingen, 1954), pp. 239, 245.

[128] Author's addition.

[129] 1QS ii. 19.

THE COVENANT FORMULARY AT THE RATIFICATION OF THE COVENANT

The explanation that in Israel a renewal of the covenant was undertaken when the covenant had been abrogated through the sin of Israel does not, however, account for a rather sizable group of texts within the OT which record a covenant renewal in greater or lesser detail.

Joshua 23

Joshua 23 is an example. The Deuteronomistic text shows clearly that it is not to be understood as recounting the original making of a covenant. It refers expressly to what is written in the סֵפֶר תּוֹרַת מֹשֶׁה (v. 6). Although we may be unable to state precisely what is meant by this phrase, the mention of Moses certainly presupposes that the 'Torah' has already been given in the context of a covenant ceremony, whether at Sinai or, possibly, as Deuteronomy suggests, before the crossing of the Jordan. In vv. 15–16, too, the covenant is not being concluded for the first time.—The promised blessing of 'peace in the land,' one of the most important parts of the Yahweh covenant, is recognized as a reality.

Nevertheless, Joshua 23 contains the solemn acceptance of an obligation by all Israel, and gives clear evidence of the covenant formulary in its structure. Scholars have therefore often suggested that Joshua 24 was the direct literary model for Joshua 23.[1] The common elements, however, are due in part to identity of literary type. In addition, there are important differences between the two chapters.

The *antecedent history* is found in Josh. 23:3–4(5). It is not composed, as in Joshua 24, as first-person speech of God, but as the speech of Joshua. It has been condensed into a brief statement: 'You have seen all that Yahweh your God has done to all these nations' (v. 3). The antecedent history remains, however, evidence of Yahweh's saving

---

[1] See Noth, *Überlieferungsgeschichtliche Studien*, vol. 1, p. 9, n. 1: 'I previously shared the generally accepted opinion that Joshua 23 was composed by the Deuteronomist after the model of Joshua 24; the basis for this view is in fact very weak. . . .' Cf. *idem*, *Josua*, pp. 10, 16; see also E. Janssen, *Juda in der Exilszeit*, FRLANT (Göttingen, 1956), p. 107.

acts 'for you' (לָכֶם [v. 3]). Verse 4 concludes with a mention of the distribution of the land to the tribes and a summary statement concerning the extent of the territory, which reaches from the Jordan to the 'Great Sea.'[2]

The *statement of substance* is introduced by: לְשְׁמֹר ... וַחֲזַקְתֶּם מְאֹד (v. 6). The essential relationship is here defined more precisely by a series of four prohibitions, each introduced by לֹא.[3] Verse 8 summarizes these prohibitions positively:

כִּי אִם־בַּיהוה אֱלֹהֵיכֶם תִּדְבָּקוּ (כַּאֲשֶׁר עֲשִׂיתֶם עַד הַיּוֹם הַזֶּה:)

No additional commandments are cited. Parallel to חֹק וּמִשְׁפָּט in 24:25, they are probably implied in v. 6:

לַעֲשׂוֹת אֶת כָּל־הַכָּתוּב בְּסֵפֶר תּוֹרַת מֹשֶׁה.

In vv. 9 and 10, what was originally a *blessing* has been transformed into a statement.[4] Thus the invocation of Yahweh becomes a confession: כִּי יהוה אֱלֹהֵיכֶם הוּא הַנִּלְחָם לָכֶם (v. 10). Before the *curse*, parallel to v. 6, v. 11 states the relationship to Yahweh once more in positive form: 'Take good heed to yourselves, therefore, to love Yahweh your God.' The introductory phrase ... וְנִשְׁמַרְתֶּם מְאֹד לְנַפְשֹׁתֵיכֶם in v. 11 corresponds to לְשְׁמֹר ... וַחֲזַקְתֶּם מְאֹד in v. 6. The substance of the curse is: 'You [shall] perish from off this good land' (v. 13; see v. 15).[5] The 'nations' will carry out the curse.

Up to this point it is easy to trace the covenant formulary. Now, however, it is located in a strange framework. Joshua's speech begins, not in v. 3, but in v. 2, with the statement 'I am now old and well

---

[2] On the omission of vv. 5 and 13a, see Noth, *Josua*, p. 133 ad loc.

[3]
7 וּבְשֵׁם אֱלֹהֵיהֶם לֹא־תַזְכִּירוּ

וְלֹא תַשְׁבִּיעוּ

וְלֹא תַעַבְדוּם

וְלֹא תִשְׁתַּחֲווּ לָהֶם

Here, too, therefore the prohibition of idolatry is among the basic stipulations. Intercourse with foreigners is once again forbidden in the same breath as the worship of foreign gods (v. 7a; cf. v. 11).

[4] For the same content in the form of a blessing, cf. Lev. 26:7–8; see also Deut. 7:24; 28:7.

[5] Cf. F 5 §21, iv. 31ff.: 'If you . . . now brea[k] these words of the document . . ., thi[s oath] shall destroy you together with your person . . ., and shall cause your seed to perish from the black earth.' According to Steuernagel, *Das Buch Josua*, HKAT (2nd ed., Göttingen, 1923), p. 296 ad loc., the use of אֲדָמָה (vv. 13, 15) in this connection is unusual. V. 16b has הָאָרֶץ! Originally, there need not have been any thought of an exile in vv. 13 and 15.

advanced in years.' And v. 14 clearly marks a new beginning, with 'And now I. . . .' In the passage that follows, Joshua announces his death, bears witness that the promised blessing has come to pass, and once more threatens the curse if the covenant is broken.[6] But what does his personal fate have to do with the covenant between Yahweh and Israel?

In Josh. 24:29, the death of Joshua is reported in an appended note. This determines at least roughly the date of the covenant ceremony described.[7] It is impossible to tell, however, whether there is any intrinsic connection between the two events. According to 24:1, Israel stands 'before God.' There is no such statement in chapter 23. It would be more correct to say that in Joshua 23 Israel stands before Joshua.—In Joshua 24, the covenant formula has the character of a liturgy; in Joshua 23, it has been completely incorporated into a sermon by Joshua. With its specific reference to the death of Joshua, however, this sermon takes on the character of a farewell discourse, Joshua's testament.

Now Joshua 23 is not the only instance of such a farewell discourse. Deuteronomy as a whole, whose intimate association with the 'covenant' we have observed, is turned by its framework into the farewell discourse of Moses. Finally, the 'testament' is a common literary form in post-biblical Jewish texts.[8] In it a great figure from Israel's past 'preaches' to his descendants in a manner similar to that of Joshua.

How does this intimate association between 'covenant' and death come about? Is it merely a literary fiction, designed to lend 'binding force to the teachings and exhortations of such a man,'[9] or was there originally an intrinsic connection, based on the *Sitz im Leben*, a connection that can still be recognized in the later literary elaboration?

In order to answer this question as fully as possible, we must back up a bit. We shall begin with a text that also contains a 'farewell discourse,' but in which reference to the death of the person speaking does not play a direct part.

---

[6] It is noteworthy that this passage does not present blessing and curse as two concurrent possibilities, but as coming in a temporal sequence.

[7] Probably the nucleus of Joshua 24 knows nothing of any impending death of Joshua (see Josh. 24:15!).

[8] See the Testaments of the Twelve Patriarchs, as well as the Testaments of Adam, Abraham, etc. For more detailed discussion, see below pp. 137ff.

[9] S. Behm, 'Διαθήκη,' in G. Kittel (ed.), *Theological Dictionary of the New Testament*, vol. 2, p. 127, referring to the testaments of philosophers.

F

I Samuel 12

This chapter belongs to a series of texts[10] that develop the Deu-teronomistic interpretation of how the monarchy began under Saul. The verdict, reached on the basis of a 'theologically defined political ideal,'[11] is negative. We may assume that the special interests of the redactor led to certain changes when the text was incorporated. These alterations, however, are not so far-reaching as to conceal the original nature of the section.

Verses 1–5 contain an exoneration of Samuel. The *antecedent history* in vv. 8–13, together with the introduction in v. 7,[12] is clearly defined. Verse 6, which comes between these two passages, is hard to explain. According to 1QS i. 18–19, we might expect a doxology before the list of צִדְקוֹת. Is v. 6 the garbled remnant of a doxology?[13] The antecedent history extends from Jacob to the suppose present.[14] It recounts Yahweh's saving acts[15] in contrast to the sins of Israel. The period down to the occupation is treated very concisely, the period of the Judges in more detail. Despite the apostasy of Israel, Yahweh has kept the promise made in the covenant—this is the tenor of the discourse. In the express listing of sins, this antecedent history is closely related to those discussed in the previous section, in the circumstances of a covenant renewal occasioned by Israel's sin.

In a departure from the structure observed elsewhere, there follows in vv. 14–15 the announcement of the *curse*.[16] These verses

---

[10] Cf. I Sam. 7:3–17; 8:1–22a; 10:18–25a; 12; 15. See A. Alt, 'Die Staatenbildung der Israeliten in Palästina,' in his *Kleine Schriften*, vol. 2, p. 14, n. 1.—On the literary problems of this chapter, cf. H. P. Smith, *The Books of Samuel* (Edinburgh, 1912), pp. 81–89; Eißfeldt, *The Old Testament*, pp. 272–73; Noth, *Überlieferungsgeschichtliche Studien*, vol. 1, pp. 59 and 5.

[11] Alt, 'Staatenbildung,' p. 13.

[12] Compare v. 7 (cf. v. 16): וְעַתָּה הִתְיַצְּבוּ וְאִשָּׁפְטָה אִתְּכֶם לִפְנֵי יהוה.... with Josh. 24:1: ...וַיִּתְיַצְּבוּ לִפְנֵי הָאֱלֹהִים.

[13] Smith, *Samuel*, p. 86: '''Jahve' so isolated cannot be right.' The following relative clause is equally strange; see Noth, *Überlieferungsgeschichtliche Studien*, p. 59, n. 3.—As a doxology, the sense would be: '(It is) Yahweh, who. . . .' See also the variant ⑤ᴸ and S, 'Yahweh alone is God' (cited by Smith, loc. cit.). Cf. the beginning of the doxology in Neh. 9:6, as well as Pss. 115:15; 121:2; 134:3; and *passim*.

[14] Quite strikingly, v. 8 reads בַּמָּקוֹם הַזֶּה at the point where, in the course of the antecedent history, we should expect the occupation.

[15] ⑤ renders the introduction in v. 7 as: ἀπαγγελῶ ὑμῖν τὴν πᾶσαν δικαιοσύνην κυρίου, ἃ ἐποίησεν ἐν ὑμῖν καὶ ἐν τοῖς πατράσιν ὑμῶν. . . . ⑤ is unable to translate the plural צִדְקוֹת!

[16] On the form, cf. Deut. 8:19.

contain antithetical conditional clauses.[17] The position of this section is itself striking; even more so is the fact that, while the curse is threatened in v. 15, there is no blessing formula such as we might expect after v. 14.[18] Probably we have here a change made by the redactor. The negative omen demanded by the context is produced by simply omitting the blessing formula.[19]

After a miraculous sign,[20] the people confess their sins. Samuel then proclaims that Yahweh will keep his covenant: 'For Yahweh will not let his people fall, for his great name's sake, because Yahweh has determined to make you a people for himself' (v. 22).[21]

Verses 20–21 contain the basic commandments demanding loyalty toward Yahweh.[22] The 'foreign gods' are here referred to as הַתֹּהוּ.

The chapter ends with a threatened curse (v. 25).

In short, the schema of the covenant renewal is preserved almost intact. All that is missing is explicit mention of a new ratification on the part of the people. According to the present text, the occasion of the covenant renewal is 'Samuel's abdication.'[23] But this abdication is itself recorded in a form that was probably not created *ad hoc*, but is based on a well-defined ceremonial.

Samuel publicly introduces the king who will succeed him in leading the nation[24] and declares of his own accord that he has become (too) old (to exercise his office). On the basis of a 'Code for

---

[17]

		14 אִם־תִּירְאוּ אֶת־ יהוה		15 וְאִם־לֹא
		וַעֲבַדְתֶּם אֹתוֹ		
		וּשְׁמַעְתֶּם בְּקֹלוֹ	תשמעו בְּקוֹל יהוה	
	אֶת־פִּי יהוה	וְלֹא תַמְרוּ	וּמְרִיתֶם אֶת־פִּי יהוה	
יהוה אֱלֹהֵיכֶם:	אַחַר	וִהְיִתֶם		

The verbs used are those typical of the general stipulations of a covenant.

[18] The same holds true for vv. 24–25.

[19] On the technique of the Deuteronomist, see Alt, 'Staatenbildung,' p. 14.

[20] Vv. 16–18. Has this sign replaced an original theophany?

[21] The translation follows Köhler, *Lexicon*, p. 358 *s. v.* יאל II; p. 614 *s. v.* נטש.

[22]

		תָּסוּרוּ מֵאַחֲרֵי יהוה	20 אַל־...
	אֶת־יהוה בְּכָל־בְּבַבְכֶם:	וַעֲבַדְתֶּם	
אֲשֶׁר ...	אַחֲרֵי הַתֹּהוּ	תָסוּרוּ [	21 וְלֹא

[23] Greßmann, *Anfänge*, p. 45.

[24] 12:2:

וְעַתָּה הִנֵּה הַמֶּלֶךְ מִתְהַלֵּךְ לִפְנֵיכֶם
וַאֲנִי זָקַנְתִּי ....

Judges,'[25] he asks and receives exoneration from the people. Like any legal act, this one must also be accompanied by an oath before witnesses.[26]

We may conclude, therefore, that in I Samuel 12 a covenant renewal is linked with a transfer of office. Concretely, we have the transfer of the leadership of Israel from Samuel, here the type of a 'Judge of Israel,' to Saul, the 'king.' It remains striking, within the context of the passage as a whole, how little the concrete circumstances have influenced the form of the text. Without doing major damage to the text, it is possible, for instance, to eliminate the passages that mention the king, or substitute a title like 'Judge' that would correspond to the office held by Samuel. Despite the uncertainty attaching to the use of the form within the total narrative as it presently stands, the question remains whether the Deuteronomist was not adhering to a fixed order with his linking of covenant renewal and transfer of office.

A study of two other 'transfers of office,' the transition from Moses to Joshua and from David to Solomon, will help clarify the picture. The two situations are quite different, and the offices are different, but there is a striking similarity between the descriptions of the transfer itself.

Deuteronomy 31–Joshua 1

Deuteronomy as a whole, in the form we have it today, evidences close relationships with the covenant formulary. Its framework characterizes it as a discourse addressed by Moses to the people

---

[25] Smith, *Samuel*, p. 84, points out that we are probably dealing with a form having meter and rhyme:

> 'Eth shor mi lakáhti
> Wa-hamor mi lakáhti
> We-eth mi'ashákti
> Eth mi raccóthi
> U-miyyad mi lakáhti kópher.'

[26] I am not completely sure that 'his anointed' (vv. 3 and 5) referred originally to 'the reigning king' (Greßmann, *Anfänge*, p. 46; et al.). Josh. 24:26; Gen. 31:13, 44–45 suggest the possibility of a pillar, Josh. 22:26–27 (cf. Numbers 7) an altar. See Smith, *Samuel*, p. 82, on v. 5: 'Nearly parallel are those passages in which a sacred object is made witness to a declaration.' Does this perhaps refer to the ark? Cf. the parallel between I Sam. 2:35 and 2:30:   35   וְהִתְהַלֵּךְ לִפְנֵי־מְשִׁיחִי

30   יִתְהַלְּכוּ לְפָנַי

(See also Josh. 7:6–7; 7:23).

If this is so, then the singular with which the passage continues n 12:5b, '(He is) witness,' would also be appropriate.

of Israel,[27] delivered not long before his death.

According to Deut. 31:2, Moses, having finished his discourse, declares:[28] 'I am a hundred and twenty years old this day; I am no longer able to go out and come in'; i.e., he can no longer function as 'duke' [in the archaic sense of 'leader'],[29] and must hand over this office to a younger person. He then introduces Joshua to the people (v. 3b), designates him as his successor, and installs him (v. 7). The train of thought in 31:1–8 is not completely clear. The structure of the verses, however, is quite simple, as comparison with the parallel passages I Sam. 12:2 and Josh. 23:2.[30] After the statement 'I am (too) old . . .,' we expect such a continuation as 'N. is the one who will go out before you.' The introduction of Joshua follow in 3b.

---

[27] See von Rad, *Studies in Deuteronomy*, p. 11.

[28] See Driver, *Deuteronomy*, pp. 333–34; Steuernagel, *Deuteronomium*, p. 110 ad loc. It is not clear what 'these words' refer to: the 'words of the covenant' that precede in the present context (see 28:69 [Eng. 29:1]; cf. 28:69–30:20 [Eng. 29–30], or Deuteronomy as a whole. Both possibilities would mean the same for our study.

Deuteronomy 31–34 has been expanded by the addition of extensive passages, and is not a unified whole. For its analysis, see Eißfeldt, *The Old Testament*, pp. 229ff. He concludes that 31:2–8; 32:48–52; 34 have nothing to do with the Deuteronomic law. 'They continue the Pentateuchal narrative, in that they tell of the appointment of Joshua as Moses' successor, of the announcement of the imminent death of Moses, and of the death itself' (p. 230). I do not agree with this conclusion, especially for 31:2–8, since the actual text argues against it. The text obviously places great importance on the connection between the ceremony described and 'all these words.'

[29] On יצא as a technical military term, see Köhler, *Lexicon*, p. 393. Cf. Num. 27:17; Josh. 14:11; I Sam. 18:16; II Sam 5:2.

[30] Josh. 23:2	וַיִּקְרָא יְהוֹשֻׁעַ לְכָל־יִשְׂרָאֵל (. . .) וַיֹּאמֶר אֲלֵהֶם	
I Sam. 12:1	וַיֹּאמֶר שְׁמוּאֵל אֶל־כָּל־יִשְׂרָאֵל (. . .)	
Deut. 31:1–2	וַיְדַבֵּר (. . .) אֶל־כָּל־יִשְׂרָאֵל: וַיֹּאמֶר אֲלֵהֶם	

Josh. 23:2–3	אֲנִי זָקַנְתִּי בָּאתִי בַּיָּמִים: וְאַתֶּם . . .
I Sam. 12:2aβ	וַאֲנִי זָקַנְתִּי וָשַׂבְתִּי וּבְנֵי הִנָּם אִתְּכֶם
Deut. 31:2a	בֶּן־מֵאָה וְעֶשְׂרִים שָׁנָה אָנֹכִי הַיּוֹם

I Sam 12:2b	וַאֲנִי הִתְהַלַּכְתִּי לִפְנֵיכֶם מִנְּעֻרַי עַד־הַיּוֹם הַזֶּה:
Deut. 31:2a	לֹא־אוּכַל עוֹד לָצֵאת וְלָבוֹא

I Sam. 12:2aα	וְעַתָּה הִנֵּה הַמֶּלֶךְ	מִתְהַלֵּךְ לִפְנֵיכֶם
Deut. 31:3a	יהוה אֱלֹהֶיךָ הוּא הָעֹבֵר לְפָנֶיךָ	
Deut. 31:3b	יְהוֹשֻׁעַ הוּא הָעֹבֵר לְפָנֶיךָ	
Deut. 31:8a	וַיהוה הוּא הַהֹלֵךְ לְפָנֶיךָ	

cf. I Chron. 23:1–2: וְדָוִיד זָקֵן וְשָׂבַע יָמִים וַיַּמְלֵךְ אֶת־שְׁלֹמֹה בְנוֹ עַל־יִשְׂרָאֵל: וַיֶּאֱסֹף אֶת־כָּל־שָׂרֵי יִשְׂרָאֵל . . .

But a theological correction has obviously been undertaken, which illustrates Israel's own view of the leader's office. Before v. 3b there has been interpolated the statement that Yahweh himself is Israel's 'duke,' whom Israel must follow wholeheartedly and steadfastly (cf. v. 8). As a result, the people bind themselves to obey, not Joshua, as we should expect, but Yahweh.[31]

The exalted position occupied by Moses and the momentousness of his words make it hard for us to realize that the succession is not absolutely guaranteed. Several other preconditions must first be met.

Deut. 31:14–15, 23[32] tell of an installation by Yahweh himself. Moses and Joshua enter the 'tent of meeting' together. The text does not allow us to decide with certainty the relation of this action to what has gone before.[33]

Now, as experience has shown, designation and possible co-regency do not automatically mean later rule.[34] The critical point is the death of the ruler. Will the successor be able to maintain his position after the death of his mighty predecessor?

What, then, will happen after the death of Moses? Will Israel fulfill its obligations toward Yahweh and freely recognize Moses' successor? This question, a cause of deep concern, is answered by Deut. 34:9[35] after the statement of Moses' death: 'So the people of Israel obeyed him [Joshua], and did as Yahweh had commanded Moses.'[36]

Up to this point we seem to have been justified in assuming a legal model as the basis for the description of the transfer of leadership

---

[31] See also Noth, *Überlieferungsgeschichtliche Studien*, vol. 1, p. 39, n. 4.—On this entire section, cf. W 2, vo. 53ff.: 'Thus (says) Mattiuaza, the king's son; thus (say) also the people of Ḫarri: if we keep this treaty [54] and oath . . ., [55] may whose gods whose names we have invoked go with us, make us great, protect us, [56] be gracious to us. May my lord Mattiuaza take the lead [as 'duke'; Weidner, *Politische Dokumente*, p. 56, n. 2]. Under his protection we shall devour a rich harvest. . . .'

[32] On treating these verses as a single unit, see Driver, *Deuteronomy*, p. 326.

[33] Cf. also the description in Num. 27:15–23, which clearly emphasizes the priestly function involved in the investiture.—The failure to mention the occupation at this point, as in Deut. 34:9 (see Noth, *Überlieferungsgeschichtliche Studien*, vol. 1, p. 191), is insignificant if we are dealing with a fixed schema for investiture, adapted to the concrete circumstances only at a few points.

[34] B. Hrozný, *Hethitische Könige* (Leipzig, 1920), p. 50: 'Although Labarnaš appoints Muršiliš as his successor, after his death . . . a certain Chattušiliš claims the throne. . . .'

Sennacherib before his death appointed Esarhaddon to be his successor. Nevertheless, after the death of Sennacherib in 681 B.C. there was a prolonged struggle for the throne.

[35] There is almost complete consensus that 7–9 belong to P. See Driver, *Deuteronomy*, p. 424; Steuernagel, *Deuteronomium*, pp. 182–83; et al.

[36] On this verse, cf. also Josh. 4:14.

from Moses to Joshua. This approach gains further support from the continuation in Joshua 1.[37]

S. Hermann has demonstrated convincingly that the so-called royal novella was a familiar form in Israel.[38] In 'its most general form,' Herrmann describes as follows the 'simple literary schema that depicts the course of a court ceremony':

'The king "appears," he informs the assembled officials of his intention, they respond with praise of the king and his wise ideas, and the performance of what has been expounded is introduced at once. A series of other elements can be adapted to this basic schema: the will of the deity can be made known to the king by a dream, which he then repeats to the officials.'[39]

We may well ask whether Joshua 1 does not record a very similar proceeding, albeit with certain changes to adapt it to the situation at hand:

1:1–9	Statement to Joshua of Yahweh's will. This comes directly, with no mention of any dream.
10–11	Instructions are given to the שֹׁטְרֵי הָעָם.
12–15	Special instructions for the Transjordanian tribes.
16–17	Response:[40] Joshua is confirmed in his office and the people state their willingness to carry out his orders.
2:1ff.	One of Joshua's commands is carried out in preparation for the occupation.

The definition of the royal novella given by A. Hermann[41] and quoted by S. Herrmann holds true with respect to Joshua 1, except that Joshua is not a king: 'In each case we are dealing with an event of overwhelming importance, whose effects last for centuries; attention centers on the king, not so much as an individual, but as a representative figure.' It is impossible to go into more detail here.

---

[37] The problem of when and by whom these pieces were brought together cannot be discussed here.

[38] S. Herrmann, 'Die Königsnovelle in Ägypten und in Israel,' *Wissenschaftliche Zeitschrift der Karl-Marx-Universität* (Leipzig, 1954), pp. 33–44.

[39] Ibid., p. 33.

[40] On the basis of the schema assumed by Herrmann, we must ask who is speaking in 1:16–17. In the royal novella, it is the officials who respond. Vv. 16–18 are quite appropriate as the response of the שֹׁטְרִים. For their function, see Exod. 5:6; Num. 11:16; Deut. 20:5.

[41] S. Hermann, 'Königsnovelle,' p. 33, citing A. Hermann, 'Die Ägyptische Königsnovelle,' in *Leipziger Ägyptologische Studien* 10 (1938).

For our study it is important to note that Yahweh's words to Joshua mention the typical content of the covenant with Israel: the gracious gift of the land (vv. 2b–4, 6), keeping the commandments (vv. 7–8a), and a blessing (vv. 5a, 8b). The deletion of particular details here is a questionable procedure.[42]

We may therefore conclude that, according to the presentation of Deuteronomy 31–Joshua 1, the transfer of the 'ducal' office from Moses to Joshua is linked with the covenant. In each of the components of the ceremony—investiture, designation, popular recognition, accession to office—a reference to the covenant and its themes plays an important role.

I Chronicles 22–29

Both the Deuteronomistic History and the Chronicler's History include much detail in their account of Solomon's succession to the throne of David. Their presentations differ in important points. Both versions, however, reveal that the covenant with Yahweh plays a role in this change of ruler.

We have selected the Chronicler's presentation because its structure is closest to the investiture of Joshua, which we have just examined.[43] We shall devote our attention particularly to question of determining what sections remain constant, as a kind of liturgical 'ordinary,' omitting as much as possible the corresponding 'proper.' In the case of Joshua, the 'proper' appears as a commission to occupy the land; in the case of Solomon, it concerns the building of the Temple.

Except for a series of lists in 23:(2b)3–27:34, I Chronicles 22–29 is a unified composition.[44]

In 23:1, we read that David is 'old and full of days';[45] he makes his son Solomon king 'over Israel'(!). For this purpose he convokes

---

[42] Steuernagel, *Josua*, pp. 209–11, starting with completely different presuppositions, necessarily makes certain deletions. Despite Noth's own criticism in *Überlieferungsgeschichtliche Studien*, vol. 1, p. 41, n. 4, we may agree with his defense of the unity of this passage in his *Josua*, p. 27. Vv. 5b and 6 can hardly stand alone as representing the primary stratum. The statement 'I will be with you' (5b) and the exhortation to keep the commandments cannot be separated from the promise of a blessing (see, for example, Deut. 26:16ff.). The mention of a written record does not need to be secondary.

[43] On the relationship of the Deuteronomistic version to the covenant, see I Kings 2:3.

[44] According to Noth, *Überlieferungsgeschichtliche Studien*, pp. 112–13, this section is a primary component of the Chronicler's History.

[45] וְדָוִיד זָקֵן וְשָׂבַע יָמִים וַיַּמְלֵךְ אֶת־שְׁלֹמֹה... Cf. Deut. 31:2; Josh. 23:2; I Sam. 12:2. See the comparison above on p. 69, note 30.

an assembly of the Israelite nobility (שָׂרֵי יִשְׂרָאֵל; v. 2). The present context does not provide an appropriate continuation, and so the verse is usually linked directly to 28:1.[46] In 28:1, however, we are clearly dealing with an assembly not only of the שָׂרִים, but of the entire people, or at least all that can bear arms.[47] I Chron. 22:17, however, presupposes an assembly of the שָׂרִים, but there is no statement of its convocation. I suggest that 23:1–2a was originally the superscription of the section 22:6–19, at whose conclusion it now stands. In many respects this section parallels 28:1ff., but the differences must also be noted.[48]

I Chron. 22:6–9 consists of two sections: the summoning and commissioning of Solomon (vv. 6–16),[49] and the obligation of the שָׂרִים to support him (vv. 17–19).[50]

As is appropriate, David delivers two speeches. The first is addressed to Solomon. He informs Solomon of the דבר יהוה that came concerning him even before his birth, according to which the covenant of Yahweh is promised to him: 'He shall be my son, and I will be his father.'[51] Yahweh has guaranteed his reign for ever. Therefore David prays, 'Yahweh be with you, so that you may succeed.' The text continues, '. . . in building the Temple.' This does, of course, represent success of a kind. Verse 12, however, which follows, has a phrase that is out of place here:[52] 'May he give you charge over Israel.' But 'May you succeed, and may he give you charge[53] over Israel, as he has spoken concerning you' goes very well

---

[46] See Galling, *Chronik*, p. 63, note 1.

[47] 28:1: חָיִל (י)וּלְכָל־גִּבּוֹרֵ ;28:2: וְעַמִּי ;28:8: כָּל־יִשְׂרָאֵל ;29:10: כָּל־הַקָּהָל.

[48] The entire passage should be compared with Deut. 31:1–8.

[49] I Chron. 22:6–7:   וַיִּקְרָא   לִשְׁלֹמֹה בְנוֹ (. . .)   וַיֹּאמֶר דָּוִיד לִשְׁלֹמֹה

Deut. 31:7:   וַיִּקְרָא מֹשֶׁה לִיהוֹשֻׁעַ   וַיֹּאמֶר   . . . אֵלָיו

In I Chronicles, the commission to build the Temple follows; in Deuteronomy 31, the commission to occupy the land.

[50] V. 17: עֹזֵר .וַיְצַו דָוִיד לְכָל־שָׂרֵי יִשְׂרָאֵל לַעֲזֹר לִשְׁלֹמֹה בְנוֹ is frequently used in the sense of 'follow obediently': I Kings 1:7; Josh. 1:14; 10:4; II Sam. 8:5; II Chron. 19:2 (parallel to אהב in the sense of a covenant agreement); 26:13; and *passim*. See especially I Chron. 12:18ff., the homage of the 'thirty' to David: 'We are yours, O David; and with you, O son of Jesse! Hail! Hail to you, and hail to him that helps you; for your God helps you' (translation following Galling).

[51] See the Nathan prophecy, especially II Sam. 7:14.

[52] Galling, *Chronik*, p. 63: 'Omit "he gives you charge over Israel," which is out of place here.'

[53] Cf. Deut. 31:14, 23; 34:9.

together, as the conclusion of the entire section in I Chron. 29:23
shows.[54] In my opinion, this detail shows once more that the preparations for building the Temple have been secondarily linked with the
investiture.[55]

The condition upon which the covenant will be maintained is
that Solomon keep the 'torah' as given through Moses (vv. 12–13).
David concludes his address to Solomon with a 'formula of encouragement,' which agrees almost word for word with that found in
Deut. 31:7,[56] although in this case the commission is different.

The address to the שָׂרִים clearly refers to the fulfilment of the
promise recorded in the covenant between Yahweh and Israel. Its
most important point is 'peace (מְנוּחָה) in the land.'[57] One minor
nuance placed in the mouth of David deserves mention: 'Yahweh
has delivered the inhabitants of the land into *my* hand!'[58] He has
therefore himself become the instrument whereby the promise to all
Israel is fulfilled.

Our observations on I Chron. 22:6–19 make it appear likely that
we are dealing with what was originally the first act of the ceremony

---

[54] 'Then Solomon sat on the throne of Yahweh as king instead of David his father;
and he prospered, and all Israel obeyed him.'

[55] We are not, however, in a position to make a definite statement concerning the date
of this linkage. According to Noth (*Überlieferungsgeschichtliche Studien*, p. 113), the 'assign-
ment of the final decision to build the Temple and of all the preparations to David' is
typical of the Chronicler.

[56] Cf. BH ad loc.; I Chron. 28:20 has been transposed.

Deut. 31:7	חֲזַק וֶאֱמָץ ׳כִּי אַתָּה תָּבוֹא אֶת־הָעָם הַזֶּה אֶל־הָאָרֶץ ...
I Chron. 22:13	חֲזַק וֶאֱמָץ
I Chron. 28:20	חֲזַק וֶאֱמַץ וַעֲשֵׂה
Deut. 31:8	הוּא יִהְיֶה עִמְּךָ לֹא יַרְפְּךָ וְלֹא יַעַזְבֶךָ
I Chron. 22:13	----------------------
I Chron. 28:20	יהוה אֱלֹהִים אֱלֹהַי עִמָּךְ לֹא יַרְפְּךָ וְלֹא יַעַזְבֶךָ
Deut. 31:8	לֹא תִירָא וְלֹא תֵחָת:
I Chron. 22:13	אַל־תִּירָא וְאַל־תֵּחָת:
I Chron. 28:20	אַל־תִּירָא וְאַל־תֵּחָת

[57] On the reinterpretation of מְנוּחָה in 28:2, which draws on Ps. 132:7, see G. von Rad,
'Die levitische Predigt in den Büchern der Chronik,' in *Festschrift O. Procksch zum 60.
Geburtstag* (Leipzig, 1934), p. 121, reprinted in his *Gesammelte Studien*, pp. 256–57.

[58] 𝔊A, 𝔙, and the Syriac are clearly taken by surprise, and substitute 'into your
hand.' See the note in BH. 𝔐 is certainly the *lectio difficilior*!

in which David 'makes Solomon king,' namely, the acceptance by the שָׂרִים of an obligation to obey Solomon.[59]

In chapter 28 it is also possible to eliminate all the passages that refer to the building of the Temple. This time the entire עָם is assembled at Jerusalem. It is they that David addresses when he speaks.[60]

Von Rad has shown how much traditional material has been assimilated in this speech.[61] The same holds true for the form. Verses 2b–7 correspond to the *antecedent history* of a covenant formulary. God's saving action in history is here his relationship with the house of David. This is shown in God's choice of David to be king and in his gift to David of a multitude of sons. The content is almost identical with that of the speech in 22:7–10, with what I think is one important difference: 28:4 shows a clear interest in associating the election of David with the destiny and the election of all Israel. In 22:7, David speaks of 'my God'; in 28:4, of 'the God of Israel.'

The antecedent history concludes with כַּיּוֹם הַזֶּה (28:7), which stands somewhat isolated in the present context, but makes complete sense within the formal schema, according to which the antecedent history extends to the present day.[62]

Seen from this point of view, the transition to the next sentence does not appear so abrupt. Here, too, וְעַתָּה (v. 8) introduces the following *statement of substance*.[63] This is divided into two parts, one addressed to all Israel, the other to Solomon personally.[64] In each case a promise is appended; in the case of Solomon, there is also a threat to reject him. The ceremony takes place in the sight of 'all Israel' (קְהַל יהוה)[65] and in the hearing of 'our God.'

A repeated 'encouragement formula' (v. 20) provides an apt

---

[59] V. 19, 'Now set your mind and heart to seek Yahweh your God,' does not agree with an interpretation that looks upon the text as a statement of fealty to Solomon. Is it an 'inconsistency' like that in Deuteronomy 31, due to the firm conviction that Yahweh —and no one else—is king in Israel?

[60] ᵍ reads: καὶ ἔστη Δαυιδ ἐν μέσῳ τῆς ἐκκλησίας (I Paral. 28:2); cf. also Ezra 10:10; Neh. 9:4.

[61] G. von Rad, 'Die levitische Predigt,' pp. 120–21 (*Gesammelte Studien*, pp. 256–57).

[62] For כַּיּוֹם הַזֶּה at the conclusion of an antecedent history, see Deut. 4:38; 10:15; Jer. 11:5. Cf. also Jer. 32:20; Dan. 9:7; Neh. 9:32.

[63] See Deut. 4:1; 10:12; Josh. 24:17; I Chron. 22:11.

[64] I do not consider it necessary to judge one of the parts secondary. The Hittite treaties witness to the mutual obligations of a ruler and the 'people of his land.' See the alternation between the second person singular and plural in the stipulations of the treaty between Ḫukkanaš and the people Ḫayaša (F 6, col. iii–iv; also W 1; W 2).

[65] This statement appears to indicate that David first had the 'nobles' swear their fealty to Solomon as representatives of the entire nation. Cf. Neh. 10:30 (Eng. 10:29).

continuation of v. 10. In the present context, it is embedded between
the account of David's giving Solomon a plan of the Temple
(28:11–19) and the account of David's provisions for the building
(29: 1–9).

The ceremony continues with a glorification of Yahweh by David.
He begins with a hymn to the greatness of God (29:10–13) and concludes with an intercession that God will 'direct the hearts' of Israel
and Solomon. David then has the entire company glorify God in
the same way (29:20). This should probably be considered a
ratification of what has taken place.—Thereupon the whole assembly
blesses Yahweh and the king (29:20). It is an open question whether
'the king' refers to David or Solomon.

On the next day follow sacrifices (v. 21), a meal 'before Yahweh'
(v. 22), and the anointing of Solomon as נָגִיד.[66]

In agreement with Deut. 34:9, I Chron. 29:23–25 explicitly
describes Israel's acknowledgment of Solomon as king. In this
statement lies the assurance that Yahweh's blessing has been transferred from David to Solomon.

After the description of David's death, the Chronicler reports the
revelation that came to Solomon in a dream at Gibeon (II Chron.
1:1–13). This is the final act of Solomon's accession to David's
throne, and so the Chronicler states at the end: 'And he [Solomon]
reigned over Israel' (1:13).[67]

In the account of the Chronicler, then, the investiture of Solomon
comprises a whole series of actions, two of which are especially
pertinent to our investigation: the oath of allegiance to Solomon
taken by the nobles, and the covenant ceremony in chapter 28,
recorded almost in its entirety. The human partners to this covenant
are the new king, the nobles, and the entire people. In both cases
David performs the ceremonial act.

The content of this covenant is closely associated with what we
have learned above of the covenant between Yahweh and Israel. The
differences, therefore, are all the more striking. In them there is a
clear attempt to show a connection between the covenant with
Israel and the covenant with the house of David.[68]

---

[66] On this title, see below, p. 83, n. 90.

[67] Cf. the discussion of Joshua 1 above. On the relationship of II Chron. 1:1–3 and
its parallel in I Kings 3:4–15 to the 'royal novella', see Herrmann, 'Königsnovelle,'
pp. 35ff.

[68] See von Rad's conclusions concerning the individuality of the Chronicler's History, in
Das Geschichtsbild des chronistischen Werkes, BWANT (Stuttgart, 1930), pp. 35, 119ff.

To give an idea of how neatly the passages referring to the building of the Temple can be removed, a translation (following Galling, with modifications) of the entire text will be set down here. The brackets mark the points at which omissions have been made.

I Chron. 23:1 When David was old and full of days, he made Solomon his son king over Israel. [2] And he assembled all the leaders of Israel.

[22:6] And he called for Solomon his son, and charged him [   ]. [7] And David said to Solomon, 'My son, [   ] [8] the word of Yahweh came to me, saying, "You have shed much blood and have waged great wars [   ]. [9] Behold, a son shall be born to you; he shall be a man of peace, and I will give him peace from all his enemies round about, for his name shall be Solomon, and I will give peace and quiet to Israel as long as he reigns. [10] [   ] He shall be my son, and I will be his father, and I will establish his royal throne in Israel for ever."

[11a] 'And now, my son, may Yahweh be with you, [11bβ] as he has spoken concerning you. [11bα] And may you be successful [   ], [12aβ] and may he give you charge over Israel. [12aα] Now may Yahweh grant you discretion and understanding, [12b] so that you may keep the law of Yahweh, your God.

[13] 'Then you will prosper if you are careful to observe the statutes and the ordinances which Yahweh commanded Moses for Israel.

'Be strong, and of good courage, and fear not, [14] [   ] [16] [   ] and Yahweh will be with you.'

[17] And David also commanded all the leaders of Israel to help Solomon his son, saying, [18] 'Has not Yahweh your God been with you? And has he not given you peace on every side? For he has delivered the inhabitants of the land into my hand, and the land is subdued now before Yahweh and his people. [19] So set your mind and heart to seek Yahweh your God [   ].'

I Chron. 28:1 And David assembled at Jerusalem all the officials of Israel, the officials of the tribes, the officers of the divisions that served the king, the commanders of thousands, the commanders of hundreds, the stewards of all the property and cattle of the king and his sons, together with the palace officials, the mighty men, and all the citizens. [2] Then King David rose and said: 'Hear me, my brethren and my people. [3] [   ] [4] And Yahweh, the God of Israel, chose me from all my father's house to be king over Israel forever; for he chose Judah as leader, and in the house of Judah my father's house, and among my father's sons it pleased him to make me king over all Israel. [5] But of all my sons (for Yahweh has given me many sons) he has chosen Solomon my son to sit upon the throne of the kingdom of Yahweh over Israel. [6] And he said to me, "It is Solomon your son [   ] that I have chosen to be my son, and I will be his father, [7] and I will establish his kingdom for ever if he continues resolute in keeping my commandments and my ordinances, as he is today."

[8] 'And therefore in the sight of all Israel, the assembly of Yahweh, and in the hearing of our God: Observe and seek out all the commandments of Yahweh your God, that you may possess this good land, and leave it for an inheritance to your children after you for ever.

[9] 'But you, Solomon my son, know the God of your father, and serve him with a whole heart and a willing mind; for Yahweh searches all hearts, and understands every plan and thought. If you seek him, he will let you find him;

but if you forsake him, he will cast you off for ever.' [11] [   ] [20] And David said to Solomon his son: 'Be strong and of good courage [   ]; fear not, be not dismayed, for Yahweh Elohim, my God, will be with you, and he will not take his hand from you or forsake you' [20b] [   ] [29:10].

[29:10] Then David blessed Yahweh in the presence of all the assembly; and David said: 'Blessed art thou, O Yahweh, the God of Israel our father, for ever and ever. [11] Thine, O Yahweh, is the greatness, and the power, and the glory, and the victory, and the majesty; for all that is in the heavens and in the earth is thine. Thine, O Yahweh, is the kingdom, and thou exaltest thyself as head above all. [12] Both riches and honor come from thee, and thou rulest over all. In thy hand are power and might [. . .] to make great and to give strength to all.

[13] And now we thank thee, Yahweh, our God, and praise thy glorious name. [14] [   ] [15] For we are strangers before thee, and sojourners, as all our fathers were; our days on the earth flee like a shadow, and there is no hope. [16] [   ] [17] And I know, my God, that thou triest the heart, and hast pleasure in uprightness, [   ] and I have seen it[69] [   ]. [18] O Yahweh, the God of Abraham, Isaac, and Israel, our fathers, keep for ever such purposes and thoughts in the hearts of thy people; direct their hearts toward thee. [19] And to Solomon, my son, give a whole heart, that he may keep thy commandments, thy testimonies, and thy statutes [   ].'

[20] And David said to all the assembly, 'Bless Yahweh, your God.' And all the assembly blessed Yahweh, the God of their fathers. And they bowed their heads, and did obeisance before Yahweh and the king. [21] On the next morning they performed sacrifices to Yahweh and offered burnt offerings to Yahweh [   ]. [22] On that day they ate and drank before Yahweh with great gladness, and they made Solomon the son of David king the second time. And they anointed him as prince for Yahweh, and Zadok as priest.

[23] And so Solomon sat on the throne of Yahweh as king instead of David his father, and he prospered, and all Israel obeyed him. [24] All the leaders and the mighty men, and also all the sons of King David, pledged their allegiance to King Solomon. [25] And Yahweh gave Solomon great repute in the sight of all Israel, and bestowed upon him such a royal kingdom as no king over Israel had had before him.

II Kings 11

The Chronicler's account of Solomon's investiture furnishes a good elucidation for what is otherwise an obscure passage in the Deutero-nomist's report of the investiture of Jehoash. The setting is the fall of Queen Athaliah (II Kings 11). There we read (v. 17):

וַיִּכְרֹת יְהוֹיָדָע אֶת־הַבְּרִית בֵּין יהוה וּבֵין הַמֶּלֶךְ וּבֵין הָעָם

לִהְיוֹת לְעָם לַיהוה

וּבֵין הַמֶּלֶךְ וּבֵין הָעָם

---

[69] In this context רָאִיתִי makes sense as a parallel to וְיָדַעְתִּי (see Eccles. 2:13, 14; 3:10, 12; cf. Exod. 3:7; I Sam. 26:12; Isa. 6:9); see Galling, Chronik, p. 70, n. 5: 'Read reḥû instead of "I have seen".'

The difficulty lies in the fact that, in its present form, the text clearly speaks of two 'covenants.'[70] But this is probably an accurate reflection of the circumstances.[71] In the one 'covenant' the people pledge their allegiance to the king;[72] in the other, the king and people together pledge themselves to be 'Yahweh's people.'[73]

But if we are to see that these statements are based on very precise concepts, originating in the legal realm, we must return once more to the Hittite treaties. Korosec describes the investiture of a vassal as follows:[74]

I. 'The basis of vassalage is the oath taken by the vassal,[75] whereby he pledges his fealty to the Great King. He becomes "subject to the oath". . . .'

II. 'The taking of the oath by the vassal is followed by a second act: the Great King invests him with dominion over the land assigned to him. . . .' The sequence of acts can be reversed, however, as in the treaty with Duppi-Tešup of Amurru: first investiture with authority, then an oath of allegiance to the Great King.[76] 'It seems

---

[70] For discussion of the problem, see von Rad, *Studies in Deuteronomy*, p. 64, n. 1. Von Rad suspects dittography in v. 17b. The same suggestion is made by H. J. Kraus, *Worship in Israel* (E.T. Oxford, 1966), p. 224, n. 99. Noth, on the other hand, assumes that the original statement was 'The priest Jehoiada made a covenant between the king and the people' ('Das alttestamentliche Bundesschließen,' pp. 442–43, reprinted in his *Studien zum Alten Testament*, p. 152).

[71] The parallel in Chronicles has what appears at first glance to be an easier text. The reason may be that, in contrast to II Kings 11:4, at the very outset of the ceremony a covenant is made with 'all the assembly' (II Chron. 23:3), which affirms that 'the king's son shall reign as Yahweh promised concerning the sons of David.' This would correspond to the second covenant in II Kings 11:17, with the people's pledge of allegiance to the king. The report in II Kings 11 seems to me historically the more probable; it speaks first of a pledge by the 'nobles.' The Chronicler has probably also introduced 'all the people' as a secondary addition in vv. 6 and 10.

[72] See above the discussion of Deut. 31:1–8; I Chron. 22:6–9.

[73] Cf. Deut. 26:18; Ezek. 37:23–24.

[74] *Hethitische Staatsverträge*, pp. 52–53 (author's numbering).

[75] The oath is based on the treaty; see W 1, W 2; cf. Korosec, *Hethitische Staatsverträge*, p. 29.

[76] As an example, we shall cite here in full the relevant passage from the treaty with Duppi-Tešup (F 1, col. 1, §7–8). i. 11 '[Wh]en, however, your father died, ac[cording to the word of your father] I [12] did not reject you. Because your father [13] had often named [you]r [n]ame [?] before the . . ., [14] therefore I showed my concern for you. You, however, [15] were overtaken by misery and disease. [16] [And] although you were sick, I, the Sun, nevertheless [17] appointed you [to] the same position as your father, and *to you* [18] *I had "your"* [sist]*er*(*s*) [?] *your brothers, and the land of Amurru take an oath.* [19] Now after I, the Sun, according to the word of your father [20] had shown my concern for you and appointed you to the position of your father, [21] behold, *I had you take an oath to the king of the land of Ḫatti, the land of Ḫatti,* [22] *and to my sons (and) to my grandsons.* [23] Now protect the oaths of the king and the power [lit. "hand"] of the king; but I, the Sun, will [24] protect you Duppi-Tešup. . . .' (author's italics; for the rest of the text, see below, pp. 182ff.).

highly probable that we are dealing with two actions that took place in close succession.'[77]

With respect to the second point: 'The enfeoffment of the vassal itself comprises two separate acts, first the framing of the document and second the investiture of the vassal.'

'The investiture of the vassal as ruler of the land assigned to him takes place when the Great King "has the land take an oath to the vassal."'[78] No further explanation of the expression 'to have the land take an oath to the vassal' is offered. Korosec suggests that we are dealing here with an oath of fealty taken by the leaders of the land in question.[79]

Thus we can reconstruct the picture of a highly developed act of international law. A double oath ceremony is clearly recognizable as the actual nucleus: an oath to the Great King taken by the vassal, and an oath taken by the people of the 'land' to the vassal. In this double ceremony, the investiture agrees completely with what we have ascertained concerning the nature of the two 'covenants' in Israel.

In the context of the present study, we are interested primarily in the covenant 'between Yahweh and the king and the people.' That the land is Yahweh's gift, i.e., fief, is a familiar concept for Israel. That the people as well as the king take an oath to Yahweh as liege lord is due to the 'legal and social structure' of Israel.[80]

Comparison with the Hittite texts therefore shows that the close connection we have observed between the 'covenant' and the

---

[77] Korosec, *Hethitische Staatsverträge*, p. 53.

'For the document of enfeoffment, three things are necessary: it must be composed (Akkadian *šaṭaru*, "write") by the Great King or at his command; the Great King must seal it (Akkadian *kanāku*); and he must hand it over (Akkadian *nadānu*, "give") to the vassal' (ibid., p. 52; cf. W 9, ro. 6). The last point is a good illustration of von Rad's thesis ('Das judäische Krönungsritual,' *ThLZ* 72 [1947], cols. 211ff.; now reprinted in his *Gesammelte Studien*, pp. 205ff.) that part of the Judahite coronation ritual was the presentation of a 'coronation protocol' in which the legitimation of the king is recorded. If this legitimation consists of a 'covenant,' in formal similarity to the Hittite form of enfeoffment, then the use of the term עֵדוּת in II Kings 11:12 appears quite appropriate.—Widengren's argument to the contrary in *Sakrales Königtum im Alten Testament und im Judentum* (Stuttgart, 1955), p. 94, n. 69 runs as follows: 'For this very reason we must reject the otherwise attractive hypothesis of v. Rad, *ThLZ* 72 (1947), pp. 211ff., to the effect that *edut* is here equivalent to "royal protocol." The word means "law"; it comes from יעד, "decree," and corresponds precisely to the Akkadian *adē*, "statutes, commandments." The לחת העדות therefore = *duppū adē*, "tablet of the laws".'— See, however, the Aramaic treaty in *Archiv für Orientforschung*, 8 (1932/33), p. 4 (translation on p. 3): 'Treaties of Bar-Ga yah, . . . with Matti'el . . .' עדי בר גאיה מלך כתך עם מתעאל. Here '*ade*' clearly does not mean merely 'statutes, commandments,' but an entire treaty. Widengren's argument can therefore not be cited against von Rad's thesis.

change in leadership in Israel need not be a late literary fiction, but is in fact determined by the *Sitz im Leben*.

Covenant Formulary and Testament

We began this section with the question of how there comes to be such an intimate association between the making of a covenant and a death, like the death of Moses or Joshua, an association that corresponds on the literary level to the connection between covenant formulary and testament. Our study has not quite yet answered this question. It is not clear, for instance, what the enthronement of Jehoash has to do with the problem. We shall now attempt to show that the coronation of Jehoash represents an exceptional case; this probably accounts for its being reported in such detail. The nature of the 'normal case' is brought out all the more plainly.

It is striking how the Hittite treaties focus on a person and not on an objective factor like an office or an anonymous institution, the 'state.' The critical point of any treaty relationship, even when the treaty is concluded 'for ever,'[81] remains therefore the death of one of the parties. Both the Great King and the vassal are concerned for what will happen to the treaty after their death. For this reason they take a series of precautions, a number of which can be determined from the texts.[82]

The Great King appoints his successor while still alive.[83] He

---

[78] Korosec, *Hethitische Staatsverträge*, p. 52. Cf. F 1 §7, i. 17–18; F 3 §4 D 29–30.

[79] Korosec refers to the oath taken by the 'princes and elders of the land of Pitašša,' ibid., p. 53.

[80] See Korosec, ibid., p. 53 (also p. 57): 'As a rule, the vassal alone appears as signatory to the treaty. In exceptional cases, however, the people of the land in question take part in the making of the treaty.' Reference is made to Akkadian *mārē* ('sons') or LÚ.MEŠ ('people') of the land.
There is an obvious similarity to the עַם הָאָרֶץ.

[81] This is not true of all treaties, but is an explicit concession on the part of the Great King, associated with the law of succession for the vassal. See Korosec, ibid., pp. 106–107.

[82] The 'vassal-treaties' of Esarhaddon are of great interest in this connection. (They have been published by D. J. Wiseman, 'The Vassal-Treaties of Esarhaddon,' *Iraq*, 20:1 [1958]. I am grateful to Prof. Scharbert for bringing these texts to my attention.)
The treaties are preserved in many copies; almost the only differences between what amount to versions of a single basic text are the various names of the vassals.
According to these treaties, Esarhaddon appointed his son Ashurbanipal as his successor in the year 672 B.C.—in other words, four years before his death. The appointment took place with great solemnity, using a form comprising a whole series of ceremonies.
'These ceremonies included the robing of the prince and his display to the people before he entered into the House of Succession (*bēt redūti*). . . . The day of Ashurbanipal's appointment as crown-price was also marked by the building of a new terrace for Esarhaddon's palace at Assur.' (Ibid., p. 4.)

G

obligates his vassal by treaty to recognize the successor.[84] He can likewise guarantee the recognition of the successor appointed by the vassal.[85] The same purpose is served by the 'oath to the presumptive successor taken by the land during the life of the reigning vassal,'[86] which the Great King initiates. Finally, the Aramaic treaty of the eighth century is concluded with three generations for similar reasons.[87]

All these measures are intended to circumvent the critical point. This is the same idea that informs the emphasis on the unbroken chain of generations in the antecedent history of the treaties.

On the basis of these observations, we may assume with some degree of probability that in Israel a change of rulers after the

---

We may also mention the oath to Ashurbanipal taken by the major officials ('the scribes, seers, diviners and other religious and palace officials'—ibid., p. 3).

The nucleus of Ashurbanipal's appointment is the fealty of all the peoples subject to the dominion of Ashur. This fealty is the subject of the treaties in question.

'Esarhaddon had assembled "the people of Assyria, high and low, from the Upper (Caspian) to the Lower (Mediterranean) Seas". . . . The whole army was present with its officers, the nobles with their sons and wives, the lulime and many representatives of subject territories. The deities were present. . . . The ceremony took place in the presence of Esarhaddon and his other sons over whom Ashurbanipal was now given precedence.' (Ibid., p. 3; cf. I Chron. 28:1.)

The succession is to be assured by treaty against all eventualities. The clauses of the treaty reveal an extensive range of possibilities for revolution, from intrigue to naked force. What is demanded is absolute loyalty to the king's successor (see, for example, lines 41–61, ibid., pp. 31ff.).

Here again the technical term for the treaties is adē (on its translation, see ibid., p. 81)!

It is typical of these treaties that they deal solely with succession to the throne. I would therefore prefer to call them 'succession treaties' to distinguish them from Hittite 'vassal treaties.' The vassal relationship is presupposed, not established.

There is no 'antecedent history' in the structure of these treaties. Mendenhall ('Law and Covenant in Israel and the Ancient Near East,' Biblical Archaeologist, 17 [1954], p. 30, n. 19) even suggests, 'The entire pattern is also radically different.' Wiseman holds a different view (ibid., p. 28). For the legal interpretation of these treaties, however, it is surely not insignificant that mention is made only of the requirement, not the performance of the 'guarantor' of the treaty. In the oath ceremony only the curse is threatened. In agreement with the usual tendency of Assyrian treaties, this section is highly developed. There is a plethora of images and 'symbolic actions' intended to illustrate the awful nature of the curse (cf. ibid., pp. 25ff.).

It is not possible to go into further details here.

[83] VAT. 13.064: 'The tablet of Tabarna, the Great King, when the Great King Tabarna became sick(?) in K(?)uššar^kι (city) and appointed his son ^mMu[ršiliš to the] kingship'; cited from Hrozný, Hethitische Könige, p. 50.

[84] F 6, col. i. 8: 'Now you Ḫukkanaš shall recognize only the Sun with respect to dominion [9] and also that son of mine whom I the Sun designate: "this one shall each recognize" [10] and in the midst (of the assembly; Hittite "ištarna," probably = an assembly of the nobles of the empire; Korosec, Hethitische Staatsverträge, p. 38) display; [11] him you Ḫukkanaš shall recognize.' Cf. I Kings 1:32ff.

[85] See W 7, col. i. 52ff.; F 1 §8, i. 24ff.; F 5 §6, A 65ff.

[86] Korosec, Hethitische Staatsverträge, p. 53; see F 3 §4, D 29–30; cf. also I Kings 1:32ff.

[87] Weidner, 'Staatsvertrag,' p. 4.

manner of the transition from Moses to Joshua and from David to Solomon was looked upon as the normal case, which was at least a goal to strive for. The successor was to take office before the death of his predecessor. We have seen, however, how intimately this succession is associated with the two covenants. The crucial act is above all the renewed ratification of the covenant with Yahweh, since it is the basis of Israel's life.

Our concept of a 'testament,' which means 'final disposition of one's estate,'[88] is certainly out of place in this context. Neither Moses nor David can hand over the covenant nor will it to an heir. It is not a piece of property that can come into another person's possession. The covenant relationship is the basis of life for the next generation, for which שָׁלוֹם shall be preserved. To put it more neatly, one might say that what matters is not death (of one generation) but life (of the next generation). It is therefore a terrible thing when the chain of generations is broken. This chain is not merely biological, as the investiture of Jehoash shows. By blood he is descended from David, but after the interregnum of Athaliah, the covenant must be concluded once again through the priest Jehoiada.

We may note, finally, that the 'chain of generations' in Israel extends beyond the head of state. It includes in like fashion generation after generation of the entire people. The Deuteronomist therefore expresses his dismay when the entire generation that had seen Yahweh's great acts of deliverance has passed away and 'another generation' has arisen that does not know Yahweh or his deeds,[89] that no longer knows the 'antecedent history of the covenant.' This knowledge, however, must be discussed in another section.[90]

[88] B. Kübler, 'Testament,' in Pauly's *Realenzyklopädie*, Reihe 2, Halbbd. 9, col. 967.

[89] See Judg. 2:6ff.

[90] Here we must point out an historical problem, although for the time being no satisfactory solution can be given.—As we have seen, the concept of the covenant is originally rooted in the amphictyony. This means that the traditions of the covenant were also handed down in amphictyonic circles. If so, however, our observation that the transfer of office in the amphictyony, as in the case of Joshua, is represented in the same way as Solomon's succession to the throne of David raises the question of how the literary type came to be transferred. Certainly the traditions of the amphictyony have different roots from those of the monarchy. But is the observed agreement merely a literary fiction, or does it correspond to a real historical development?

On this problem, see also A. Alt, 'Gedanken über das Königtum Jahwes,' in his *Kleine Schriften*, vol. 1, pp. 345ff., especially p. 356.

To what extend did the kingship become an amphictyonic office? The relevant data include such texts as II Sam. 5:1-3. The act by which elders transfer the kingship to David can easily be imagined as taking place according to the forms discerned in Deuteronomy 31-Joshua 1, as well as in II Kings 11 and I Chronicles 22-29.—It is striking that in both II Sam. 5:2 and I Chron. 29:22 the title נָגִיד is expressly used. Are its original roots in the amphictyony or the monarchy?

V

THE RECITATION
OF THE COVENANT FORMULARY

In Section III we placed some restrictions on the instances in which a covenant renewal in the strict sense was undertaken. We considered it unlikely that the covenant was renewed on a regular basis, at least before the Exile. If this restriction is correct, however, the question at once arises of how we are to explain the broad influence exerted within Israel by the forms and content associated with the covenant.[1]

Here, too, I think the Hittite texts contribute to our understanding of how the 'covenant' works. As was mentioned above, a Hittite treaty contains an explicit stipulation concerning the regular *recitation* of the treaty formulary. In the treaty with Alakšanduš,[2] we read: 'Furthermore, this tablet, which I have set [forth] for you, Ala[kšanduš], shall be re[cit]ed to you three times each year, and you Alakšanduš shall know it.' Or, again, in the treaty with Mitanni:[3] 'In the land of Mitanni, also, (a duplicate) is deposited before Tešup, the lord of the *kur*[*i*]*uni* of Kaḫat. 'Repeatedly'[4] may it be recited before the king of the land of Mitanni and before the people of the land of Ḫarri.'[5]

The purpose of the recitation is therefore that the text of the treaty may be 'known'[6] or 'kept.'[7] The recitation of the 'tablet' includes the stipulations, the historical introduction, and the sanctions. Korosec therefore suspects a 'politico-legal reason' for this stipulation. On the one hand, the vassal is 'to be reminded of his treaty obliga-

---

[1] Alt, *Kleine Schriften*, vol. 1, p. 325, in the course of studying Joshua 24 states the following basic principle: 'Only in the context of oft-repeated situations in the life of a people can a literary type achieve the consistency of form and content without which its development in new directions is inconceivable.'

[2] F 5 §19, col. iii. 73–75. See also the note on this passage in Friedrich, *Staatsverträge*, part 2, p. 76, n. 4: KUB i. 16 (= 2 Bo TU 8) iii. 56–57: 'These [word]s shall be recited to you each month.'

[3] W 1, vo. 36–37.

[4] See Weidner, *Politische Dokumente*, p. 29, n. 3. The translation 'repeatedly' is not certain.

[5] This corresponds to W 2, vo. 7–8; see also F 3 §30, J 1–2. 'A semi-annual recitation of the treaty documents is found in a treaty fragment published by Forrer'; see Korosec, *Hethitische Staatsverträge*, p. 101.

[6] F 5 §9, col. iii. 75.

[7] F 3 §30, J 3.

tions, but also of the evidences of Hittite good will that he has already received and for which he is obligated to be grateful.'[8] On the other hand, the legitimacy of the vassal is confirmed once again before the nobles by the content of the treaty.[9]

According to Deut. 31:9ff., Moses decrees a recitation of the תּוֹרָה.[10] This is to take place every seven years, on the occasion of the Feast of Booths in the year of release. The purpose of the recitation is given as follows:[11]

12   לְמַעַן יִשְׁמְעוּ וּלְמַעַן יִלְמְדוּ
וְיָרְאוּ אֶת־יהוה אֱלֹהֵיכֶם
וְשָׁמְרוּ לַעֲשׂוֹת אֶת־כָּל־דִּבְרֵי הַתּוֹרָה הַזֹּאת

Formally, then, the significance of the recitation does not differ from what we ascertained above with respect to the recitation of the treaties.

On Deut. 31:9ff., Alt writes:[12] 'Although the expression may be unusual, the recitation of the apodictic law, which places the entire assembly of the people under obligation, at the Feast of Boots in the seventh year amounts in fact to a regularly repeated renewal of the covenant between Yahweh and Israel, the covenant that, in the mind of this people, called them to life.'—The considerations just outlined, however, show that, legally speaking, we are not in fact dealing with a renewal of the covenant. The covenant is concluded once and for all. Its duration does not depend on a natural cycle and the calendar. The antecedent history refers to historical events. The validity of the covenant can be put in question only by historical events. The covenant does not 'decay.' As a matter of fundamental principle it is concluded עַד עוֹלָם.[13]

---

[8] Korosec, *Hethitische Staatsverträge*, p. 102.

[9] Ibid.

[10] According to Steuernagel, *Deuteronomium*, p. 161, in v. 9 'הַתּוֹרָה הַזֹּאת in D²c refers to the entire legal discourse, not just chapters 12–26; cf. 4:44.'

On the text, see especially Kraus, *Worship*, pp. 74–75; also Kutsch, *Herbstfest*, pp. 19ff., 140ff.

[11] Driver, *Deuteronomy*, p. 336, translates: 'That they may hear, and that they may learn and fear Jehovah your God.'

[12] Alt, *Kleine Schriften*, v. 1, p. 328.

[13] See also Korosec, *Hethitische Staatsverträge*, pp. 106–107; Section V, 'The Duration of the Treaties': 'The parity treaties are concluded for eternity; there is not even a mention of any necessity for renewing the treaty.'

On this point, our study arrives at the same conclusion as E. Kutsch, who starts from quite different presuppositions: 'In all probability, to the extent the available evidence allows us to determine, there was never an annual covenant renewal ceremony to be celebrated at the Feast of Booths or even a Feast of Booths that might have been considered a covenant renewal festival' (*Herbstfest*, p. 158).

A different view is espoused by Mowinckel, who says of the autumn festival in Israel: 'And at the same time it is the feast of renewal of the covenant. We have seen that every cultic celebration is an act that creates, renews, and maintains a covenant.'[14]

H. J. Kraus[15] has objected to this definition on the grounds that it interprets the Old Testament statements concerning the covenant by the criterion of a 'phenomenological approach to the cult.' Now of course there can be no doubt that Israel borrowed cultic forms that were familiar to the rest of the ancient Near East. Mowinckel has assembled much material to illustrate this point. But even when Mowinckel has given special attention to the connection between myth and cult, the 'covenant' still, with respect to form, appears to have a closer relationship to history and international law.

According to Neh. 8:1, at the Feast of Booths Ezra recites from the סֵפֶר תּוֹרַת מֹשֶׁה אֲשֶׁר־צִוָּה יהוה אֶת־יִשְׂרָאֵל.[16] Verse 18 explains more precisely what Ezra recited 'day by day, from the first day to the last day.' Here, too, the purpose of the recitation is knowledge of the תּוֹרָה, on the part of both the people as a whole (8:12)[17] and especially the nobility (8:13).

Hölscher[18] considers the text a literary composition by the Chronicler based on the synagogue worship of his time. Rudolph, on the contrary, writes: 'In fact, Nehemiah 8 was the prototype that was later imitated, down to specific details, in the synagogue . . . and was therefore also probably able to serve as a model in this respect in the time of the Chronicler.'[19] It is hardly necessary, however, to assume literary dependence. The similarities are more likely due to the common *Sitz im Leben*.

Finally, the Mishna (Soṭa vii. 8) speaks of a recitation on the Feast of Booths. Here it is the king who does the reading.[20] This

---

[14] S. Mowinckel, *Décalogue*, p. 123.

[15] *Worship*, pp. 19ff.

[16] For a discussion of what is meant by this סֵפֶר, see Galling, *Chronik*, p. 233; Galling suggests the Pentateuch. According to Rudolph, *Esra*, pp. 145, 74, it is 'the Jewish Yahweh Torah as found at that time in Babylon.'

[17] For details (the function of the Levites, translation, etc.), see Rudolph, *Esra*, pp. 144ff. On v. 8, see E. Kutsch, 'מִקְרָא,' *ZAW*, 65 (1953), pp. 247ff.; p. 252, esp. n. 8.

[18] 'Die Bücher Esra und Nehemia,' in Kautzsch, *Heilige Schrift*, vol. 2, pp. 542–43.

[19] *Esra*, p. 149.

[20] Widengren, *Sakrales Königtum*. Widengren draws the conclusion that in Deut. 31:10ff. we are also dealing with a 'royal passage' (p. 95, n. 81).—This conclusion is not convincing. As our study has shown, we need not assume that the covenant is linked to a specific political form.

text is important for us because it also gives more details of what was recited, at least in the period of the Mishna. The passages are Deut. 1:1–6:3; 6:4–6; 11:13ff.; 14:22ff.; 26:12ff.; and portions of the blessings and curses from 27–28.[21]—The recitation therefore included not only legal sections of Deuteronomy, but also historical portions as well as blessings and curses. The nature of the material read therefore agrees with the recitation of a covenant formulary.

The passages that argue for a recitation of the תּוֹרָה are not numerous enough to allow us to draw further conclusions. One can certainly argue to the contrary by saying that in Israel 'knowledge of the covenant' formed part of the covenant. That this idea is not merely a product of the late period has been demonstrated by H. W. Wolff in a study of Hosea.[22] To 'elucidate the function of priestly דעת,'[23] Wolff cites this very passage (Deut. 31:9ff.). Following Alt, he considers it possible that Deut. 31:9ff. originally ordered the recitation of the series of apodictic laws. His study of Hosea shows, however, that for the latter priestly דַּעַת cannot be restricted to apodictic law.[24] Hosea cites the 'basic message of ancient Israelite covenant law expressly in 13:4 as the very core of Israel's "knowledge,' following the formulation of Exod. 20:2: "I, Yahweh, am your God from the land of Egypt; you know no God but me, and besides me there is no savior."'[25] 'His [Hosea's] polemic against the Baal cult, however, shows that we must not seek the object of that lost knowledge merely, or, according to Hosea, even primarily, in the ancient theocratic law, but rather in God's actions as they have been revealed.'[26] 'As giver of the land, Yahweh should have been known by the people from the climactic sentence of the ancient Credo.'[27] On Hos. 8:1b–2, Wolff writes: 'Israel, in its prayers of lament,[28] maintains that it has knowledge of its God. But the prophet's word disputes the truth of this quoted assertion by showing that the major content of the דעת, namely Yahweh's covenant (ברית) and Yahweh's teaching (תורה), has been rejected; thus the blessing (טוב) prepared by Yahweh has been repudiated.'

[21] According to Driver, *Deuteronomy*, p. 336, n. 1.

[22] H. W. Wolff, "'Wissen um Gott' bei Hosea als Urform von Theologie," *Evangelische Theologie*, 12 (1952/53).

[23] Ibid., p. 544; see also p. 538.   [24] Ibid., p. 544.

[25] Ibid., p. 546; cf. also Hos. 12:10.   [26] Ibid.

[27] P. 546, with reference to Hos. 2:10 (Eng. 2:8); see below.

[28] Here once more we find the distress depicted twice, once by the people and once by the prophet. According to Hosea, we are dealing with a curse consequent to the breaking of the covenant; see Hos. 8:1b.

The 'knowledge' that Hosea demands equally of priests and people can, however, be set perfectly parallel to the individual elements of the covenant formulary:[29] bestowal of the land, statement of substance, individual stipulations, and blessings and curses.

The Psalms show in like fashion that there was an obligation to know the 'covenant' and hand on this knowledge.[30] This holds true especially for the content of the antecedent history and the legal section. The Psalms also show, however, that, quite apart from official proclamation, this content was known in various forms to a group of considerable size[31] as well as to individuals.[32]

In the context of the present study, we must restrict ourselves to these references. The occurrence of similar stipulations in the Hittite treaties suggests to me that there is generally no justification for assigning a late date to all the traditions that mention a recitation of the תּוֹרָה and instruction concerning its content.[33] It is quite possible that in Israel, too, 'knowledge of the words of the covenant' was from the very outset a part of the covenant. The evidence cited in this chapter shows that this knowledge was not limited to the laws and their individual stipulations, but included above all knowledge of the history of Israel, of Yahweh's mighty acts.[34]

---

[29] See the passages cited by Wolff, 'Wissen,' p. 549.

[30] Weiser in particular has pointed this out (*The Psalms* [E.T. Philadelphia, 1962], pp. 25ff.). See, for example, Pss. 40:6–11 (Eng. 40:5–10); 78:1–7; 81:4ff. (Eng. 81:3ff.); 105:1–5; 111:4; 135:13.

[31] Pss. 107:1–2, 43; 118:1–4; 102:19–23 (Eng. 102:18–22); 75:2 (Eng. 75:1).

[32] Pss. 118:17; 77:12 (Eng. 77:11); 143:5.

[33] I therefore do not think that the stipulation in Deut. 17:18–19 is necessarily a fiction.

[34] Deut. 31:24ff. illustrates how the document of the covenant with Yahweh was also deposited in a sacred spot like a treaty: 'When Moses had finished writing the words of this "law" in a book, to the very end, Moses commanded the Levites who carried the ark of the covenant of Yahweh: "Take this 'book of the law' (סֵפֶר הַתּוֹרָה הַזֶּה), and put it by the side of the ark of the covenant of Yahweh your God, that it may be there for a witness against you. . . .' Cf. also Deut. 27:2ff.; Josh. 24:26–27. See W 1, vo. 35–36: 'A duplicate of this tablet has been deposited before Šamas of Ari[nn]a, since Šamas of Arinna directs kingship and queenship. [36] In the land of Mitanni, also, (a duplicate) has been deposited before Tešup, the lord of the "kur[i]nnu" of Kaḫat. . . .'

C

SUMMARY

Our study has shown that the covenant formulary in Israel exhibits a close association with the international treaties of the ancient Near East. The treaty form was developed using the Hittite vassal treaties as an example. Comparison revealed that such different literary elements as historical narrative, territorial description, laws, blessings, and curses together constitute a coherent whole. The parallelism of the literary types suggested that the making of the covenant, its renewal, ratification, and recitation took place in a fashion similar to that of an international treaty.

In the Old Testament texts, the treaty schema has been more or less altered. It appears, for example, in the stylized form of an address or turned into a narrative; in other words, the schema has been subjected to literary assimilation. The question is whether we should merely think in terms of acquaintance with the schema or assume that it was utilized directly.

According to Alt,[1] 'Only in the context of oft-repeated situations in the life of a people can a literary type achieve the consistency of form and content without which its development in new directions is inconceivable.' The texts we have examined show both that the form remains remarkably constant and that, where it has been altered, the alteration has been made with real appreciation of its meaning. Signs of acquaintance with the 'covenant formulary' were found in texts of widely varying origin (historical and prophetical texts, psalms, etc.). I consider it likely that we must also think in terms of direct utilization. But where do we find a *Sitz im Leben* that could preserve such a form so long? I cannot imagine this consistency of form except by assuming that it was used in worship. At the moment I cannot muster adequate support for this hypothesis. Only in a single instance can the use of the formulary as part of a liturgy be illustrated: in the liturgy of 1QS. But the Old Testament does not contain any liturgy for worship, nor would the nature of the text lead us to expect any. The late date of 1QS need not argue against early use of the formulary in worship.

---

[1] *Kleine Schriften*, vol. 1, p. 325.

This hypothesis is closely associated with the question of when the form came to be used in Israel. I think Joshua 24 gives us a clue. This text reproduces the schema particularly well, both in general structure and in its details. The reproduction is more exact than in a series of other texts, e.g., those of the Deuteronomist and Chronicler. This argues against the assumption that Joshua 24 has been subjected secondarily to a stylized revision reflecting better knowledge. If this text, however, is considered early—and few exegetes dispute an early dating—, then there is little reason to date the initial use of the schema very late.

The assumption that Israel had a concept of a covenant with Yahweh, which was later connected with the 'schema,' I consider unlikely. How should we conceive the realization of the 'covenant idea' without a form?

It must be expressly stated that the present study has been intended to explain only one kind of 'covenant.' It has been shown that בְּרִית taken by itself, like the English 'treaty' or 'contract,' is a strictly formal concept; it is necessary to specify in addition what kind of בְּרִית we are dealing with. The fully developed Hittite formulary was utilized in international law. This provided a good parallel to the covenant between Yahweh and his people. We must distinguish this type of בְּרִית from treaties between private individuals or contracts, which were certainly also found in Israel.[2]

To Noth[3] belongs the credit for pointing out the 'various kinds of covenant' that 'we must assume for the Old Testament from the very beginning.' I think it is possible that the legal concepts of the Hittite treaties can also contribute to our understanding of the formulas and concepts used in the Old Testament in connection with בְּרִית.

It will always be a remarkable fact that Israel experienced and came to understand its relationship with its God in such an objective and dispassionate form. This form is intimately associated with both history and law. This point distinguishes Israel from what was considered 'religious' in the world around it:[4] there the gods are represented primarily in the cycles of nature and cultic myths. Israel,

---

[2] See, for example, the treaties concerning pasturage and water rights: Gen. 21:22ff.; 26:26ff.; 31:43ff.

[3] In 'Das alttestamentliche Bundschließen,' *Gesammelte Studien*, pp. 142ff.; 153.

[4] According to an oral communication from Prof. Falkenstein, the concept of a treaty between a people and its own God is unknown outside of Israel.

in contrast, confesses that Yahweh has revealed himself in history. Israel knows that Yahweh is a God of law, not of caprice.[5]

The outcome of our primarily formal investigation and its limits must be seen in the light of this confession on the part of Israel. We shall cite several points to illustrate this statement.

The Israelite covenant is as far removed in content from the international treaties as it is closely related in form. The historical portions of the treaty formulary and the covenant formulary can be compared on the basis of their form. The history that they record, however, is incomparable and unique. The 'antecedent history' of the covenant formulary tells of God's acts among his people from generation to generation—ultimately, in fact, from eternity.[6] These acts are saving acts, 'demonstrations of Yahweh's righteousness.' Israel's loyalty to its Lord, its keeping of the commandments, is a response to God's acts of grace in history.

If, however, history is of such crucial importance for the covenant, we may well imagine the distress that arises when God's action in history can no longer be discerned.—Up to the occupation of Canaan, history is for Israel clearly a history of salvation. This period is therefore also the least variable element of the 'Credo.' The memory of the period of the Judges is already clouded by the sin of Israel. The accounts of the introduction of the kingship show that it was judged ambivalently. This ambivalence is disguised once more through the figure of David, whom all Israel recognizes as the anointed of the Lord. To later ages, however, the clarity of Israel's history and the clarity of the parallel between secular political history and saving history was by no means obvious. To them, the clarity was already obscured by the 'division of the kingdom.' The Deuteronomistic History shows the scandal caused by this event. The Chronicler tries to restore uniformity by disregarding the history of

[5] I would therefore not share Kraetzschmar's remonstrance (*Bundesvorstellung*, p. 180) 'that [the covenant concept] gave primacy of place in Israelite religion to an element that did not exactly add to its profundity: legalistic evaluation of religious matters.'

[6] I think it is possible, taking this observation as our point of departure, to connect form-critical study with the conclusions of literary criticism of the Pentateuch. Form-critical study might explain why there was a need to retell the history of Israel and interpret it afresh in various sources and successive redactions. In origin, at least, the reason cannot be literary. Knowledge of history is necessary because the basis of Israel's life in the covenant with Yahweh depends on this knowledge. It might also be possible to draw a more exact picture of the *Sitz im Leben* of the great historical works of the Old Testament. They function as expanded 'antecedent histories,' corresponding to the antecedent histories in Joshua 24 and Nehemiah 9.

the Northern Kingdom,[7] but the results show how problematic this attempt is. The Exile, finally, marks the most crucial turning point. Nehemiah 9 and Psalm 106 show how historical retrospect turns increasingly into a review of the history of Israel's sins. Even in Egypt the fathers sinned (Ps. 106:7). History becomes clouded.[8] This is made clear at its most extreme in IV Esdras. On the other hand, history may die out completely, yielding to exemplary narrative.[9]

The very structure of the covenant formulary shows how grave the silence of history proper must have been for the understanding of the covenant between Yahweh and his people. Noth has pointed out that a consequence was the 'exaltation of the law to independent and absolute status.'[10] The consequences of this development must be traced in the post-canonical literature. The structure of the covenant, in which history and law are intimately connected, allows us to understand how this process became necessary.[11]

Almost the exact opposite happens to the element of 'blessings and curses' in the covenant formulary. The borrowing of this element of the alien form is probably the most dubious aspect of its adoption, theologically speaking.[12] It is all too easy to arrive at the conclusion that blessing and curse, in the form of reward and punishment, follow automatically upon the fulfillment or non-fulfillment of the conditions of the covenant. There is a real danger that such 'automatism' will impugn God's freedom.[13] This is the limit to which the conception of the covenant as a 'treaty with God' must come.—Our study has shown that, when the form was borrowed, it was the element of 'blessings and curses' that was subjected to the most extensive changes. The most momentous change was the 'historicizing' of this element. Originally, the blessings and curses referred primarily to phenomena in the realm of nature, such as life and death, sickness

---

[7] See von Rad, *Geschichtsbild*, p. 135.   [8] Cf. Ezekiel 20!

[9] Noth, *Gesetze*, p. 72: 'Though this group (the post-exilic community) still continued to preserve and value the ancient narrative tradition of the history of Israel, it was henceforth understood as a collection of historical examples for human conduct with respect to the law and its consequences.'—Cf., for example, the utilization of the patriarchal narratives in the Testaments of the Twelve Patriarchs and the Book of Jubilees (see below, part II, pp. 144ff.).

[10] *Gesetze*, p. 79.

[11] In the New Testament, in contrast, the events of the present are acknowledged once more to be 'saving history'! Cf. Paul's speech in Acts 13:16ff.; also Acts 7:2ff., esp. vv. 51–53. Here the 'antecedent history' is traced all the way to Jesus.

[12] See Noth, 'Die mit des Gesetzes Werken umgehen, die sind unter dem Fluch,' in his *Gesammelte Studien*, p. 155, and esp. p. 171.

[13] See also M. Buber, *Two Types of Faith* (E.T. London, 1951), pp. 143f.

and health, offspring, etc. As early as Joshua 24 we found the beginnings of the development whereby blessings and curses ceased to stand juxtaposed as neutral possibilities. The present is perceived as as time of salvation; the curse threatens in the future. When disaster strikes Israel, this situation is reversed. The present becomes the period of the curse, and the period of blessing is awaited in the future. In this way, however, the element of 'blessings and curses' becomes the basis for a speculative interpretation of history. On this point, too, the post-canonical writings show a further development of this beginning.[14]

The circle of men addressed in the covenant underwent momentous sociological changes in the course of history, constituting first a tribal league, then a nation, and finally a cultic community. In the comparison to the revolutionary nature of these changes, their influence on the covenant form remained strikingly small. A study from the perspective of content would probably yield a different picture.

The conception of a covenant, as developed in a simple literary formulary, served to render the relationship between God and man comprehensible in human form. The criticism leveled by the prophets[15] shows, however, the danger of misusing this form. In a study of the meaning of the covenant within its total context, these prophetical voices must also be heard.

The present study has been intended to help elucidate one section of the greater question concerning the 'Old Covenant.' In the second part, which follows, we shall attempt to use the results of form-critical analysis of Old Testament texts to aid in understanding the structure of Jewish and Christian texts.

---

[14] See, for instance, the eschatological sections of the Testaments of the Twelve Patriarchs: Test. Sim. 5:2–6; Lev. 4; 10; Jud. 23:3ff.; Iss. 6:1ff.; Dan 5 (see below, Part II, pp. 153ff.).

[15] See, for example, Isa. 28:15; Amos 5:14; Hos. 8:1; Mic. 3:11.

Part Two

THE COVENANT FORMULARY
IN JEWISH AND EARLY CHRISTIAN TEXTS

A

INTRODUCTION

Our form-critical study in the first part of the present work demonstrated the existence of the 'covenant formulary' as a literary type in Old Testament texts. In part two, we shall trace the history of this literary type beyond the Old Testament.

We shall first summarize briefly once again the most important conclusions of the first part:[1]

The structure of the covenant formulary follow that of ancient Near Eastern international treaties. In its most simple form, it comprises the following elements: (1) 'antecedent history,' (2) statement of substance concerning the mutual relationship of the parties to the covenant, (3) the individual stipulations of the covenant, and (4) blessings and curses.[2]

Like an international treaty, the covenant formulary constitutes the basis of the covenant between Yahweh and Israel.

The conditions of the covenant include automatically 'knowledge of the covenant.' We must probably think in terms of regular public recitation of the covenant formulary. The connection with worship explains, among other things, the widespread occurrence in the Old Testament of the traditions associated with the covenant.

By its very nature the covenant is concluded 'for ever.' A renewal of the covenant is necessary when it has been broken. For such a covenant renewal, a penitential confession is inserted into the basic formulary.

Ratification of the covenant must be distinguished from renewal of the covenant. Such a ratification is undertaken when there is a change of leaders in Israel. The use of the covenant formulary on such occasions explains the later transformation of the formulary into a 'testament.'

Form-critical study of Jewish and Christian texts is subject to the difficulty that they very rarely contain literary types preserved in pure form. By the nature of the case we are dealing with highly

---

[1] See the author's article 'Das Bundesformular, sein Ursprung und seine Verwendung im Alten Testament,' *ThLZ*, 83 (1958), col. 585.

[2] See Part One above, pp. 10, 19ff. Two elements, the 'preamble' and 'invocation of witnesses,' can be ignored here.

H

developed and degenerate forms. In such texts it is therefore much more difficult to determine what is a mark of the literary type, what a peculiarity of the text at hand. Our study is made easier, however, by the fact that we do not have to work out the basic schema of the literary type and its typical characteristics on the basis of the relatively late texts.

We shall first of all be concerned to demonstrate that the same structures occur in these texts. We shall pay particular attention to where and how the original literary type of the 'covenant formulary' has been transformed. It is in the variations that we can best comprehend their underlying purpose.

Methodologically, we shall attempt to determine and define the literary type of larger units. As in Part One, our study will not be content with working out the 'smallest units'; it will attempt to show that it is possible to give a form-critical explanation for the assembly of literarily diverse elements, belonging originally to different literary types, to form a larger whole. This would provide a counter-example to Eißfeldt's statement:[3] 'Gunkel's own proposed method shows that his way of examining and presenting the material in literary-historical terms can only be applied to the smallest units —the single narrative, the single legal statement, the single saying, the single poem and so on. It cannot deal with the larger units and is quite unable to deal with the books as we have them.'

The texts under discussion are examples that were selected and brought together for methodological reasons. It is impossible here to enter into a discussion of the historical and theological relationship of the texts.

[3] *The Old Testament*, p. 4.

B. I

THE COVENANT FORMULARY
IN JEWISH TEXTS

1. The Manual of Discipline

We shall begin our study with a text from the so-called Manual of Discipline.[1] The section in question is iii. 13–iv. 26, a section well marked off from its context. It is preceded by an account of the conditions for admission to the community.[2] In iii. 13 the text begins with a new superscription:

למשכיל להבין וללמ' את כול בני אור...

The manuscript of the text as it has been preserved also shows that a new section begins at this point. The 'teaching' concludes with iv. 26. There follows in column v a kind of directory for the community, beginning with the superscription: וזה הסרך לאנש' היחד...

The section iii. 13–iv. 26 is structured as follows:

I. Dogmatic Section (iii. 15–iv. 1).[3]

This section could be termed a dogmatic theology *in nuce*. Statements are made concerning God and creation, man and his destiny. Special emphasis is placed on the dualism created by God between light and darkness, truth and depravity. These are represented by the prince of light and an angel of darkness.

Apart from its special subject matter, in the present context we are interested in the formal characteristics of this portion.

In the Old Testament covenant formulary, the 'antecedent history' occupies this position. An historical retrospect recounts Yahweh's mighty acts, which form the basis for the covenant relationship. Josh. 24:2–13[4] is an example of such an 'antecedent history.' This antecedent history begins, it is true, מֵעוֹלָם (v.2), but this refers

---

[1] For the text, see M. Burrows, ed., *The Dead Sea Scrolls of St. Mark's Monastery* (New Haven, 1950–51), vol. 2, fasc. 2. The text is cited as 1QS.

Roman numerals refers to the columns of the manuscript, Arabic numerals to the lines.

[2] This account includes, among other elements, a detailed liturgy for a covenant renewal ceremony (i. 18–ii. 10; ii. 18). See below, pp. 168–69, 189ff.

[3] On the superscription in lines 13–14, see below, pp. 108–09. On the structure of the text, compare the facsimile edition at each point. The structure agrees generally with the paragraphs of the manuscript.

[4] See above, pp. 19–20.

to the time when the fathers dwelt 'beyond the (Euphrates) River,' and therefore remains within the framework of history. The antecedent history is introduced by the preamble as the words of Yahweh, the 'God of Israel.' The latter formula is therefore a title, but there is nowhere any discussion of the 'existence of Yahweh himself.'

The text in Nehemiah 9, which is related in terms of literary type,[5] presents a somewhat different picture. It contains a confession of praise ...מִן־הָעוֹלָם עַד הָעוֹלָם (v. 5). But the statement 'Thou, O Yahweh, art the God who didst choose Abram' (v. 7) is preceded by praise of Yahweh for his creation:

> 'Thou, O Yahweh, art alone,
> Thou hast made heaven
> And the heaven of heavens with all their host,
> The earth and all that is on it,
> The seas and all that is in them.
> Thou preservest all that lives,
> And the host of heaven worships thee.' (Neh. 9:6)[6]

The creation and preservation of the world are here the beginning of God's saving acts. These statements are much more static than those found in the other Old Testament historical retrospects. Even the preference shown for nominal sentences exemplifies this characteristic. Such a statement as וְאַתָּה מְחַיֶּה אֶת־כֻּלָּם presupposes a higher degree of abstraction than the demonstration of how Yahweh has preserved life in particular instances throughout the generations of the fathers. From v. 7 on, however, Nehemiah 9 follows the traditional outline of *Heilsgeschichte*.

The sequence in Psalms 135 and 136 corresponds to that in Nehemiah 9: first praise of Yahweh in creation, then historical retrospect.[7] It is striking that, in the description of creation, Psalm 135 can employ the beginning of an onomasticon.[8] Once this step is taken, further development of this section is immediately conceivable.[9]

---

[5] See above, pp. 47ff.   [6] The translation follows Galling, *Chronik*, p. 235.

[7] The process as depicted corresponds to the placing of the primal history before the stories of the patriarchs in Genesis 1–12.

[8] 'Heaven, earth, seas, deeps, clouds, lightnings, rain, wind'; see G. von Rad, 'Job xxxviii and Ancient Egyptian Wisdom,' in his *The Problem of the Hexateuch* (E.T. New York, 1966), pp. 281–91.

[9] See hymn A I, according to A. Dupont-Sommer, 'Le Livre des Hymnes' (1QH), in *Semitica*, 7 (1957), pp. 26–27 (= 1QH i. 1–20). Cf. I Clement 20! See also the Clementine liturgy from the Apostolic Constitutions (H. Lietzmann, ed., *Die Klementinische Liturgie aus den constitutiones apostolorum VIII*, Bonn, 1910, p. 12, line 28; p. 21, line 25).

Comparison with the Old Testament text makes the character of the text in the Manual of Discipline clearer. As in the biblical texts, creation is discussed. We find this concern for creation in such statements as 'He created man to rule over the whole earth' [ברא!] (iii. 17–18). It has therefore been suggested that the text refers consciously to Genesis 1.[10] The original function of the section in the total structure of the form can be heard in the statement 'The God of Israel and the angel of his faithfulness help all the sons of light' (iii. 24–25). But there is here no trace of any confession of the acts of God in history. A general description of providence in cosmic events replaces history.[11] It is impossible to imagine in this context a sentence like that found in Josh. 24:15, 'Choose this day whom you will serve,' which demands a free response to God's free election. Despite this change in content, which corresponds to a change in theological outlook, the function of this element of the literary type remains the same. To bring out this change, however, it would be better to refer to this element as the 'dogmatic section,'[12] rather than as the 'antecedent history.'

II. Ethical Section (iv. 2–6, 9–11).

The beginning of the ethical section is clearly marked by the statement: ואלה דרכיהן בתבל... (iv. 2).[13] The first point to notice is the position of this section. It differs from the preceding section in both style and form. The reflective statements of the first section are replaced by long series of qualities. The sections clearly belong to different literary types. They are not, however, merely juxtaposed without any relationship to each other. The catchword דרך has already attracted our attention in the first section.[14] The second

---

[10] S. P. Wernberg-Møller, *The Manual of Discipline* (Grand Rapids, 1957), p. 67: 'The echo of biblical phraseology is not confined to the word "*twldwt*" (Lambert), but the use of words like "*myn*" (L. 14), "*br'*" (L. 17), and "*ld't twb(wr')*" (IV, 26) suggests that the whole of the essay is based on Gen. 1ff.'

[11] It is likely that this section also reveals especially markedly the presence of foreign influence on the sect (see K. G. Kuhn, 'Die Sektenschrift und die iranische Religion,' *Zeitschrift für Theologie und Kirche*, 49 [1952], pp. 296–316). This influence shows up especially in the strict determinism and the dualism of the text. Here, of course, the dualism is part of creation. The terms used raise the question of possible Hellenistic influence; see, for example, the statement: מאל הדעות כול הווה ונהייה (iii. 15).
According to Bardtke (*Die Handschriftenfunde am Toten Meer*, Berlin, 1953, p. 90), we should translate: 'All being and all happening (come) from the knowing God.'

[12] In the discussion to follow, we shall retain the term 'dogmatic section.'

[13] See also the facsimile.

[14] iii. 20   בדרכי אור יתהלכו
     iii. 21   ובדרכי חושך יתהלכו
     iv. 1   וכול דרכיה

section is clearly intended to spell out in detail the 'way of light' and the 'way of darkness.'

It can also be shown on the basis of the form as a whole that the two sections belong together and that the second is intended to be the logical consequence of the first. In the Old Testament, the 'antecedent history' is followed by statement of substance and individual stipulations.[15] In the statement of substance, the relationship between Yahweh and Israel, which is based on Yahweh's saving acts, is stated expressly once more. It can be reduced to the formula 'I will be your God, and you shall be my people.'[16] The conduct required of Israel can then be described in more detail. In Josh. 24:14, we read: 'Now therefore fear Yahweh, and serve him in sincerity and in faithfulness; put away the gods which your fathers served beyond the River, and in Egypt, and serve Yahweh.' Frequently a series of infinitives is used at this point to describe the basic relationship. Nehemiah 10:30 reads:[17]

לָלֶכֶת בְּתוֹרַת הָאֱלֹהִים...

וְלִשְׁמֹר

וְלַעֲשׂוֹת אֶת־כָּל־מִצְוֹת יהוה אֲדֹנֵינוּ

וּמִשְׁפָּטָיו

וְחֻקָּיו

Then, with Neh. 10:31 (Eng. Neh. 10:30), there follow directly the individual stipulations of the covenant, such as the prohibition of mixed marriages (v. 31 [Eng. v. 30]) and the obligation to pay taxes for the Temple (vv. 33–34 [Eng. vv. 32–33]). In Deuteronomy, instead of 'לָלֶכֶת בְּתוֹרַת הָאֱלֹהִים' (Neh. 10:30 [Eng. 10:29]), we read: לָלֶכֶת בִּדְרָכָיו (Deut. 30:16).[18]

Formally, the text of the Manual of Discipline agrees with what we found in the Old Testament: a close association with the preceding dogmatic section, description of the ethical section as 'ways,'[19]

---

[15] Cf. Josh. 24:14; Exod. 19:5–6a; Deut. 4:1ff.; 29:8; Exod. 34:11a, 12–16, 17–26.
[16] On the formula, cf. Exod. 6:7; Lev. 26:12; Deut. 29:12; II Sam. 7:24; Isa. 51:15–16; Jer. 7:23; 11:4; 24:7; 30:22; 31:1, 33; 32:38; Ezek. 11:20; 14:11; 34:30; 36:28; 37:23, 27; Hos. 2:25 (Eng. 2:23); Zech. 8:8; 13:9; I Chron. 17:22; see also especially Deut. 26:16–19.
[17] Cf. Deut. 10:12–13; 11:22, 28.
[18] The suffix in בִּדְרָכָיו refers to יהוה אֱלֹהֶיךָ. Cf. also Deut. 5:33; 9:12; 10:12; 11:12, 28.
[19] As in the Old Testament, this is still a technical term. See W. Michaelis, 'ὁδός,' in Kittel, Theological Dictionary, vol. 5, pp. 42ff., esp. 50ff.

followed by individual stipulations. The content, however, reveals once more some clear changes of emphasis. In the series of infinitives, the beginning of the ethical section with a series of general infinitives, one would expect a paraphrase of the basic conduct required of men. Since, however, the first section expresses a determinism destining man to good or to evil, the second section cannot simply speak of man as an active agent. In 1QS iv. 2–3, the subject of the infinitives:

ל ה א י ר בלבב איש

ו ל י ש ר לפניו כול ד ר כ י צדק

ו ל פ ח ד לבבו במשפטי אל

must, from the context, probably be 'the angel of his truth,' who helps all the sons of light ('to illuminate . . . to level . . . to terrify').[20] This and similar additions hardly make the language of the passage smooth.[21] It is possible that we are dealing here with exigencies of the form, for there is a similar difficulty in Neh. 10:30 (Eng. 10:29). Here, too, it is not immediately apparent what the infinitives (see above) depend on. In Nehemiah 10, however, the construction is smooth if the infinitives refer to:[22] וּבְכָל־זֹאת אֲנַחְנוּ כֹּרְתִים אֲמָנָה.

In iv. 3–6 and 9–14,[23] the text of the Manual of Discipline contains a catalog of virtues and vices. It is unlikely that the catalog was composed for this text ad hoc; the author probably interpolated it here.[24] The two halves are no longer completely parallel. The series of virtues reveals the peculiar nature of the sect more strongly. The point at which this catalog has been interpolated, however, is note-worthy. In Exodus 34, for example, the same position in the structure of the basic form is occupied by the so-called 'cultic' decalog. Nehemiah 10 contains obligations placed upon Israel to guarantee its distinction from the Gentiles, together with the obligation to carry out the Temple cult. In place of objective divine commands (in

[20] See the good translation of Wernberg-Møller, *Manual of Discipline*, p. 7: '. . . to make his heart fear God's statutes.'

[21] W. H. Brownlee, *The Dead Sea Manual of Discipline* ('Supplements to *BASOR*,' 10–12, New Haven, 1951), p. 15, n. 2, suggests: 'The heading to the first list has been lost through accidental scribal omission, or through oversight on the part of the author.' He supplies: 'The way of the Spirit of truth is to enlighten. . . .' See Wernberg-Møller, *Manual of Discipline*, p. 73: 'It is clear that something is missing in the headline in IV, 2; the phraseology of l. 9 suggests that we should supply *lrwh 'mt* (cf. Dupont-Sommer).'

[22] See Rudolph, *Esra*, p. 174 ad loc.

[23] On the appended blessings and curses, see below, pp. 104ff.

[24] See G. von Rad, 'The Early History of the Form-Category of I Corinthians XIII. 4–7,' in his *Problem of the Hexateuch*, pp. 309–10.

Exodus 34) or cultic obligations (in Nehemiah 10), the Manual of Discipline describes the subjective disposition of the believer. Of course this description implies certain demands; but these demands refer far less immediately to the individual or the community than do the demands in the Old Testament commandments. The catalog of the Manual of Discipline describes the pious believer as a type.[25]

In this case, the difference in literary type of the smallest units is obvious: in the first case, we have a 'decalogue'; in the second, regulations for the cultic community; in the third, a catalog of virtues and vices. In the larger unit, all three have the same function, to express an obligation. Since they occupy the same position, however, the change in ideology behind the texts is all the clearer.

It is of course possible to say that the interpolation of the catalog of virtues and vices at this point within the Manual of Discipline is fully appropriate to the form. It shows, among other things, that the form itself is not yet completely petrified, but is still subject to meaningful alteration at this point.

The part of the formulary that refers to the ethical conduct of the individual will be called the 'ethical section' in the discussion to follow. It comprises the 'statement of substance' together with the 'individual stipulations' of the Old Testament formulary.[26] The 'individual stipulations' of the Manual of Discipline are not restricted, however, to instructions for the devout individual. There are also stipulations that refer to the community as a whole. These, however, are comprised in a special 'corpus of legal stipulations.'[27]

III. Blessings and Curses

The blessing and curse formulas show clearly that we may reasonably speak in terms of borrowing an ancient form rather than assume the completely free creation of a new form on the part of the supposed author, a form that could not be assigned to any literary type. This means that our original designation of this element as 'blessings and curses' still holds as an initial description.

In the case of the blessing formula (iv. 6b–8), we must certainly think in terms of a special viewpoint on the part of the author of the Manual of Discipline. The conclusion in particular is reminiscent of his special style, as found elsewhere: 'A crown of glory with a robe

---

[25] Ibid., p. 307.
[26] See the discussion of the Didache below, pp. 127ff.
[27] See below, pp. 100ff.; 118; 130.

of splendor in eternal light (they will receive)' (lines 7–8).[28] With regard to the first element of the blessing, 'למרפא,' different interpretations are possible: it may be understood 'eschatologically' from the outset, or it may originally have meant merely 'healing.'[29] In the promise of 'fulness of peace through the length of days, fruitfulness of offspring together with all lasting blessings and everlasting joy through lasting life,'[30] we can still recognize clearly ancient formulas of blessing. Here, too, the words can be interpreted according to the doctrines of the sect: the writer, for example, probably no longer understood 'עולם' in its Old Testament sense, 'everlasting time,' but as 'eternity' in the metaphysical sense.[31] The interpretation of the promise of 'abundant posterity' in this context remains difficult, especially in its position following a catalog of virtues. This detail, I think, shows clearly the formal constraints brought about by the borrowing of what was originally a blessing formula. Methodologically, therefore, it is impossible to draw immediate historical conclusions from the details of such a blessing formula. Brownlee, for example, concludes from the mention of posterity: 'This would seem to indicate that the sect married. . . .'[32] The unique nature of the text is most easily explained as a consequence of the borrowing and reinterpretation of an ancient blessing formula.

The same holds true for the curse (iv. 12–14) that follows the catalog of vices.[33] We have here a series in which the threatened

[28] Bardtke's translation, following Brownlee.

[29] See Wernberg-Møller, *Manual of Discipline*, p. 79, n. 2: 'The word "*mrp*", is used in the O.T. as referring to eschatological salvation, visualised as "healing" (cf. Jer. 8:15; 14:19; Mal. 3:2). The conception is common in pseudepigraphical literature. . . .'— But the passages from Jeremiah (see also Jer. 33:6) need not be understood 'eschatologically'; they contain promises of blessing after Yahweh turns aside the curse.

[30] ‎...למרפא ורוב שלום באורך ימים
‎ופרות זרע עם כול ברכות עד
‎ושמחת עולמים בחיי נצח וכליל כבוד
‎עם מדת הדר באור עולמים

[31] On this point, see E. Jenni, *Das Wort 'olam im Alten Testament* (Berlin, 1953), esp. pp. 50ff.

[32] Brownlee, *Dead Sea Manual of Discipline*, p. 15, n. 14.
See the methodologically similar suggestion by Bardtke, *Handschriftenfunde*, p. 91, n. 2. Bardtke translates מרפא as 'calmness.' 'Compare also the description by Josephus with reference to the calmness and steadfastness of the Essenes in times of persecution (*Jewish War* ii. 8. 10).'

[33] 'All who walk in this (spirit) will be afflicted with many plagues at the hand of the angels of pestilence, with eternal ruin through the furious wrath of the avenging God, with lasting terror and eternal humiliation—altogether, the ignomiy of destruction in the fire of the dark places. All their times in their generations will be in grievous mourning and bitter misfortune until their complete destruction, nor shall any remnant escape' (following Bardtke, *Handschriftenfunde*, pp. 91–92).

disaster is described in terms of various concepts.[34] At the end comes
'complete destruction, nor shall any remnant escape.' This last turn
of phrase is typical of the curses in the context of a covenant.[35]

The mention of the 'angels of pestilence' in the series of curses is
striking. These angels presuppose a conception of the curse that
scarcely appears in the Old Testament texts mentioning the curse
when the covenant is broken. Their significance is clear, however, in
any comparison with texts of treaties outside the Bible. There, before
the blessings and curses, the 'gods of the oath' are invoked as
witnesses and guarantors of the treaty. If the treaty is broken, it
falls to them to execute the sanctions against those that have broken
their oath. They 'pursue' the guilty 'until they are completely
destroyed.'[36] In the present text, the 'angels of pestilence' have
clearly replaced the 'gods of the oath.'[37] The mention of the 'angels
of pestilence,' even though they stand in parallel with the 'avenging
God,' at this precise point in the Manual of Discipline can hardly be
considered accidental. This raises several questions, however. The
treaty formulary was early adopted as the form for the covenant with
Yahweh; when this took place, invocation of Yahweh himself
replaced invocation of the 'gods of the oath.' The Old Testament
texts show this clearly. Were there also, besides the Old Testament
form that has been preserved for us, 'uncensored' forms in which the
'gods of the oath' continued to exist under the guise of 'angels of
pestilence'? Does such a form make its appearance once more here

---

[34] Cf. the series in Job. 36:10ff.

[35] See, for example, Deut. 28:45, concluding the first part of the list of curses:
'All these curses shall come upon you
    and pursue you
    and overtake you,
    until they destroy you,
because you did not obey the voice of Yahweh your God, to keep his commandments and
his statutes. . . .'

[36] Cf. the treaty between Šuppilulimaš and Mattiwaza (Weidner, *Politische Dokumente*,
pp. 33–34), vo. 59ff.: 'If you Mattiuaza . . . and you people of Ḫarri do not keep the
words of this treaty, may . . . the gods, the lords of the oath, destroy you.' Also ibid.,
p. 35, vo. 63: '. . . and these gods, who are the lords of the oath, shall ordain misery and
impoverishment for you.'
    Cf. Friedrich, *Staatsverträge*, Teil I, pp. 119–20, §10 D, 25; p. 125, §15, C 23ff.; p. 129,
§17, C 21; p. 131, §18, B iii 30; Teil II, pp. 113–14, col. ii, 2ff., §10.

[37] A connecting link can be found in such texts as Enoch 100:10–13 (see above, p. 24).
Here 'the angels in heaven, from the sun, the moon, and the stars search out deeds with
respect to sin.' 'Clouds, mist, dew, and rain will be made witnesses against the trans-
gressor.' At the end, we read: 'In those days, when the frost and snow with their cold and
all the snow-winds with all their plagues fall upon you, you will not be able to withstand
them' (v. 13).

and in other related late texts? Or are we dealing with foreign influences in the late period? If the latter, the interpolation was performed with remarkable intelligence.

Finally, we must recall once more the peculiarity that in our text the catalog of virtues and vices is associated with series of blessings and curses.

The section from iv. 5 to the end of the column repeats, with minor changes, ideas that have already occurred in the previous sections. In particular it draws its content from section one. The theology of the sect is once more expressed with special clarity. But it is the piling up of temporal expressions that gives the sections its special character.[38] The temporal sequence[39] shows that we are dealing with an *eschatological* passage: 'until then' (for the present; line 23), 'until the final end' (16–17), 'until the determined time of judgment' (19–20), 'then . . . then . . .' (followed by a future tense!), 'until he creates something new' (25), 'for an "eternal" covenant' (22). The present age is contrasted with another, new age. Between the two ages comes the 'judgment,' to damnation and to salvation. End and judgment are comprehended in the 'mysteries of the wisdom of God.'[40]

The negative and positive perspectives of eschatology, damnation and salvation, link the whole section closely with the preceding blessings and curses. The term פקודה, 'visitation,' furnishes another connection.[41] Blessing and curse are referred to as פקודה, as is the last judgment. In their original form, blessing and curse present alternatives, an 'either/or.' In contrast to the blessing and curse, the eschatological section is based from the very outset on the temporal sequence 'now/then.' In the structure of the formulary, this turns the element of 'blessings and curses' into an 'eschatological section.'

---

[38]

עד קץ אחרון	16		לכול קצי עולמים	16
לעד ואז... 20 ואז...	19		אל...נתן קץ	18
לברית עולמים	22		עד מועד משפט	19
עד קץ...ועשות חדשה	25		עד הנה	23
			[...]. לכול קצי	25

[39] Taken according to the sense, not in the order of the text!

[40] ...אל ברזי שכלו ובחכמת כבודו נתן קץ להיות עולה 18

It is interesting to note that at this very point the term 'רז' is used. Within the Old Testament it occurs only in Daniel 2. Ⓖ translates it 'μυστήριον'! (Cf. Dan. 2:18–19, 27–30.) Dan. 2:28: ἀλλ' ἔστι θεὸς ἐν οὐρανῷ ἀνακαλύπτων μυστήρια, ὃς ἐδήλωσε τῷ βασιλεῖ Ναβουχοδονοσορ, ἃ δεῖ γενέσθαι ἐπ' ἐσχάτων τῶν ἡμερῶν.

[41] iv. 6 in the introduction to the blessing; iv. 12 in the introduction to the curse. Cf. in the eschatological section iv. 19 and iv. 26.

Terminology for the Elements of the Literary Type on the Basis of the Text

In the case of Old Testament texts, one is usually compelled to determine the literary type by deriving the structure of the text and the boundaries of its constituent units from an examination of the text itself. Terms from modern literary criticism are often used to give names to the literary types. It is therefore easy to object that the methods of form criticism enmesh the text in a network of structures alien to the text itself, which were quite unknown to its ancient author. Above all, alien categories are used to designate the literary types. The introduction of the text we are now studying shows very clearly that the author himself was aware of the structure we have derived from our examination of the text.[42] In addition, it is possible to derive the author's terms for the units from the introduction.

First the *Sitz im Leben* and function of the text are given (iii. 13): למשכיל להבין וללמד את כול בני אור. Determining the meaning of למשכיל involves some difficulties. It is usually translated 'for the wise.'[43] 'The wise' can refer either to every member of the community[44] or specifically to a teacher of the community.[45] The verbs that follow, which describe a teaching function, together with the parallel in the Damascus Document (13:7ff.), in my opinion support the second possibility: 'the one who makes prudent.' According to this superscription, the text that follows contains the teaching binding upon the community of 'sons of light.'

The content of this teaching, according to the superscription, is threefold (iii. 13–15).

I.	(ללמד ...)[46] בתולדות כול בני איש לכול מיני רוחותם
II.	באותותם למעשיהם בדורותם[47]
III. (a)	ולפקודת נגיעיהם
(b)	עם קצי שלומם

Such an organization, however, corresponds to the structure of the text resulting from our detailed examination.[48] The 'dogmatic section' is called תולדות. This term is usually translated here as

---

[42] We have already pointed out the general agreement between this structure and the division of the manuscript by the scribe.

[43] Bardtke, Wernberg-Møller, and Brownlee adopt this translation.

[44] This interpretation is suggested by Wernberg-Møller, *Manual of Discipline*, p. 66, n. 39.

[45] Brownlee, *Dead Sea Manual of Discipline*, p. 13, n. 21: 'The word "*maskil*" may well be drawn from Dan. 11:33 where the same verb for "instruct" is used as here (cf. also Dan. 12:3). Being of Hiph'il formation the word means not so much one who is

'sequence of generation.'[49] This translation emphasizes the course of history. Strangely enough the term thus is less appropriate to this text than to the 'antecedent history' of the original covenant formulary, which depicts the acts of Yahweh through the sequence of generations down to the present.[50] The text from the Qumran sect eliminates a genuine account of history in favor of a strict determinism, and is therefore much more static. It is possible that the author of the Manual of Discipline is here using a technical term that no longer really suits his purposes.

The correspondence between part two of the superscription and the content of the 'ethical section' is well expressed in the translation of Wernberg-Møller: 'with the (different) characters of their actions in their generations.'

Part three of the superscription shows once more what our detailed study suggested: the author of the Manual of Discipline did not clearly distinguish the blessings and curses from the eschatological section.[51] The opposed concepts 'plagues' and 'peace' correspond to 'curses and blessings.' Part three of the superscription as a whole must certainly be understood eschatologically. Characteristically, in contrast to the text itself blessings and curses are transposed. Now the 'time of salvation' comes at the end.

---

wise in and of himself but one who is able to teach wisdom.' Dupont-Sommer suggests a similar interpretation.

[46] The arrangement of the individual ideas is disputed. See Wernberg-Møller, *Manual of Discipline*, p. 66, n. 39: 'The style of the first two lines of the essay [referring to iii. 13ff.] is stilted and turgid and has given rise to a variety of translations.' But the structure is not in fact so difficult if we follow Wernberg-Møller (ibid., n. 42) in construing the preposition 'ב' as introducing the object of ללמד; then, however, the second 'ב' (in באותותם) must also be taken with ללמד in the sense of an enumeration.

[47] On this as a 'periphrastic genitive construction,' see ibid., p. 67, n. 44: 'The characteristic of this construction is that the "nomen rectum" is anticipated by a suffix and introduced by the preposition "*l*".'

[48] This organization is repeated, I think, at iv. 15ff. in the text:

I.   באלה תולדות כול בני איש
                      ובמפלגיהן ינחלו כול צבאותם לדורותם
II.   ובדרכיהן יתהלכו
           וכול פעולת מעשיהם במפלגיהן לפי נחלת איש...

What follows constitutes the 'eschatological section.'

[49] Bardke and Brownlee translate '(succeeding) generation'; Wernberg-Møller, 'the genealogies.'

[50] The Priestly Document especially uses תולדות in this extended meaning.—See also above, pp. 21, 29, 89.

[51] A more thorough analysis with special attention to content would here have to take into account the deterministic influences in the Manual of Discipline (see especially iv. 15ff.).

The Corpus of Legal Stipulations in the Manual of Discipline (v–ix?)

The portion of the text under discussion (iii. 13–iv. 26) is followed immediately by the corpus of legal stipulations in the Manual of Discipline.

Ludwig Köhler has said of Deuteronomy:[52] 'This Deuteronomy has been called a legal code. This name is wrong. It is a legal collection in which ancient statues obviously alternate with quite recent ones. . . . A legal code is a collection of statutes that comes into being when the lawgiver draws up his individual statutes with a very specific legislative purpose and according to a pervasive and uniform concept of law. A legal collection, however, relinquishes precisely this uniform, pervasive, legislative purpose, bringing together ordinances both ancient and modern, which are intended to remain in force, so that the legislative basis need not be uniform, and usually is not.'

In my opinion, comparison with Deuteronomy can also help us understand the special nature of the Manual of Discipline. It does not contain a single uniformly conceived rule for the community, but is rather a collection. Various smaller corpora were probably brought together in the process. This would explain the multiplicity of super-scriptions (or colophons?),[53] all of which refer in similar fashion to 'legal ordinances.' A few parallel passages occur, e.g., regulations concerning admission (and readmission?) to the community.[54] The content of these regulations cannot in every case be reduced to a single denominator. The examination of the candidate, for example, is undertaken in one case by the 'multitude,' in another by a specifically authorized individual.[55]

---

[52] *Der hebräische Mensch*, Anhang 'Die hebräische Rechtsgemeinde,' (Tübingen, 1953), pp. 165–66.

[53]

וזה הסרך לאנשי היחד	v. 1
אלה תכון דרכיהם על כול החוקים האלה	v. 7
באלה יתהלכו בכול מגוריהם	vi. 1
הזה הסרך למושב הרבים	vi. 8
ואלה המשפטים	vi. 24
ואלה המשפטים	viii. 20
אלה החוקים	ix. 12
אלה תכוני הדרך	ix. 21

Cf. 1QSa i. 1 and 6.

[54] v. 20–25; vi. 13–23; vii. 18–21; viii. 16–19. Cf. i. 1ff.; 1QSa i. In v. 20ff., admission to the community is referred to as admission to the 'covenant':

וכיא יבוא בברית לעשות ככול החוקים האלה ....

[55] v. 20ff. and vi. 13ff.

Within the corpus itself, the sections with the designation סרך or חוק are distinct from those that contain משפטים.

The section vi 24–ix. 11 is primarily a collection of משפטים.[56] It could be called the 'criminal law' as opposed to the 'civil law' of the 'community rule.' It contains typical casuistic ordinances. Each is introduced by (אם (ימצא בם איש...,[57] האיש אשר,[58] or merely אשר.[59] Then follows a brief outline of the 'case' and the degree of punishment.

סרך and חוק make up the community rule proper.[60] This includes regulations concerning such matters as admission to the community; 'separation,' i.e., the relationship of the community to the surrounding world; the forms of liturgical life; and the structure of the community with its various 'classes' and offices. Here, too, we can observe similarities in the structure of the major units. A superscription such as זה הסרך is usually followed by a series of infinitives, which describe life within the community in general terms.[61] Some of these introductions agree even in vocabulary with the characteristics of the statement of substance in Old Testament texts.[62]

---

[56] Following the organization of the manuscript: vi. 24–viii. 4; viii. 4–19; viii. 20–ix. 5; ix. 5–11.

[57] E.g., vi. 24.

[58] See the series in vii. 15ff.

[59] vii. 12ff.

[60] Roughly the following major units can be distinguished: v. 1–vi. 23 (v. 1–13; 13–25; v. 25–vi. 23 according to the manuscript); ix. 12–x. 8. Cf. i. 1–iii. 12 and 1QSa.

[61] Cf. i. 1 (according to the emendation suggested by Brownlee and confirmed by more recent discoveries; see *Qumran Cave I*, p. 107).

(i. 1–2)   סרך היחד

לדרוש· לעשות· לאהוב· לשנוא· לדבוק· לעשות· ללכת

(v. 1–2)   וזה הסרך

לשוב· להחזיק· להבדיל· להיות

(ix. 12–13)   ואלה החוקים

להתהלך· לעשות· למוד· להבדיל· לשקול· להחזיק· לעשות

[62] See above, pp. 21, 28–29, 35, especially pp. 37ff, and *passim*. Cf., for example, Deut. 10:12–13 (see also 11:22):

וְעַתָּה יִשְׂרָאֵל מָה יהוה אֱלֹהֶיךָ שֹׁאֵל מֵעִמָּךְ

כִּי אִם־לְיִרְאָה   אֶת־יהוה אֱלֹהֶיךָ

לָלֶכֶת   בְּכָל־דְּרָכָיו

וּלְאַהֲבָה אֹתוֹ

וְלַעֲבֹד   אֶת־יהוה אֱלֹהֶיךָ בְּכָל־לְבָבְךָ...

לִשְׁמֹר   אֶת־מִצְוֹת יהוה וְאֶת־חֻקֹּתָיו...

In the following individual stipulations there appear series of imperatives and jussives, as well as series negated with 'לא.'[63]

The corpus of legal stipulations—like the corpus of laws in Deuteronomy—is a self-contained unit. Its framework, however, associates it intimately with the rest of the Manual of Discipline. The legal stipulations are binding upon 'Israel as the community of the eternal covenant.'[64]

2. The Damascus Document

Like the Manual of Discipline, the Damascus Document is a 'collection.'[65] For it, too, this hypothesis explains the many over-lappings, and especially the repeated superscriptions. In this case the two fragments, A and B, still show that there were different recensions of the same work. Texts A and B generally parallel each other, but may, for instance, provide different scriptural citations for the same idea.[66]

Although only fragments have been preserved, the structure of the whole is still easily discernible.

1. Dogmatic Section ('Antecedent History') : 1–6:11

In contrast to the section iii. 15–iv. 1 in the Manual of Discipline, we are dealing here with a very extensive section. As expected, it stands at the beginning of the text. It is itself composed of several pieces: 1:1–2:1, 2:2–13, and 2:14–21 have almost parallel intro-ductions.[67]

The first part, 1:1–2:1, comprises a brief historical retrospect from the time that God 'gave Israel into the hand of Nebuchadnezzar, the King of Babylon,' to the rise of the community ('the New Covenant'). The history of the community, together with the 'awakening of the

---

[63] See v. 14–20; cf. i 13ff.

[64] v. 5–6: לישראל ליחד ברית עולם

The catchword ברית occurs several times in the corpus (see v. 2–3, 8, 9, 10, 11, 12, 18, 19, 20, 22, and *passim*).

[65] Eißfeldt, *The Old Testament*, pp. 649ff. For bibliography on the Damascus Document, see ibid., p. 649. The edition of the text used in the present study is: L. Rost, *Die Damas-kusschrift*, 1933. The citations refer to the page and line number of Schechter, which follows the manuscripts; see Rost, *Damskusschrift*, p. 7, n. 1.

[66] A 1 has a quotation from Isaiah in 7:10ff., whereas B gives a quotation from Zachariah in 19:7ff.

[67] 1:1–2:   ועתה שמעו כל יודעי צדק ובינו במעשי אל
2:2–3:   ועתה שמעו אלי כל באי ברית ואגלה אוזנכם בדרכי רשעים
2:14–15:   ועתה בנים שמעו לי ואגלה עיניכם לראות ולהבי במעשי אל

teacher of righteousness,' is depicted, albeit in a fashion not quite comprehensible. In the manner of Deuteronomistic theology, historical disaster is seen as a curse consequent on transgression of the covenant.[68]

The second part, 2:2–13, corresponds best in form and content to the 'dogmatic section' in the Manual of Discipline. The chapter begins with a passage '*de deo*.' The character of the confessional formulas becomes clear when they are compared with corresponding formulas in the Old Testament, which they echo sometimes word for word.[69] First stands, instead of 'God's goodness and mercy,' 'knowledge of wisdom, counsel, prudence, and understanding.' These concepts are almost personalized. God has 'placed counsel before him'; prudence and understanding 'serve him.' 'Repentance' is mentioned expressly as prerequisite for forgiveness. Punitive justice is stressed. The 'angels of pestilence'[70] are mentioned once more as instruments of wrath.

The rest of this portion, like the corresponding passage in the Manual of Discipline, speaks of election (מקדם עולם!), providence, and God's predestination for all time. Understanding comes to the

[68] 1:16ff.:   למען הדבק בהם את אלות בריתו להסגירם
לחרב נקמת נקם ברית בעבור...

There follows, like a catalog of vices, a series of twelve points, each marking a transgression of the covenant. Cf. Nehemiah 9.

[69] Cf. Exod. 34:6; Num. 14:18; Joel 2:13; Jonah 4:2; Nahum 1:2ff.; Pss. 86:5; 103:8; 145:8; Neh. 9:17; Ecclus. 2:13. See above, p. 35.

2:3–5:   אל אהב דעת חכמה ותושייה הציב לפניו ערמה ודעת הם
ישרתוהו ארך אפים עמו ורוב סליחות לכפר בעד
שבי פשע וכוח וגבורה וחמה גדולה בלהבי אש

Exod. 34:6   אֵל רַחוּם וְחַנּוּן אֶרֶךְ אַפַּיִם וְרַב־חֶסֶד וֶאֱמֶת:
נֹצֵר חֶסֶד לָאֲלָפִים נֹשֵׂא עָוֹן וָפֶשַׁע וְחַטָּאָה
וְנַקֵּה לֹא יְנַקֶּה פֹּקֵד עֲוֹן אָבוֹת עַל־בָּנִים וְעַל־בְּנֵי בָנִים...

Jonah 4:2:   אֵל־חַנּוּן וְרַחוּם אֶרֶךְ אַפַּיִם וְרַב־חֶסֶד
וְנִחָם עַל־הָרָעָה

Neh. 9:17:   אֱלוֹהַּ סְלִיחוֹת
חַנּוּן וְרַחוּם אֶרֶךְ־אַפַּיִם וְרַב־חֶסֶד

Ecclus. 2:13:   (ἐμβλέψατε εἰς ἀρχαίας γενεὰς καὶ ἴδετε . . .)
διότι οἰκτίρμων καὶ ἐλεήμων ὁ κύριος
καὶ ἀφίησιν ἁμαρτίας καὶ σῴζει ἐν καιρῷ θλίψεως.

[70] See above, pp. 106–107.

I

faithful in all ages through 'his anointed.'[71] All in all, here too history retreats in favor of metaphysical speculation concerning the 'ages.'[72]

The third part, 2:14–6:11, is closest to the 'antecedent history' in the Old Testament in structure, content, and function.[73] The presentation follows the traditional scheme of the 'antecedent history.' The text begins with the fall of 'the guardians of heaven,'[74] mentions the Deluge, and continues the series: Noah's sons, Abraham, Isaac, Jacob, the sons of Jacob, their sons, Egypt, the desert, Kadesh. To this point obedience or disobedience to the commandments of God is gauged in each case, with distinct stress on apostasy and its consequences.[75] As in Neh. 9:26–31, there follows a summary of the further course of history: 'God's wrath was kindled against their community; therefore their sons perished, and their kings were destroyed, their mighty men therefore perished, and their land was therefore devastated; therefore those generations became guilty that first entered into the covenant, and they were consigned to the sword, because they forsook the covenant of God. . . .'[76]

In what follows, the 'renewal of the covenant of God with Israel for ever for the remnant of those that hold fast to the commandments'[77] probably refers to the history of the sect and no longer to the ancient history of Israel. The same is true of the statement: 'He built a house for them' (3:19). The very scope of the description from 3:12 on, in contrast to the terse outline that precedes, shows that the author is especially interested in this section of Israel's history.

In the form of this whole passage the history of the sect clearly lays claim to being the legitimate continuation of the history of Israel. This claim is also expressed in the way a number of passages from Scripture are interpreted as referring to the sect (Ezek. 44:15 and Isa. 24:17, among others). The commentary on these passages

---

[71] 2:12.

[72] See especially 2:9–10:

ידע את שני מעמד ומספר ופרוש קצהם
לכל הוי עלמים ונהויית עד מה יבוא
בקציהם לכל שני עולם...

Cf. 1QS iii. 15.

[73] See especially Nehemiah 9.   [74] 2:18: עירי השמים.

[75] It is striking that the text does not mention the incident of the Golden Calf in this context. What does the 'eating of blood' refer to, which is stressed as being especially abominable?

[76] 3:8–11.   [77] 3:12ff.: הקים אל את בריתו לישראל עד עולם...

follows the model of a '*pesher*.' The following figures from Israel's history are also mentioned: Levi, David, Eleazar, Joshua and the elders, Zadok, Moses, Aaron, Jachin and his brothers. Further details cannot be discussed here.

The author concludes in 5:20ff. with a description of his own time, which he clearly looks upon as the 'last days of wickedness,'[78] 'until the Teacher of Righteousness comes at the end of days.'[79] Since the 'antecedent history' is traced down to the author's own time, it fulfills precisely the function of the 'antecedent history' in the structure of the Old Testament covenant formulary.

II. Ethical Section: 6:11–7:4

The ethical section begins with a passage that formally resembles the Old Testament statement of substance. As is typical in the introduction of the basic commandments, we find a formula beginning with שמר, followed by infinitives.[80] The author, however, has first inserted a commandment 'for all those that enter into the covenant' (6:11), 'that none of them enter the sanctuary to kindle the altar for "nothing".' This commandment to break off all relationship with the official cult is obviously especially important. In the Old Testament, the basic commandment that occupies this position is the prohibition against worship of alien gods.

The series of commandments in the form of dependent infinitives is expanded to sixteen members. It is hard to determine the boundary between the basic commandments in the statement of substance and the individual commandments. At any event, the commandments cited in this section differ from the individual stipulations in the corpus proper of the Damascus Document. Their fundamental quality predominates. These commandments include the requirement that 'each shall love his brother as himself' (6:20–21). There is no parallel requirement here 'to love God.' The commandment to sustain 'the widow, the orphan, and the stranger' is fully biblical. There is a striking emphasis on the 'poor and needy.'[81]

---

[78] 5:20: ובקץ חרבן הארץ
6:10 (see Ezek. 21:30): ... בכל קץ הרשיע
[79] 6:10–11: עד עמד יורה הצדק באחרית הימים
[80] אם לא ישמרו לעשות כפרוש התורה לקץ הרשע
ולהבדל מבני השחת ולהנזר מהון הרשעה ...
(לגזול, להיות, להבדיל, לטהור, להודיע, ולשמור, להרים,
לאהוב, להחזיק, לדרוש, להזיר, להוכיח, לא לנטור, להבדיל)
[81] 6:16: עני ואביון ;6:21: עני עמו

Three times a commandment is expanded by the addition of the phrase: 'according to the interpretation (made by the sect).'[82] These are the commandments relating to the Torah, the Sabbath, and the sacred offerings. Feasts and fasts are regulated by the directives of those who 'have entered into the new covenant in the land of Damascus' (6:19).[83] There are also special משפטים (7:2, 3) for guarding against unchastity and keeping free of impurity. These are probably the very points that define the 'heresy' of the sect.

III. Blessings and Curses

The blessing follows section two immediately. Here it consists only of the brief formula: 'All who walk in perfect holiness, according to all the principles of the covenant with God, have assurance that they will live for a thousand generations'[84] (7:4–6).

The curse section is greatly expanded in the Damascus Document. In fact, a brief formula corresponding to the blessing would suffice, something on the order of: 'And all who reject the commandments and ordinances, their wickedness will be requited when God punishes the earth';[85] or: 'And so it is right for all who have entered into his covenant but do not keep these ordinances—he will punish them to destruction through Belial.'[86]

The present instance, especially through comparison of the two recensions A and B, illustrates clearly how the expansion of a simple form-element, here the curse, comes about. Both recensions follow the first sentence of the curse (see above) with a scriptural quotation. Recension A quotes Isa. 7:17: 'There will be brought upon you and upon your people and upon your father's house such days as have not come since the day that Ephraim departed from Judah.'[87] Recension B cites instead Zech. 13:7, almost word for word: 'Awake, O sword, against my shepherd and against the man of my company, says God; strike the shepherd, that the sheep may be scattered; I have turned my hand against the little ones.'

---

[82] 6:14: 'כפרוש התורה לקץ הרשע'; cf. 6:18 and 20.

[83] 6:19: באי הברית החדשה בארץ דמשק. Cf. Jer. 31:31; Luke 22:20; I Cor. 11:25; II Cor. 3:6; Heb. 8:8; 9:15.

[84] The translation follows G. Molin, *Die Söhne des Lichtes*, Wien, 1952, p. 49. Cf. B 19:1–2.

[85] This follows recension B 19:5–6; cf. recension A.

[86] B 19:13–14; cf. A. See also B 19:13: 'Those that remain will be delivered to the sword, which performs the vengeance of the covenant.'

[87] The divine name has been omitted at the beginning. Isa. 7:17 reads: 'Yahweh will bring upon you. . . .'

In recension A, a scriptural catena follows Isa. 7:17; Amos 5:26; 9:11; Num. 24:17 (repeated). Each of these passages is interpreted as referring to the history of the sect. Recension B is considerably shorter. It interprets הַצֹּעֲרִים of Zech. 13:7 as עֲנִיֵי הַצֹּאן, referring to the sect, and, contrary to the original meaning of the text, finds in its deliverance 'at the end of God's visitation.' At the conclusion, B appends a brief quotation from Ezek. 9:4.

There is hardly any difference in content between the two recensions, but each cites different scriptural proof for the same idea.

The conclusion of the Damascus Document, in its present form as it has been preserved, follows immediately upon the curse. It comprises quite diverse elements. The train of thought is not always clear. We must probably think if terms of successive composition and revision.[88] It is plain, however, that here, as in the eschatological section of the Manual of Discipline, blessing and curse are understood temporally. The curse that follows because 'they have entered into the covenant but have not departed from the way of the faithless'[89] is effected in history by the 'head of the kings of Javan, who will come upon them to perform vengeance' (B 19:23–24; cf. A 8:11–12). The curse is therefore understood as operating within history.

On the other hand, the sect is conscious of living 'in the last days of the faithlessness of Israel' (20:23). It awaits judgment upon the evildoers: 'All of those that have entered into the covenant and have transgressed the boundaries of the Torah, when the glory of God appears over Israel they will be separated from the camp and together with them all the evildoers of Judah, in the days of its testing' (20:25ff.). Then those that do penance 'will rejoice and be glad . . . and they will see his salvation. . . .'[90] This means, however, that deliverance and damnation are awaited in a coming eschaton.[91] In the Damascus Document as in the Manual of Discipline, blessing and curse are linked with an *eschatological* section.

---

[88] According to 20:28 (see also 20:32), they are to 'listen to the voice of the Teacher of Righteousness.' According to 19:35–20:1, they are to base their reckoning 'on the day that the teacher of the community(?) was "taken away".' See also 20:13–14.

[89] 19:16–17. There follows a list of sins!

[90] At this point comes a series of Hebrew imperfects; these indicate the future perspective of the section. Cf. also the similar series in 20:15ff.: אז . . . ובקץ ההוא

[91] See also the phrases describing the time:
B 19:10: בקץ הפקדה (here contrasted to the 'first visitation').
B 19:10–11: בבוא משיח אהרן וישראל
B 20:1: עד עמוד משיח מאהרן ומישראל

The Corpus of Legal Stipulations: 9:1–16:20

Like the Manual of Discipline, the Damascus Document contains an actual corpus of laws regulating the life of the community. The state of preservation of the Damascus Document, however, unfortunately does not allow us to say with assurance where this corpus should be placed. Taking the Manual of Discipline as a parallel, one might simply think of it as tacked on at the end of the preserved portion of A or B.[92]

We are dealing once again with a collection of stipulations.[93] No specific order is recognizable. Among other things, the collection contains stipulations referring to entrance into the community (15:7ff.); in this connection, there is mention of being listed in a kind of 'community roster' (14:4–5). There are also stipulations concerning bathing (10:10–13), the Sabbath (10:14–11:18), ritual purity (11:18–12:18), the structure of the community (13:2ff.), and individual offices (judges, 10:4–10; the 'camp inspector,' 13:7–14:2?). To the extent that the passage is intelligible, 14:12ff. contains a kind of 'collection order.' A fund consisting of two days' income per month on the part of each member of the community is built up to support (חזק Hiphil!) the 'poor and needy,' as well as the aged, lepers, prisoners in foreign lands, etc.

The stipulations differ in formulation. There are sections of considerable length containing several stipulations dealing with a single theme. The catchword comes at the beginning, introduced by 'על': על הטהר במים (10:10, concerning purification with water); על הש[ב]ת... (10:14, concerning the Sabbath . . .). Then follow series of jussives, negated by means of 'אל.'

Individual legal decisions are introduced by:

9:1   כל אדם אשר...

9:2   כל איש מביאי הברית אשר...

9:13   כל אשם מושב אשר...

---

[92] In A 7:6ff. (cf. B 19:2ff.), 'And if they live in the camp according to the order (סרך) of the land . . .,' we have a passage strangely intruded between blessing and curse. It is possible that this once constituted the beginning of the corpus.

[93] Here, too, there is a striking accumulation of superscriptions or colophons (12:19–13:2).

12:19   סרך מושב ערי ישראל על המשפטים האלה ל...

12:20   ואלה החקים למשכיל להתהלך בם...

12:21–22   וכמשפט הזה יתהלכו...

12:22   וזה סרך מושב המחנת יתהלכו באלה...

There follows a description of the case and its resolution. This form comes closest to the משפטים of the Manual of Discipline.

The stipulations regulating the offices of the community are termed סרך. They begin with the title of the office-holder:

10:4   ...וזה סרך לשפטי העדה

13:7   וזה סרך המבקר למחנה

Terminology for the Elements of the Literary Type on the Basis of the Text

Here, too, the superscription in 2:14 shows how the author of the text conceived its function and structure.[94]

ועתה בנים שמעו לי ואגלה עיניכם לראות ולהבין...

The direct personal address distinguishes the Damascus Document from the Manual of Discipline, which is composed neutrally in the third person. In the sections that follow, however, this direct address is not maintained. We are probably dealing here with a secondary stylization.

Two influences merge here and in the parallel superscriptions: (1) The influence of preaching. This is suggested by the personal address directed toward those 'who have knowledge of righteousness' (1:1), 'who (enter or) have entered into the covenant.' (2) The influence of wisdom discourse.[95] This is suggested especially by the stated intention of teaching 'understanding' (1:1; 2:14) and of 'opening' ears and eyes. Here, too, probably belongs the address to 'sons,' although wisdom literature usually employs the phrase 'my son.'

This superscription differs hardly at all in content from the superscription in 1QS iii. 13. The superscription in 2:14–16 names two types of subject matter for the following section:[96]

[94] Cf. 1:1   ועתה שמעו כל יודעי צדק ובינו במעשי אל

2:1   ועתה שמעו אלי כל באי ברית ואגלה אזנכם בדרכי רשעים

[95] On this point, see W. Baumgartner, 'Die literarischen Gattungen in der Weisheit des Jesus Sirach,' *ZAW*, 34 (1914), pp. 161–98, esp. p. 164: 'Where a new section begins, where Sirach addresses himself to a new theme, is often not specially indicated. . . . Occasionally, however, we find a kind of superscription that suggests the new theme: "Hear, you sons, the just words of your father" (3:1; cf. 23:7; 41:14*a*). More impressive are the personal introductions like that in 16:24–25: "Hearken to me and receive understanding and attend to my words. I will cause my spirit to gush forth by weight and proclaim my knowledge by measure" (cf. 24:32ff.; 36:16*a*–30:27; 39:12). Usually, however, a very short introductory formula suffices: "My son" (2:1; 3:17; 4:1, 20; 6:18; 10:28; 11:10; 18:30; 21:1; 37:27; 38:16; 40:28) or "Hear, my son" (6:23).' The influence of wisdom elements on the Manual of Discipline and the Damascus Document should be examined in more detail.

[96] Cf. also 3:15–16 in the Damascus Document, which is in part similar:

ודרכי אמתו רחפצי רצונו אשר יעשה האדם וחיה בהם

I   (להבין) במעשי אל

II   ולבחור את אשר רצה

ולמאוס כאשר שנא

להתהלך   תמים בכל דרכיו

ולא לתור במחשבות יצר אשמה ועני זנות

The deeds of God (I) are compared with the conduct of man (II), which is intended to correspond to the former. Here, then, we have once more the association of 'antecedent history' with 'statement of substance.' Apart from the fact that the superscription does not mention 'blessings and curses,' the superscription fits the text that follows it in every point examined above.

Section II contains the requirement, corresponding to the statement of substance, 'to walk perfectly in all his ways and not "to explore" the thoughts of a guilty mind.'[97] Remarkably, this requirement is almost more suitable to the parallel passage in the Manual of Discipline iv. 2–14, with its catalog of virtues and vices, than to 6:11–7:4 of the Damascus Document. Here the parallelism required by the literary type goes so far that individual elements of the form can exchange places.

In the portion of the Damascus Document that deals with offices, we find the following concerning the 'inspector'[98] (13:7–8):[99]

'This is the regulation concerning the camp inspector:
(a) He shall instruct the multitude concerning the acts of God
and shall cause them to understand his mighty wonders
and enumerate before them what has taken place since all eternity
with all interpretations.
(b) And he shall have mercy upon them
like a father with his children
and (shall take away) all their offences.
Like a shepherd of his flock he shall loose all the bonds with which they are bound,
(lest there be) oppressed and broken members in the community.'

[97] On 'mind' as a translation of יצר, see von Rad, 'Form-Category,' p. 312.

[98] Interestingly, Koehler (*Lexicon*, p. 144b) connects מבקרא with בקר, a Nabatean priestly title.

[99] The translation follows Molin, *Söhne des Lichts*; the organization in (a) and (b) is the author's.

                       וזה סרך המבקר למחנה   13:7–8

במעשי אל   ישכיל את הרבים

בגבורות פלאו   ויבינם

נהיות עולם   ויספר לפניהם

בפרתיה

The task assigned the 'inspector' in (b) can best be thought of as the 'office of the keys.' In the present context, however, the material in section (a) is especially interesting. In my opinion, it describes precisely the function and content of an 'antecedent history.' The 'antecedent history' is 'instruction.' We find once again the verb שכל and בין both in the Hiphil.[100] Nothing could better describe the content of the Old Testament recapitulations of *Heilsgeschichte* than the phrase 'the acts of God and his mighty wonders.'[101] The retrospect goes back to 'all eternity' (עולם). This can be understood historically after the example of Josh. 24:2 ('Your fathers lived of old . . .') and as parallelism to the 'acts of God.' But the phrase נהיות עולם is also eminently suitable for a beginning with creation, like that found in the 'dogmatic section' of the Manual of Discpline (iii. 15–iv. 1)[102] and the similar passage in the Damascus Document, 2:14–6:11. It is the 'inspector's' duty not only to pass on the tradition, but also to interpret it (בפרתיה). Damascus Document 2:14–6:11, as we have shown, is a good example of such 'interpretive' exposition of the 'antecedent history.'

It is striking that the instructions pertaining to the office of the 'inspector' refer with such precise restrictions to his responsibility

---

[100] Cf. 1QS iii. 13; Damascus Document 1:1; 2:14.

[101] Cf. especially Psalm 78, with the superscription: מַשְׂכִּיל לְאָסָף.

1 'Give ear, O my people, to my teaching (here: תּוֹרָתִי);

  incline your ear to the words of my mouth.

2 I will open my mouth for a parable;
  I will utter riddles from of old (חִידוֹת מִנִּי־קֶדֶם).

3 What we have heard and known, what our fathers have told us,
4 we will not hide from their children,
  we will tell of it to another generation:
    the glorious deeds of Yahweh and his might (תְּהִלּוֹת יהוה וֶעֱזוּזוֹ),

    and his wonders that he has done (וְנִפְלְאוֹתָיו אֲשֶׁר עָשָׂה).

5 He established his testimony in Jacob,
  and appointed a law in Israel,
6 that another generation might learn of them,
  the children yet unborn, when they arise,
  they shall tell them to their children,
7   so that they may set their confidence in God
  and not forget the works of God (מַעַלְלֵי־אֵל)

  and keep his commandments.
8 They should not be like their fathers. . . .'
  The translation follows H. Schmidt, Die Psalmen, HAT (Tübingen, 1934), pp. 147–48. This introduction is followed by a retrospect of the history of Israel from the Exodus to the election of David.

[102] Cf. the beginning, iii. 15.

for passing on and interpreting the 'antecedent history,' but say nothing of any responsibility on the part of the 'inspector' for, say, exposition of the 'laws.' We must reckon with the possibility that in this respect there has been a kind of division of labor among various offices. According to Damascus Document 14:6–8, the 'priest who conducts the examination'[103] must 'be familiar with the book [. . .] and all the ordinances of the Torah,'[104] in other words, assume a special responsibility for the law.

[103] The translation follows Molin, *Söhne des Lichts*.

[104]

14:6–8   והכהן
אשר יפקד אשר הרבים...
מבונן בספר [...] בכל משפטי התורה
לחברם כמשפטם

II

THE COVENANT FORMULARY
IN EARLY CHRISTIAN TEXTS

In this chapter we shall attempt to study several early Christian texts in the light of our previous conclusions.[1]

1. THE EPISTLE OF BARNABAS

'The so-called Letter of Barnabas is a didactic and edifying discourse clothed in the form of a letter (i.e., an epistle).'[2] The stylized use of direct personal address throughout is due to the epistle form.[3] As we have seen, the Manual of Discipline is composed in the neutral third person throughout; in the Damascus Document only the 'antecedent history' takes the form of direct address.

Despite the 'lack of perspicuity and logical continuity,'[4] the formulary can still be clearly discerned.

I. Dogmatic Section

The introduction in chapter 1 is followed in chapters 2–17 by a 'section of dogmatic polemic.'[5] Its nature can best be described by the instructions relating to the 'antecedent history' in Damascus Document 13:7–8, mentioned above: 'He [the inspector] shall instruct the multitude concerning the acts of God . . . and enumerate before them what has taken place since all eternity, with all interpretations.' Here the clear sequence of the retrospect is even more overgrown with interpretation than in the corresponding section of the Damascus Document. A wealth of Old Testament quotations are

---

[1] It must be stated expressly at the outset that the author is neither in a position nor competent to enter into the extensive scholarly discussion of these texts. Our immediate purpose is simply to try out a specific methodological approach. Perhaps, however, this study can assist our understanding of the texts.

[2] K. Bihlmeyer, *Die apostolischen Väter* (2nd ed., Tübingen, 1955), p. xxi. The author's translation follows that of H. Veil in E. Hennecke, *Neutestamentliche Apokryphen* (2nd ed. Tübingen, 1924), pp. 503ff.

For a commentary, see H. Windisch, *Der Barnabasbrief*, HNT, Die Apostolischen Väter, III (Tübingen, 1920). On the other early Christian texts, see also H. Köster, *Synoptische Überlieferung bei den Apostolischen Vätern, Texte und Versuchungen*, 65 (Berlin, 1957).

[3] 'Sons and daughters' (1:1); 'my brothers' (3:6; 5:5); 'you children of love and peace' (21:9).

[4] Bihlmeyer, *Apostolischen Väter*, p. xxi. The passage continues: 'The literary clumsiness of the author is a sufficient explanation.'

[5] Ibid.

interpreted in allegorical and typological fashion.[6] But within the almost baroque embellishments and artful interlacing of quotations some themes stand out. The section 5:1–7:2[7] expounds in particular a relationship between creation and the passion of Christ. Abraham, Isaac, and Jacob are mentioned.[8] The name of Moses appears most frequently of all.[9] He is the prophetical lawgiver.[10] The battle with the Amalekites is interpreted.[11] The covenant at Sinai was received by Moses, but forfeited at once by Israel.[12]

An essay on the Sabbath[13] and another on the Temple[14] bring the first section to a close.

Remarkably, therefore, this section does contain once more the most important data of *Heilsgeschichte*.[15] But the character of this section as 'antecedent history' in the sense of the covenant formulary is also well expressed in the words of the Epistle of Barnabas itself.

[6] On this type of exposition and concatenation of quotations, see K. Stendahl, *The School of St. Matthew* (Philadelphia, 1968), esp. pp. 207ff.: 'Did Matthew make use of Testimonies?' Stendahl also gives additional bibliography.

[7] One may inquire whether the 'antecedent history' proper does not begin here, with 5:1. In this case chapters 2–4 would still be part of the introduction, suggesting the themes to be taken up in the following section but not going into detail. The 'scriptural proof' in 5:2–4 interprets 5:1. In 5:5ff. the text continues: 'And furthermore, my brothers, when the Lord took it upon himself to suffer for our soul, he, the Lord of the whole world, to whom God said immediately after the foundation of the world, "Let us make men after our image and after our likeness!"—hear then how he came to take it upon himself to suffer at men's hand. . . .' The quotation from Genesis 1:26 is taken up again in 6:12 and expanded (see also 6:9): 'It is we, then, to whom reference is made in the Scriptures, where he [God] says to his Son, "Let us make men after our image and after our likeness, to rule over the beasts of the earth and the birds of the sky and the fish of the sea." And referring to his, his excellent creature, the Lord said, "Increase, and multiply, and fill the earth." As those words were addressed to the Son, so I will show you also how he [Christ], as a word to us, effected at the last a second creation. . . .' —After another quotation, from Gen. 1:28, in 6:18, the section concludes with 7:1–2: 'Know, therefore, children of joy, that the merciful Lord has made all this known to us in advance, that we may know to whom in all things we owe our thankful praises. . . .

[8] Barn. 8:4; cf. 6:8; chapter 9 mentions Abraham in the context of the circumcision story. See also the series: Isaac—Rebecca—Jacob—Joseph—Ephraim—Manasseh in chapter 13, which deals with the 'heritage of the covenant.'

[9] See 10–15:1.

[10] Barn. 10:11–12: 'Now you see how excellent a lawgiver Moses was. But how could those men have comprehended this and understood it? We, however, have rightly understood the commandments, and proclaim them as the Lord desired.' Cf. 6:8; 10:2, 9.

[11] Barn. 12:2–7, 9; cf. Exod. 17:8ff.

[12] Barn. 14:1: 'Knowing this, we shall now also examine whether he really gave the covenant that he had sworn to the fathers he would give to their nation. Of course he gave it; but on account of their sins they were not worthy to receive it.' There follow quotations from Exod. 24:18; 31:18; 32:7, 19.

[13] Chapter 15. Barn. 15:1: 'Furthermore, as concerns the Sabbath. . . .' This chapter is linked to what precedes by a reference to the ten commandments given at Sinai.

[14] Chapter 16. Barn. 16:1: 'As regards the Temple, then. . . .'

[15] Even the occupation is mentioned! See 6:8 and 12:8–9.

The author concludes this section by saying: 'To the extent, therefore, that it was within my power and appropriate in a simple presentation to provide you with information, my soul hopes that in my efforts I have omitted nothing *that pertains to salvation*.[16] For if I write concerning things that are just now in view or belong to the future, it will be hard for you to understand them, because they are contained in parables. Enough then on this matter' (17:1–2).[17]

In the Old Testament formulary, too, the 'antecedent history' contains 'what pertains to salvation.'[18]

II. Ethical Section

In the light of our study so far, it is hardly surprising that the Epistle of Barnabas continues (18:1): 'But let us now pass on to another kind of knowledge and teaching. There are two *ways* of teaching and efficacious power, the *way of light* and the *way of darkness*. . . .'[19] Next, following the schema of the two ways, comes a catalog of virtues and vices. As in the Manual of Discipline, the schema of the two ways is linked with a cosmic dualism.[20] Over the way of light are placed the 'illuminating angles of God'; over the way of darkness, the 'angels of Satan.'[21]

In the late texts it is certainly difficult to draw a line between

---

[16] '. . . παραλελοιπέναι τι τῶν ἀνηκόντων εἰς σωτηρίαν.'

[17] Cf. 1:7–8.

[18] Also of interest in this connection is the beginning of the Epistle (1:2), which follows the salutation formula: 'Μεγάλων μὲν ὄντων καὶ πλουσίων τῶν τοῦ θεοῦ δικαιωμάτων εἰς ὑμᾶς. . . .' According to Windisch, *Barnabasbrief*, p. 303 ad loc., 'In Barn. δικαιώματα usually = "requirements," "commandments" . . .; here (and in 4:11), on account of μεγάλων . . . καὶ πλουσίων and τῆς δωρεᾶς πνευματικῆς χάριν, it must mean "revelations of deliverance," "demonstrations of grace" . . . .' Windisch cites the similar beginning of Cyprian's *De op. et eleem.* i: 'Multa et magna sunt, fratres carissimi, beneficia divina, quibus in salutem nostram Dei patris et Christi larga et copiosa clementia et operata sit et semper operetur.' In these passages, therefore, δικαιώματα (= 'beneficia' in Cyprian) corresponds in meaning to the Hebrew צְדָקוֹת, which serves to designate the content of the 'antecedent history' in the covenant formulary. See I Sam. 12:7: אֶת (וְאִוָּדְעָה לָכֶם) כָּל־צִדְקוֹת יְהוָה אֲשֶׁר־עָשָׂה אִתְּכֶם. For a more detailed discussion, see above, p. 66, n. 15; cf. also 1QS i. 21: והכוהנים מספרים את צדקות אל (see the further discussion below, pp. 168, 190).

[19] Μεταβῶμεν δὲ καὶ ἐπὶ ἑτέραν γνῶσιν καὶ διδαχήν.
'Ὁδοὶ δύο εἰσὶν διδαχῆς καὶ ἐξουσίας,
ἥ τε τοῦ φωτὸς καὶ ἡ τοῦ σκότους.

[20] See Siegfried Wibbing, *Die Tugend- und Lasterkataloge im Neuen Testament*, Dissertation, Heidelberg, 1955, p. 144.

[21] Barn. 18:1. The next sentence, in 18:2, has the effect of a theological correction. The dualism exists only in the present age of unrighteousness, not prior to creation: 'καὶ ὁ μέν ἐστιν κύριος ἀπὸ αἰώνων καὶ εἰς τοὺς αἰῶνας, ὁ δε ἄρχων καιροῦ τοῦ νῦν τῆς ἀνομίας.'

statement of substance and individual commandments. But when we
read in 19:2: 'Love him who created you, fear him who formed
you, glorify him who redeemed you from death. Be simple of heart
and rich in spirit. Do not consort with those that walk in the way of
death; hate everything that is displeasing to God, hate all hypocrisy.
Do not neglect the commandments of the Lord,' the scope of these
commandments corresponds to that of a statement of substance. First
of all we find the verbs[22] 'love,' 'fear,' 'do not consort,' 'hate,' 'do
not neglect' that occur again and again in the statements of substance.[23] In addition, we find the usual twofold structure: first a
positive statement with reference to God ('love . . .'), then a negative
statement concerning what is 'displeasing' to God. In the Old
Testament, a renunciation of foreign gods would stand in this place.

There follows a long series of commandments, each introduced
with οὐ. They are interrupted only rarely by positive commandments,
at least down to v. 6. Here, unlike the Manual of Discipline, the
dependence of the commandments on the Decalogue is still clearly
discernible.[24] This almost makes it impossible to speak of a 'catalog
of virtues.'—With more accuracy one can call the corresponding
'way of the black one' or 'way of eternal death' a 'catalog of vices.'
It brings together simple concepts. Nevertheless, it begins the list
with the prohibition of 'idolatry,' which was lacking in the statement
of substance.

III. Blessings and Curses

Barn. 21:1 provides once more a general summary of the commandments: 'Now whoever has learned all the requirements of the
Lord, as they stand written, it befits him to walk according to
them.'[25]

A blessing is then promised: 'Whoever follows them will gain
glory in the kingdom of God.'

---

[22] See also the preceding sentence: 'ἔστιν οὖν ἡ δοθεῖσα ἡμῖν γνῶσις τοῦ περιπατεῖν
ἐν αὐτῇ τοιαύτη.'
[23] See, for example, Deut. 10:12–13; 11:22–23.
[24] 5 'οὐ μὴ λάβῃς ἐπὶ ματαίῳ τὸ ὄνομα κυρίου.
ἀγαπήσεις τὸν πλησίον σου ὑπὲρ τὴν ψυχήν σου.
οὐ φονεύσεις τέκνον ἐν φθορᾷ, οὐδὲ πάλιν γεννηθὲν ἀποκτενεῖς . . .
6 οὐ μὴ γένῃ ἐπιθυμῶν τὰ τοῦ πλησίον σου,
οὐ μὴ γένῃ πλεονέκτης . . .
4 οὐ πορνεύσεις, οὐ μοιχεύσεις, οὐ παιδοφθορήσεις . . . .'
[25] 'Καλὸν οὖν ἐστίν, ματόντα τὰ δικαιώματα τοῦ κυρίου, ὅσα γέγραπται, ἐν τούτοις
περιπατεῖν. . . .'

Finally comes the curse: 'But whoever chooses that (evil conduct) will perish with all his works.'

Blessing and curse are here understood eschatologically. This is especially noticeable as the passage continues: 'Therefore there is a resurrection, therefore there is recompense . . .' and (v. 3): 'Near is the day in which all things will perish with the evil; near is the Lord and his reward.'[26] In comparison to other texts, the brevity of the section 'blessings and curses' is striking. Barn. 21:4–9 comprises the conclusion of the Epistle.

2. THE DIDACHE

Viewed in the light of our hypothesis, the Didache presents a peculiar picture.[27] With slight exaggeration, one could say that, with respect to its literary type, the Didache is a torso. In contrast to the Manual of Discipline, the Damascus Document, and the Epistle of Barnabas, the Didache lacks an 'antecedent history.' The structure of the formulary would lead one to expect this antecedent history before the opening sentence: 'There are *two ways*, one that leads to *life* and one that leads to *death*.' This omission raises new questions concerning the origin of the Didache. It is possible, of course, for a single element of a literary type to take on independent life and undergo further independent development. This would mean that the Didache reflects a secondary stage of development. The Epistle of Barnabas, for example, would then preserve the earlier form.[28] If this is so, I question whether it is permissible to see in the Didache—or its precursors—the prototype of a Jewish or early Christian 'catechism.' It is not natural but remarkable that we have here ethical instruction without 'antecedent history,' i.e., without a recapitulation of or even reference to God's saving acts, in any form.[29]

---

[26] 'ἐγγὺς ἡ ἡμέρα, ἐν ᾗ συναπολεῖται πάντα τῷ πονηρῷ. ἐγγὺς ὁ κύριος καὶ ὁ μισθὸς αὐτοῦ.'

[27] The text of the Didache follows Bihlmeyer, *Apostolischen Väter*, pp. 1–9; and H. Lietzmann, *Die Didache* ('Kleine Texte für Vorlesungen und Übungen,' 6 [5th ed., Berlin, 1948]).

The translation follows that of E. Hennecke, *Neutestamentliche Apokryphen* (Second edition, Tübingen, 1924), pp. 555–65.

For a commentary, see J.-P. Audet, *La Didachè, Instructions des Apôtres* (Paris, 1958), including extensive bibliography. See also especially M. Dibelius, 'Die Mahlgebete der Didache,' in his *Botschaft und Geschichte* (Tübingen, 1956), vol. 2, pp. 117–27.

[28] Such a conclusion does not in itself enable us to say anything about the absolute date of the two documents and their mutual relationship.

[29] Bihlmeyer, *Apostolischen Väter*, p. xiii: 'The document can generally be termed a handbook on the religion of early Christianity. . . . The first [part], comprising chapters 1–10 or 1–6, contains first of all an outline of moral theology (ethical catechism) like that to be inculcated upon the baptismal candidates. . . . Cultic regulations follow. . . .'

There is also another possibility: it may be only accidents of textual transmission that have preserved the Didache for us in such isolation. The manuscript evidence should be examined once again to find the context in which the Didache is embedded and how it is connected with its context. The published editions, unfortunately, give little information on this point, since their preconceived goal is to present the text of a Didache free of all 'accretions.'

The Didache contains a series of details that are of interest in the context of our present study.

II. Ethical Section

In contrast to all the texts so far studied, the 'two-ways schema' is not linked with any 'dualistic cosmology'[30] and its angelology.[31] This association is the really new element in the ethical section of the non-OT texts. In this respect the Didache is closer to Deut. 30:15ff.[32]

This time the statement of substance is clearly set off (1:2):

'Η μὲν οὖν ὁδὸς τῆς ζωῆς ἐστιν αὕτη
πρῶτον ἀγαπήσεις τὸν θεὸν τὸν ποιήσαντά σε
δεύτερον τὸν πλησίον σου ὡς σεαυτόν.
πάντα δὲ ὅσα ἐὰν θελήσῃς μὴ γίνεσθαί σοι,
καὶ σὺ ἄλλῳ μὴ ποίει.

It is interesting that the 'Golden Rule' is cited at this point. In 1:3–6, the statement of substance is interpreted with reference to New Testament texts.[33] This is shown by the introduction (1:3): Τούτων δὲ τῶν λόγων ἡ διδαχή ἐστιν αὕτη. . . .' This statement is accurate; even in the Old Testament the statement of substance is

---

[30] See Wibbing, *Tugend- und Lasterkataloge*, p. 144; Wibbing refers to K. G. Kuhn in *Zeitschrift für Theologie und Kirche*, 1950, p. 207.

[31] The Teaching of the Twelve Apostles contains it also, albeit in a modified form: 'Viae duae sunt in saeculo, vitae et mortis, lucis et tenebrarum, in his constituti sunt angeli duo, unus aequitatis, alter iniquitatis' (Teaching 1).

The 'teaching' refers to the basic form of the 'ways' represented in the Latin translation. For a discussion, see Audet, *Didachè*, pp. 131ff., 154. The text of the Teaching is taken from the apparatus of Lietzmann, *Didache*.

[32] Deut. 30:15: 'See, I have set before you this day life and death, good and evil.' Deut. 30:16: 'If you obey the commandments of the Lord. . . .'

Deut. 30:19: '. . . I have set before you life and death, blessing and curse; therefore choose life, that you and your descendants may live.' Then follows the repetition of a statement of substance (Deut. 30:20): 'Loving Yahweh your God, obeying his voice, and cleaving to him. . . .'

[33] This interpretation (1:3–6) is not found in the Teaching nor in the Apostolic Constitutions. See H. Achelis, 'Apostolische Kirchenordnung,' in *Realenzyklopädie für Protestantische Theologie und Kirche* (3rd ed., Leipzig, 1896), vol. 1, p. 732.

given in such a way as to take on concrete form in particular cases.

Following a superscription, 'Δευτέρα δὲ ἐντολὴ τῆς διδαχῆς' (2:1), 2:2 contains additional individual commandments. As in the Epistle of Barnabas, there are unmistakable echoes of the Decalogue at the beginning.[34] The parenetic element, however, is stronger; it is especially emphasized by the repeated address 'τέκνον μου' (3:1; 4:1). The strict prohibition form is not adhered to.

Although here, too, the 'way of life' can hardly be termed a 'catalog of virtues,' the corresponding 'way of death' in chapter 5 contains once again a true catalog of vices. The mere listing of abstract concepts in 5:1 is given up again in v. 2 in favor of a listing of persons 'from whom one should be preserved.'

III. Blessings and Curses

In this section, the text presents us with a riddle. V. 6:1 concludes the 'teaching' with a summary: '"Ορα, μή τίς σε πλανήσῃ ἀπὸ ταύτης τῆς ὁδοῦ τῆς διδαχῆς, ἐπεὶ παρεκτὸς θεοῦ σε διδάσκει.' Then follows (v. 2): 'εἰ μὲν γὰρ δύνασαι βαστάσαι ὅλον τὸν ζυγὸν τοῦ κυρίου, τέλειος ἔσῃ.' The statement 'You will be perfect' can still be understood as a promise. Therefore one would expect the corresponding 'εἰ δ' οὐ δύνασαι' (2b) to be followed by a corresponding threat. Instead, the text continues: 'ὃ δύνῃ, τοῦτο ποίει'. This seems at first glance to be a statement of astounding moderation, in violent contrast to the decision demanded by the rest of the text between 'life and death.'[35] The present recension of the Didache, however, is probably concerned here with distinguishing between a maximum requirement ('bear the whole yoke of the Lord . . . be perfect') and a minimum requirement, which then also includes the dietary regulation in 6:3.[36]

Now the parallel text in the Teaching of the Twelve Apostles concludes much more smoothly from the point of view of the literary type. The corresponding passage in the Teaching reads (vi) 'et vide, nequis te ab hac doctrina avocet, et si minus, extra disciplinam doceberis [4] haec in consulendo si cottidie feceris, prope eris vivo

---

[34] See 2:2ff. (the omitted verbs supplement the commandments of the Decalogue with related concepts):
  'οὐ φονεύσεις, οὐ μοιχεύσεις . . . , οὐ κλέψεις. . . .
  οὐκ ἐπιθυμήσεις τα τοῦ πλησίον . . . .
  οὐ ψευδομαρτυρήσεις. . . .'
[35] Did. 1:1; 4:14; 5:1.
[36] Cf. Acts 15:29. On the basis of the introductory formula 'Περὶ δὲ τῆς βρώσεως,' 6:3 could constitute the first part of the following section!

K

deo; quod si *non* feceris, longe eris a veritate. [5] haec omnia tibi in animo pone et non decipieris[37] de spe tua. sed per haec sancta certamina pervenies ad coronam, [6] per dominum Iesum Christum regnantem et dominantem cum deo patre et spiritu sanctu in saeculo saeculorum. amen.'[38]

In the Teaching, the twofold structure has been preserved: positive actions and negative actions, each with their consequences. Of course the statements 'prope eris vivo deo' and 'longe eris a veritate' scarcely still show that at one time powerful blessings and curses came at this point in the formulary. The promise is reminiscent of the blessing formula that follows the catalog of virtues in the Manual of Discipline: 'and eternal joy in everlasting life and a crown of glory together with the robe of splendor in eternal light.'[39]

The *eschatological* portion of the Didache comes at the end of the actual corpus of the community rule. This section should not be considered a part of the community rule.[40] In the 'last days' lawlessness will have the upper hand. The 'deceiver of the world' will perform signs and wonders. Those who hold fast to the faith will be saved. 'Then the signs of truth will appear . . .' (16:6). 'Then the world will see the Lord coming on the clouds of heaven' (16:8).[41]

The Corpus of Legal Stipulations in the Didache

The corpus of the Didache contains a collection of regulations ordering the life of the community, with special reference to various points in its worship, together with instructions for individual offices. The parallel with the corresponding corpora in the Manual of Discipline and the Damascus Documents warns us against placing too much weight on these directives. For the same reason, it is unlikely that we have here a complete rule. If it is a collection, early and late material can very easily stand juxtaposed.[42]

There are also parallels in the formulation of the individual regulations that show that the Didache stands in an ancient legal tradition. For example, the section of the Didache dealing with baptism may be compared with the section of the Damascus Docu-

---

[37] F* reads 'deceperis'; F¹, 'decipieris.'

[38] This concludes the entire Teaching; it therefore does not include the 'dietary regulation' at all.

[39] 1QS iv. 7–8; the translation follows Molin.

[40] See Köster, *Synoptische Überlieferung*, pp. 160, 173, 189–90.

[41] On the series 'τότε 5 . . . καὶ τότε 6 . . . τότε,' see 1QS iv. 19–20: . . . ואז . . . ואז; on 'ἐν τῷ ἐσχάτῳ καιρῷ . . .,' cf. קץ אחרון in 1QS iv. 16.

[42] See above, p. 110, Köhler's definition with regard to Deuteronomy.

ment dealing with immersion.[43] It is clear from the outset that there is a fundamental difference between this immersion and baptism. An examination of their content would make the difference even clearer. Here our interest is first of all in the formal structure. First, the theme is mentioned in a kind of superscription: 'concerning baptism' (Didache); 'concerning purification in water' (Damascus Document).[44] In the Didache, there follows (with the baptismal formula interpolated!) the instruction to baptize in running water. This is followed in turn by a listing of several cases in which running water is not available, with a ruling as to what should be done in each case.

On the basis of the literary type, we may say that the interpolation of the baptismal formula at this point is form-critically secondary. It merely interrupts the listing of the various 'cases.' This observation is similar to that made by Dibelius with respect to the table prayers of the Didache. The Damascus Document also contains a series of cases, albeit with merely negative rulings, stating what sort of water does not suffice.[45]

In each case we are clearly not dealing with a complete order for the entire complex; specific—probably disputed—cases are decided. Therefore in this and the parallel passages we are dealing with collections of legal decisions, arranged by subject, which come thereby to apply beyond the individual case.[46]

There is also a parallel for another form. Several passages occur that (a) are introduced by 'And whoever . . . ,' followed by a specification of the person concerned. Then follows (b) what 'he' does

[43] See Did. 7:1: 'Περὶ δὲ τοῦ βαπτίσματος, οὕτω βαπτίσατε· ταῦτα πάντα προειπόντες εἰς τὸ ὄνομα τοῦ πατρὸς καὶ τοῦ υἱοῦ καὶ τοῦ ἁγίου πνεύματος ἐν ὕδατι ζῶντι. 2. ἐὰν δὲ μὴ ἔχῃς ὕδωρ ζῶν, εἰς ἄλλο ὕδωρ βάπτισον· εἰ δ' οὐ δύνασαι ἐν ψυχρῷ, ἐν θερμῷ. 3. ἐὰν δὲ ἀμφότερα μὴ ἔχῃς, ἔκχεον εἰς τὴν κεφαλὴν τρὶς ὕδωρ [εἰς ὄνομα . . .].'
Dam. 10:10–13: על הטהר במים
אל ירחץ איש במים צואים ומעוטים מדי מרעיל איש
אל יטהר במה כלי וכל גבא בסלע אשר אין בו די מרעיל

[44] See also the superscriptions 'περὶ δὲ τῆς βρώσεως' (6:3); 'περὶ δὲ τῆς εὐχαριστίας' (11:1); 'περὶ δὲ τῶν ἀποστόλων καὶ προφητῶν' (11:3). Cf. Dam. 10:14: על השׁ[ב]ת; 16:3: על משפט ה[נ]דב[ות.

[45] Cf. also 1QS iii. 4–5, where the following sequence occurs: 'He must not sanctify himself in the sea and rivers; neither is he purified by any water that washes away impurity.' The rulings in Dam. 10:10–13 elucidate the meaning of 'any water.' See also 1QS iii. 9.

[46] Cf. Hag. 2:11–13; Zech. 7:3ff. In Haggai the priests are asked for a ruling; in Zechariah, 'the priests of the house of Yahweh of hosts and the prophets.' Who holds the corresponding office in the Didache? Cf. also Did. 8:1, on 'fasting,' with the fasting inquiry in Zech. 7:3.

and finally (*c*) how he is to be dealt with.[47] This is the simplest case. It is possible, of course, for additional eventualities to be taken into account under both (*b*) and (*c*). This is done by adding 'but if . . .' (11:9) or 'but whoever . . .' (11:12).

This corresponds to the structure of a series of passages from the Damascus Document. In Dam. 12:2–3, for example, we read: (*a*) And whoever (is ruled by the spirits of Belial), (*b*) so that he preaches apostasy, (*c*) shall be judged like one who engages in necromancy and soothsaying.[48] There are also longer series discussing the most diverse eventualities.[49]

The legal decision is also clearly recognizable in this form.

3. THE SO-CALLED SECOND EPISTLE OF CLEMENT

The Second Epistle of Clement[50] is especially important in this context, since it still illustrates the original *Sitz im Leben*. In the case of other texts, e.g., the Testaments of the Twelve Patriarchs, one may assume the presence of sermonic forms; the literary structure so dominates the picture, however, that such forms cannot be precisely determined. In the case of II Clement, however, it may be considered certain 'that the purported epistle is in fact a homily, the earliest Christian sermon that has been preserved, intended by its author to be read publicly during worship immediately after the Scripture reading (19:1).[51]

We cannot here go into the particulars of the subject matter. Our interest focuses first of all on the formal structure. Most scholars assume that the text shows no clear arrangement.[52] The sermon is admittedly not constructed logically, with a clear train of thought, but rather according to a formal principle. The individual points are cited on the basis of a predetermined schema. We shall attempt

---

[47] Did. 11:7: 'καὶ πάντα προφήτην λαλοῦντα ἐν πνεύματι οὐ πειράσετε οὐδὲ διακρινεῖτε. . . .'

[48] Dam. 12:2–3:   כל איש אשר ימשלן בו רוחות בליעל
ודבר סרה
כמשפט האוב והידעוני ישפט   וכל אשר...

[49] See Dam. 9:1ff.: .כל אדם אשר...וכל איש...וכל...אם...

[50] The text follows Bihlmeyer, *Apostolischen Väter*, pp. 71–81. The translation follows that of H. von Schubert in Hennecke, *Neutestamentliche Apokryphen*, pp. 588–95.

[51] Bihlmeyer, *Apostolischen Väter*, p. xxix.

[52] '. . . is a homily not based on a specific text and not conforming to a specific pattern' (Schubert, in Hennecke, *Neutestamentliche Apokryphen*, p. 589).

'The content is rather general, the organization loose' (Bihlmeyer, *Apostolischen Väter*, p. xxix).

to show that this is the same basic schema found in the texts so far examined.

I. Dogmatic Section (Chapters 1–2)

The section begins appropriately with '*de deo*.' Since, however, we are dealing with a genuinely Christian sermon, the very first sentence makes an equation: 'We should think of Jesus Christ as of God.' First, however, let us point out the traditional 'topoi' of this section. The 'demonstrations of God's grace' are recalled.[53] The Old Testament would continue at this point with a retrospect of the 'demonstrations of grace,' like those found in Exod. 34:10; Pss. 105: 12–44; 135:8–12; Neh. 9:7ff. Instead II Clement makes only a general statement: 'For he has given us the light, like a father he has addressed us as sons, he has saved us when we were lost' (1:4); or: 'For he had mercy upon us and, since it grieved him, he saved us, since he saw much error and corruption among us, and that we had no hope of salvation except through him' (1:7). But these statements can also be taken as summaries of Old Testament texts like Ps. 106:4–46; Dan. 9:4–19; Neh. 9:34ff. That the preacher can proceed in so summary a fashion where one would expect more detailed exposition may be explained by the fact that, as mentioned above, the sermon was preceded by the Scripture reading in the worship service. Neither is it probably by accident that the listing of 'demonstrations of grace' begins with (1:4): 'τὸ φῶς γὰρ ἡμῖν ἐχαρίσατο,' and that 1:8 reads: 'ἐκάλεσεν γὰρ ἡμᾶς οὐκ ὄντας καὶ ἠθέλησεν ἐκ μὴ ὄντος εἶναι ἡμᾶς.' If the latter statement in particular is read out of context, bracketing the 'ἡμᾶς' as necessary, it will sound to the unbiased listener as though the creation is being discussed. In 1QS iii. 13ff., a parallel passage according to literary type, we find almost the same catchwords: 'light,' 'before they came into existence,' 'as soon as they came into existence.'[54] In the latter

---

[53] II Clem. 1:3: 'πόσα δὲ αὐτῷ ὀφείλομεν ὅσια;'
Cf. 1QS i. 21–22, which corresponds exactly in the structure of the formulary: 'And the priests shall recount the demonstrations of God's righteousness in his mighty deeds and bear witness to all his gracious demonstrations of favor upon Israel' (חסדי רחמים). In the ⑥ of Isa. 55:3, 'τα ὅσια' translates חסדים! Cf. also the introductions in Pss. 78:1–9; 105:1–6; 106:1–3.

[54] The translation follows Molin.

1QS iii: מאל הדעות כול הווה ונהייה ולפני היותם   15
הכין כול מחשבתם...
והואה ברא אנוש לממשלת תבל...   17
והואה ברא רוחות אור וחושך...   25

passage, however, the connection with creation is still unmistakable.[55]

Our study has shown how the 'antecedent history' in post-OT texts comes more and more to take up the theme of creation and preservation, with the result that 'history' in the strict sense almost vanishes. In II Clement we can observe a development that is almost precisely the reverse. Both the context and the interpolation of 'ἡμᾶς' make it appear likely that statements originally associated with the creation are now made to refer to redemption in Christ.

Chapter 2 adds scriptural proof of the dogmatic section. Isa. 54:1 is interpreted after the manner of a *pesher* so as to apply to the present.[56] After the introduction: 'καὶ ἑτέρα δὲ γραφὴ λέγει, ὅτι . . . ,' Matt. 9:13 (and parallels) is added and interpreted, to provide a New Testament quotation.

The dogmatic section closes with 2:7: 'Thus the Christ also sought to save what was lost, and saved many, since he came and called us who were already lost.' Now the author of II Clement can be chided for his 'simplicity' or 'naiveté.' But the immense claim of his message can be gauged by the structure of his sermon. For him there is once more a true 'antecedent history,' on which man's relationship to God is based. For him God's 'gracious acts' have become real in Christ. 'Keeping the commandments' as he lives his life is only a consequence of a relationship to God that has been renewed through God's mercy. As he so thinks and lives, a part of the message of the Old Testament is fulfilled. The structure of his sermon also shows that this fulfillment does not depend on a scriptural proof that seems to us more or less debatable.

II. Ethical Section

(a) Statement of Substance (3–4:2)

The function of the statement of substance as a link between the 'antecedent history' and the individual commandments can be clearly observed in II Clement. The first sentence summarizes the 'antecedent history' once more: 'Such great mercy therefore he has shown toward us.' 'πρῶτον μέν, ὅτι . . .' (3:1) corresponds to the introduction to the statement of substance in the Didache: "Η

---

[55] See also Shepherd of Hermas i: 'Πρῶτον πάντων πίστευσον ὅτι εἷς ἐστιν ὁ θεός, ὁ τὰ πάντα κτίσας καὶ καταρτίσας καὶ ποιήσας ἐκ τοῦ μὴ ὄντος εἰς τὸ εἶναι τὰ πάντα, καὶ πάντα χωρῶν, μόνος δὲ ἀπώρητος ὤν.' Cited from M. Whittaker, 'Der Hirt des Hermas,' in *Die Apostolischen Väter I*, (Berlin, 1956). For a commentary, see M. Dibelius, 'Der Hirt des Hermas,' in *Die Apostolischen Väter IV*, HNT (Tübingen, 1923), pp. 497–98.

[56] 2:1: 'ὁ εἶπεν . . . ἡμᾶς εἶπεν.' 2:2, 5 'τοῦτο λέγει. . . .'

μὲν οὖν ὁδὸς τῆς ζωῆς ἐστιν αὕτη· πρῶτον. . . .' In the Didache there follows the commandment to love God; in II Clement, the commandment 'not to sacrifice to dead gods and not to worship them.' In the Old Testament, both commandments are frequently found together in the statement of substance. The one is the negative side of the other. Josh. 24:14, in the statement of substance, 'Now therefore fear Yahweh and serve him in sincerity and in faithfulness; put away the gods . . . ,' requires acknowledgment of the Lord 'who brought our fathers up from the land of Egypt, out of the house of bondage . . .' (Josh. 24:17); in II Clement, it is acknowledgment of him 'through whom we have been saved.'

The series of infinitives can still be recognized: 'to do . . . to hearken to his commandments . . . to honor him. . . .' Here, though, the series is parenetically expanded and interpreted.

(b) Individual Commandments

In the Didache, this section has the superscription (2:1): 'Δευτέρα δὲ ἐντολὴ τῆς διδαχῆς . . .'; here we have instead a transitional formula (4:3): 'Now, therefore, brethren, let us acknowledge him in works. . . .' The Didache contains direct commandments; here the series of infinitives is continued. Echoes of the Decalogue can still be heard in the sequence: '. . . not to commit adultery, not to speak evil against one another, not to covet.'[57] Here the commandment 'to love one another' comes first, before 'not to covet.' One would actually expect it to appear in the statement of substance. Is it here merely a version of the commandment 'not to kill'? Or does ἀγάπη take first place as the 'cardinal Christian virtue'? Other 'virtues' are named: '. . . to be moderate, merciful, kindly.' In 4:4–5:4 the simple listing form is dropped. But in this the form itself shows how the point of pressing concern to the preacher—steadfastness in persecutions—makes itself heard. In 5:6ff. there appear once more the catchwords common to this section: 'to walk holily and righteously,' 'to desert the right way.'[58] Finally, 6:4 comprises a short catalog of vices.

III. Eschatological Section (6:7–7:6)

Promise and threat are presented in the briefest possible form in 6:7: 'For if we do the will of Christ we shall find peace; but nothing will deliver us from eternal punishment if we do not obey

---

[57] Cf. also the lists in Köster, *Synoptische Überlieferung*, p. 164.
[58] II Clem. 5:7: ἡ ὁδὸς τῆς δικαίας.

his commandments.' The rest of the text, to 7:6, uses traditional phrases and images to describe eschatological salvation and damnation.[59]

In the light of the formulary that we have assumed to be present, the sermon could end at this point. What follows is essentially a series of minor units almost all of which follow the same schema: a general exhortation is linked with an eschatological promise and threat. In brief form, this structure is found, for example, in 11:1: 'But now let us serve God with pure hearts'—'and we shall be righteous'—'but if we do not serve him, because we do not believe God's promise'—'we shall be in misery.' This simple schema is expanded in various ways by means of scriptural quotations and their interpretation, as well as through parenetic application. The series of minor units is linked together with the catchword 'repentance.'[60]

Our study has shown that, at least in chapters 1–7, the structure of II Clement is by no means 'loose,' but probably follows a preconceived schema very closely. It turns out that the formulary we have hypothesized could also form the basis of a sermon.[61] We shall have to return to this conclusion when we consider the question of how the literary type could have remained so constant until well into the Christian era. We are able to date II Clement fairly accurately within a few years of A.D. 140. But II Clement does not give the impression of marking the first use of the form as a sermon.

---

[59] The quotation from Ezekiel 14 is strikingly appropriate at this point, for there a curse is threatened involving 'sword, famine, evil beasts, pestilence' (14:21). It is strange, however, that in Ezekiel the otherwise frequent mention of 'captivity' is lacking (v. 22?), while it is the only element mentioned in II Clem. 6:8.

[60] 8:1, 2; 9:8; 13:1 (twice); 16:1; 17:1; 19:1.

[61] At least with respect to the form of II Clement, we must disagree with the statement of H. von Schubert ('Einleitung zum sogen. 2. Clem. brief,' in Hennecke, *Neutestamentliche Apokryphen*, pp. 588–89): 'The growth of a sermonic literature, finally, presupposes that, for the purposes of effective presentation, the speaker has selected from the multitude of his thoughts those that seemed appropriate, arranged them, and given them fixed form. The preliminary stage of this process should be sought not so much in the Jewish synagogue lecture or the prophetical outpourings of the early Christians as in the lectures of the Cynic and Stoic teachers, who, like Epictetus, had practical goals in the realm of religious ethics, i.e., offered "pastoral guidance".'

III

THE COVENANT FORMULARY
AS A 'TESTAMENT'

In the Old Testament, there is a close association between covenant formulary and testament.[1] This association comes about because the covenant must be confirmed when Israel undergoes a change of leadership. Literarily, the 'testament' comprises the elements of a 'normal' covenant formulary. At the beginning of the 'testament' there usually stands a statement that the present bearer of the office has become too old, and therefore designates his successor.[2] Within the formulary there is an important change: blessings and curses become promises and threats.[3] In the Old Testament, the stylization of all Deuteronomy as 'Moses' farewell address' is an impressive example of the use of the covenant formulary as a 'testament.'

In its specialized form as a testament the covenant formulary also continued to exert its influence far beyond the Old Testament. This influence may be able to explain a series of peculiarities in the extensive 'testament literature.' The following portion of our study will be devoted to this purpose.

1. JUBILEES

In the farewell addresses of Abraham, Isaac, and Jacob, Jubilees contains a form of the testament that has undergone little literary development. Furthermore, the direct relationship to the Old Testament is very close throughout. The simple structure of the testament is therefore all the more recognizable.

A good example is 'Abraham's last words to Isaac' in Jubilees 21.[4]

A preamble first states the date and persons concerned: 'And in the sixth year of the seventh week of years of this (42nd) Jubilee, Abraham summoned his son Isaac, and commanded him, saying. . . .'

Next comes the statement concerning Abraham's age: 'I have

---

[1] See above, pp. 63, 81ff.
[2] See Deut. 31:1–3; Josh. 23:2; I Sam. 12:1–2; I Chron. 23:1.
[3] See, for example, Josh. 23:14ff.; I Sam. 12:25.
[4] The translation, based on the Ethiopic text, follows that of E. Littmann in E. Kautzsch, *Apokryphen und Pseudepigraphen*, vol. 2, pp. 75ff. See also H. Rönsch, *Das Buch der Jubiläen* (Leipzig, 1874), pp. 28ff. The corresponding last words of Isaac and Jacob will be referred to in the notes when they provide important supplementary material.

grown old and do not know the day of my death and am satiated with my days. And behold, I am 175 years old.'[5]

I. The 'antecedent history' begins with a retrospect of the life of Abraham:

> For all the days of my life I have been mindful of God,
> and have striven with all my heart to do his will and to
> walk uprightly in all his ways.
> My soul has hated idols,
> that I might pay heed to do the will of my creator. (21:2, 3)

Abraham thus bears witness to his devotion; but this personal 'antecedent history' also leads up to an extended statement of faith:

> A   living God is he,
> and holy   is he,
> and faithful   is he above all others,[6]
> and with him there is no respecting of persons
>   or accepting of bribes;
> but
> a   just God is he,
> and he brings to judgment all who transgress his commandments
>   and those who despise his *covenant*. (21:4)

This statement of faith corresponds to the 'dogmatic section' with its 'de deo' theme in the texts we have previously studied.[7]

II. (*a*) The rest of the text in Jubilees 21 follows the assumed formulary quite regularly. The *statement of substance* reads:

> But you, my son, observe his commandment
>   and his ordinance
>   and his judgment,[8]
> and do not follow after the unclean
>   or after carved images
>   or after cast images. (21:5)

The Latin version has turned 'following foreign gods' into 'abire post abominationes.' The text goes on to explain, among other things, what is meant by 'unclean.' This detail shows how a minor change can produce a new interpretation of the ancient formula. It explains

---

[5] At this point the testament of Isaac (Jub. 36:1ff.) also includes the announcement of Isaac's impending death and his request for burial: 'My children, I shall go the way of my fathers into the house of eternity, where my fathers are. Bury me close beside my father Abraham in the double cave in the field of Ephron the Hittite.'

[6] The Latin fragment groups the words somewhat differently: '. . . et justus et ex omnibus non est apud eum accipere personam. . . .'

[7] See especially above, pp. 99ff., 112–13.

[8] It is probably better to read the plural, with the Latin version: 'custodi praecepta eius et mandata eius et iudicia eius . . .' = Hebrew לשמר מצותיו וחוקותיו ומשפטיו.

the rather awkward juxtaposition here of 'following after' and 'uncleanness.'[9]

II. (b) The Corpus of Individual Stipulations.

The corpus contains primarily stipulations concerning the 'peace offering' (21:7ff.), the wood to be used for the burnt offering (21:12ff.), regulations concerning purity (21:16), and a collection of stipulations based on the catchword 'blood' (21:17–20).

The zeal with which detailed regulations concerning the wood for the sacrifices are laid down, going beyond the biblical tradition, suggests that the stipulations are based on priestly tradition. In the discussion of the 'peace offering' reference is made to Leviticus 3 and 7. Minor changes may also be present here, although the state of textual transmission does not admit many definite conclusions.[10]

The section concerning 'blood' (21:17ff.) is of interest because of the literary technique employed. The catchword 'blood' occurs in the context of regulations concerning purity: 'And let no blood appear on you or on your clothing.' This is followed by various regulations, such as: 'Bury blood,' 'Eat no blood,' and 'accept no bribe for human blood.' This last regulation is recorded in Jub. 21:19, 20 in two versions.

III. In the concluding section of his speech, Abraham states:

> I see, my son, all the works of the children of men,
> how they are sin and wickedness. . . . (21:21)

This is followed by a negative warning:

> Take care that you do not go upon their way. . . .

This is followed in turn by a threatened curse:

> Else he (the supreme God) will hide his countenance from you,
> and will deliver you into the hand of your sin,[11]

---

[9] It is hard to decide whether the prohibition against eating blood is still a part of the statement of substance—the catchword is taken up again in 21:17ff.—or whether it belongs to the sacrificial torah that follows, since the prohibition in Lev. 7:26 occurs in the context of the peace offering. The boundary between the stipulations in the statement of substance and the corpus of individual stipulations is here somewhat fluid.

[10] According to Jub. 21:8, for example, 'the liver with the kidneys' is to be offered; Leviticus 7 speaks of the 'appendage of the liver.' Lev. 7:15 requires that 'the peace offering for thanksgiving' be eaten on the same day; only the 'votive offering' and 'freewill offering' may still be eaten on the following day. Jub. 21:10 states quite generally: 'And eat its flesh on this day and on the second day.' Cf. also Jub. 21:11 and Lev. 2:13. What does Jub. 21:7 refer to, where we read that the offering is to be 'cooked in oil' ('confectum in oleo')?

[11] Here the 'angels of pestilence' are once again clearly eliminated (see above, pp. 106–107, 109). The ancient curse formula, however, is still easily recognizable.

and will efface you from the earth,
as well as your seed under the heavens,
and your name and your seed will perish from the whole earth.[12]

Then comes a corresponding positive commandment:[13]

And observe the ordinances of the supreme God,
and do his will,
and deal justly in all things. (21:23)

This leads up to a promise of blessing:

And he will bless you in all your works,
and will call forth from you a plant of righteousness
  upon the whole earth through all the races of the earth,
and my name and your name will not be forgotten under the heavens
  throughout all days. (21:24)[14]

Isaac is dismissed with a benediction (21:25):

Go, my son, in peace. . . . And may the supreme God, my God and your
God, strengthen you to do his will.

The conclusion is strange, since we are dealing with the 'last
words of Abraham to Isaac':

'And he departed from him in joy' (21:26).[15]

Jubilees does not exhibit any literary pretensions. Large sections, in
fact, do nothing but repeat Genesis 1–Exodus 12. The narrative and
legal expansions make 'the patriarchs appear as pedantic observers
of the law.'[16] There is a close connection with the Qumran writings,
as similarities of content and the finds themselves show.[17] The more

---

[12] Cf. the curse in Jub. 36:9ff., especially the mention of the 'day of confusion and of
the curse and of anger and of wrath. . . .'

[13] Jub. 20:7 interpolates at this point an invocation of witnesses (see above, pp. 23ff,
esp. 25):

I make you witnesses, my children;
love the God of heaven,
adhere to all his commandments,
and do not follow after their idols,
and   after their uncleanness. . . .

The ancient formula 'to follow after idols' is here interpreted as 'following after their
uncleanness.' In 21:5, the 'idols' have been omitted completely. Cf. the 'adjuration' in
35:21ff.; 36:7.

[14] See the ancient blessing formula in 20:9: '. . . that he may have pleasure in you and
grant you his mercy and cause the morning and the evening rain to fall for you.' (See also
the continuation.)

[15] Jub. 23:1 concludes: '. . . and he covered his countenance and extended his feet
and slept the eternal sleep and was gathered to his fathers.' There follows a dirge and
burial.

Jub. 35:27 mentions a farewell meal, as does 36:17: '. . . and he ceased commanding
them and blessing them, and they ate and drank before him.'

[16] Eißfeldt, *Old Testament*, p. 607.

[17] Ibid., pp. 607–608, with bibliography.

the individuality of the author recedes into the background, the easier it is to recognize the forms that have been adopted. Using the 'last of words of Abraham' as an example, we have demonstrated both the adoption of the formulary and its connection with the 'testament' form. The text showed that the original covenant formulary can have interpolated into it not only community rules, as in the Manual of Discipline and the Damascus Document, but also 'quite specific injunctions about the offering of sacrifices,'[18] i.e., explicitly priestly traditions.

The features of the literary type which we have worked out also are of assistance in understanding a literarily much more complex form of the 'testament' in the 'Testaments of the Twelve Patriarchs.'

2. THE TESTAMENTS OF THE TWELVE PATRIARCHS

The Testaments of the Twelve Patriarchs[19] became once more a topic of lively debate after 1947.[20] The occasion was the discovery of the Qumran texts, in which similarities to and agreements with the Testaments were evident at the first glance. Finally, some fragments of the Testaments were even discovered in Qumran caves 1 and 4.[21] This raised the old question once more: are the Testaments of the Twelve Patriarchs a Jewish document, a Christian document, or a Jewish document with Christian interpolations?[22]

The thesis that the Testaments of the Twelve Patriarchs is a Christian document composed about 200 A.D. has recently received new support from de Jonge.[23] He denies any possibility of eliminating interpolations on the basis of manuscript variants, and attempts to

---

[18] Ibid., p. 607.

[19] For the text, see R. H. Charles, *The Greek Versions of the Testaments of the Twelve Patriarchs* (Oxford, 1908). The sigla for the manuscripts are given there, p. lx. The names of the twelve patriarchs are abbreviated to their two or three initial letters. The translation follows that in E. Kautzsch, *Apokryphen und Pseudepigraphen*, vol. 2, pp. 458–506.

[20] See, for example, the bibliography in Eißfeldt, *Old Testament*, pp. 631–32.

[21] D. Barthélemy and J. T. Milik, *Qumran Cave I* ('Discoveries in the Judaean Desert,' I [Oxford, 1955]), pp. 87–91. Cf. J. T. Milik, 'Le Testament de Lévi en araméen,' *Revue Biblique*, 62 (1955), pp. 398–406; Starky, *Revue Biblique*, 63 (1956), p. 66.

[22] The first scholar to publish the Testaments, J. E. Grabe (*Spicilegium patrum*, I, 1698), argued for Jewish origin and Christian interpolations. His thesis was subsequently adopted by F. Schnapp (*Die Testament der 12 Patriarchen untersucht*, Halle, 1884). W. Bousset restricted the extent of the interpolations and attempted to define them more precisely by comparing the Greek text with the Armenian text, which he believed had not undergone Christian revision ('Die Testamente der 12 Patriarchen,' *ZNW*, 1 [1900], pp. 141–75, 187–209).

[23] Marinus de Jonge, *The Testaments of the Twelve Patriarchs* (Assen, 1953).

demonstrate the presence of Christian ideas in large sections of the Testaments.[24] It is impossible to discuss this thesis here; H. Aschermann has given good reasons for disputing it.[25] In Aschermann's view, the differences of textual tradition in the 'Christian passages' in the various manuscript groups and translations can be explained in this way: 'These versions represent various stages in the christianization of the Testaments. This of course eliminates the possibility of assuming a Christian author.'[26] This following study will in part confirm Aschermann's conclusions on the basis of other evidence. Aschermann's interest centers primarily on the smaller forms of the parenetic passages, with special reference to the New Testament.[27] Our primary concern will be to show how the ancient testament form has been utilized in the Testaments. The differences will illustrate more clearly the unique characteristics of the Testaments.

---

[24] 'If the conclusion reached in this chapter are right, the Testaments may become of great importance as a source for our knowledge of the beliefs and interests of the Christian Church at the end of the second century and the beginning of the third century A.D. Written by a pious Christian for ordinary Christians, they may bring us nearer to the life in the Christian communities of that time than any more theological treatise' (ibid., p. 128).

[25] H. Aschermann, *Die paränetischen Formen der Testamente der 12 Patriarchen und ihr Nachwirken in der frühchristlichen Mahnung*, Dissertation, Berlin, 1955. See also Eißfeldt, *Old Testament*, pp. 634–35.

It seems to me that de Jonge often confuses cause and effect. According to him, for example, the following passages refer to Christ: '. . . we find a number of passages where hardly any distinction seems to be made between Christ and God. So we read in T.N. VIII 3 ". . . ὀφθήσεται Θεὸς κατοικῶν ἐν ἀνθρώποις ἐπὶ τῆς γῆς. . . ."

'T. Iss. VII 7 even says: "ἔχοντες μεθ' ἑαυτῶν τὸν Θεὸν τοῦ οὐρανοῦ συμπορευόμενον τοῖς ἀνθρώποις ἐν ἁπλότητι καρδίας" (*Testaments*, p. 126).'

Compare, however, such passages as Ps. 77:60 (𝔊): 'σκήνωμα αὐτοῦ, οὗ κατεσκήνωσεν ἐν ἀνθρώποις.'

Isa. 8:18: '. . . παρὰ κυρίου σαβαωθ, ὃς κατοικεῖ ἐν τῷ ὄρει Σιων.'

Lev. 26:12: '. . . καὶ ἐμπεριπατήσω ἐν ὑμῖν καὶ ἔσομαι ὑμῶν Θεός.'

𝔐: . . . וְהִתְהַלַּכְתִּי בְּתוֹכְכֶם וְהָיִיתִי לָכֶם לֵאלֹהִים

Note that 'ἐν ἁπλότητι καρδίας' in Test. Iss. 7:7 does not refer grammatically to the 'God of heaven' but to 'the men' who are 'simple of heart.'

The concepts and their formulations are, in themselves, by no means necessarily 'Christian.' That they could be *interpreted* to yield a Christian meaning is shown by the early Christian use of the Old Testament for scriptural proof. De Jonge shows how the Testaments can be understood in a Christian sense and were in fact so understood.

As the Qumran texts show, a mere mention of the 'anointed one' (χριστός) need not be a Christian feature (see also K. G. Kuhn, 'Die beiden Messias Aarons und Israels,' *ThLZ*, 79 [1954], cols. 760–61). To this extent, de Jonge's evaluation of the numerous interpolations, *pace* Bousset, is accurate, as is his thesis of the unity of the text, albeit the unity is of the opposite kind that he seeks to demonstrate.

[26] Aschermann, *Paränetischen Formen*, pp. 20–21.

[27] What de Jonge calls an 'analysis of the composition of the Testaments along form-critical lines' (*Testaments*, p. 38) is by and large an examination of the tradition and its themes.

Preamble and Conclusion

A synopsis of the framework of the Testaments shows that they are based on a uniform schema that changes only in minor details or receives only small additions.

The sequence is roughly this:

(a) The preamble: 'A copy of the words [or: the testament] of (name of the patriarch), which he recited to his sons before his death in the . . . year of his life.[28] He was healthy [or: sick], assembled his sons, kissed them, and said to them, "Hearken, my children, to (name of the patriarch) your father, and hear his speech; I. . . ."'

(b) The conclusion: 'When he had said this, he died [or: stretched out his feet and rested in a good sleep]. And his sons laid him in a coffin. After (some time) they brought his bones to Hebron and buried him with his fathers.'

The uniformity of this framework stands in contrast to the remaining content of the Testaments, which suggests that it was imposed on the material all at once. De Jonge once more concludes: 'They [the framework passages] must have been written by the Christian author himself. . . .'[29] One may ask, however, whether this framework is not itself the translation of a Hebrew or Aramaic original, rather than an original composition in Greek.[30]

[28] It is striking that in the Test. Reuben, Simeon, and Zeb. the chronological relationship to the death of Joseph is also given.

[29] *Testaments*, p. 110.

[30] To confirm this hypothesis it would be necessary to examine the framework of the Testaments with respect to manuscript variants. For example:

Test. Reuben reads:	καὶ ἔθεντο αὐτὸν	ἐν σορῷ
Test. Simeon:	καὶ ἔθηκαν αὐτὸν	ἐν θήκῃ ξυκίνῃ
Test. Zeb.:	καὶ ἔθηκαν αὐτὸν . . . εἰς θήκην ξυλίνην	
Test. Benj.:	καὶ ἔθηκαν αὐτὸν	ἐν παραθήκῃ

These variants may perhaps be explained on the basis of an original בָּאָרוֹן. The ⑤ translates this word in Gen. 50:26 as 'ἐν τῇ σορῷ.' 'ἐν θήκῃ ξυλίνῃ' would be a periphrastic translation. אָרוֹן also refers to the 'money chest' (II Kings 12:10–11; II Chron. 24:8–9). This might explain the text in Test. Benj.: 'παραθήκη' = 'depositum.'

Test. Reuben reads:	ἀνενέγκαντες	αὐτὸν
Test. Simeon:	ἀνήγαγον	αὐτὰ
Test. Zeb.:	ἀναγαγόντες	
Test. Dan.:	ἀπήνεγκαν	τὰ ὀστᾶ αὐτοῦ
Test. Gad:	ἀνήγαγον	αὐτὸν
Test. Asher:	ἀνήγαγον	αὐτὸν
Test. Joseph:	συνήγαγον	τὰ ὀστᾶ Ἰωσήφ
Test. Benj.:	ἀνήγαγον	τὰ ὀστᾶ τῶν πατέρων αὐτῶν
Test. Benj. c:	ἄραντες	τὸ σῶμα αὐτοῦ

All these Greek forms might be based on a Hebrew text that corresponds to Exod. 13:19: וְהַעֲלִיתֶם אֶת־עַצְמֹתַי מִזֶּה אִתְּכֶם . . .

I. Narrative Sections

We shall devote our attention first to the narrative sections at the beginning of the individual testaments.[31] Besides these, minor narrative passages occur in the ethical and didactic sections. Each of the patriarchs recounts stories from his life. They usually begin with an explanation of their names, illustrating a particular characteristic or a unique experience. The biblical tradition is borrowed, especially Genesis 49 and Deuteronomy 33, but then expanded by the addition of a wealth of haggadic details.[32] Sometimes the catchword of the didactic section to follow is mentioned, sometimes there is only a loose connection. The patriarch tells of his life as an example or a warning. The many references to Joseph in this connection are striking;[33] in fact, Test. Benj. gives the impression of being almost more concerned with Joseph than with Benjamin.[34]

The narrative sections could be called 'biographical confessions or examples for admonition.'[35] But comparison with the texts previously examined suggests a more important element in these narrative passages.

Test. Joseph is an example. It begins with a confession of 'what the Lord has done for him.'[36] As the Testament continues, it recounts each of the many dangers into which Joseph fell, and tells how he stood the test. It always states, however, that God delivered him. The Test. Joseph is not unique in this respect. In the case of Test. Joseph,

---

[31] These appear clearly in Test. Simeon, Judah, Iss., Zeb., Dan, Naph., Gad, Benj. In Test. Reuben and Joseph they are not so clearly distinguished. Test. Asher has no narrative section. Test. Levi must be examined separately.

[32] See the description of their content in Eißfeldt, *Old Testament*, pp. 632–33.

[33] For example, the phrase 'περὶ 'Ιωσὴφ' occurs once in Test. Reuben (4:8), six times in Test. Simeon, ten times in Test. Iss., three times in Test. Dan, three times in Test. Naph., eight times in Test. Gad. See also the index in Charles, *Greek Versions*, p. 311.

The repeated references to Joseph must be distinguished from the sharply defined 'Levi-Judah' passages at the end of several Testaments. The context of these latter passages is quite different. One may ask whether a kind of 'Joseph literature' did not provide material for the Testaments.

[34] See also Test. Gad.

[35] See Aschermann, *Paränetischen Formen*, pp. 6–7.

[36] 1:3–5: 'Εγὼ εἶδον ἐν τῇ ζωῇ μου τὸν φθόνον καὶ τὸν θάνατον.
Καὶ οὐκ ἐπλανήθην ἀλλ' ἔμεινα ἐν τῇ ἀληθείᾳ Κυρίου.
Οἱ ἀδελφοί μου οὗτοι ἐμίσησάν με,   'Ο δὲ Κύριος ἠγάπησέ με.
Αὐτοὶ ἤθελόν με ἀνελεῖν,   'Ο δὲ Θεὸς τῶν πατέρων μου ἐφύλαξέν με.
Εἰς λάκκον με ἐχάλασαν,   Καὶ ὁ ὕψιστος ἀνήγαγέν με.
'Επράθην εἰς δουλείαν,   Καὶ ὁ πάντων δεσπότης ἠλευθέρωσέν με.
Εἰς αἰχμαλωσίαν ἐλήφθην,   Καὶ ἡ κραταιὰ αὐτοῦ χεὶρ ἐβοήθησέ μοι·
'Εν λιμῷ συνεσχέθην,   Καὶ αὐτὸς ὁ Κύριος διέθρεψέ με . . .
See also 3:4; 4:8; 9:5.

one might claim the the biblical narrative itself suggests that the story of Joseph is a story of God's guidance, although in the Bible, in contrast to Test. Joseph, the miracle of God's guidance is seldom expressed directly.

Simeon was angry with Judah for five months[37] because Judah had spared Joseph. Therefore Simeon's hand was half paralysed for seven days. He did penance and prayed to God that his hand might be restored.[38]

The 'spirit of understanding of the Lord' came upon Levi (2:3), and he prayed to the Lord to deliver him (2:4). To Judah the Lord gave 'grace in all that he did in the field and in the house' (2:1).[39] Issachar gave the fruits of his labor first to the Lord through the Lord's priest, then to his father, and only then to himself. Therefore the Lord doubled his possessions in his hand (3:7).[40] Dan was prevented by 'the God of Jacob his father' from doing evil (to Joseph) (1:9).

It therefore does not suffice to say that the patriarchs recount their lives as examples of virtue and as warnings against their vices. They are also and above all exemplary in their relationship with God. On this point the Testaments stand completely in the tradition of 'Israel's wisdom,' that the 'fear of God' is the beginning of wisdom. Indisputably, however, there is more pronounced interest here in the personal element, even in the psychological make-up of the individual. The piety recommended here is practical, not meditative. A statement like that in Test. Iss. 3:7 is very revealing: 'ὅτι ὁ θεὸς συνεργεῖ τῇ ἁπλότητί μου.' The actions of God and the actions of man stand in equilibrium. God is on the side of the devout man, and the devout man is the virtuous man; the virtues naturally include prayer, fasting, and almsgiving. The question of Job seems to have vanished without a trace.

The extent to which theological ideas and the understanding of life have changed becomes especially clear when we realize at what point these 'ideal biographies' of the patriarchs occur. They are

[37] Test. Simeon 2:11ff.

[38] Test. Simeon 2:13–14: '. . . καὶ μετανοήσας ἔκλαυσα καὶ ηὐξάμην Κυρίῳ τῷ Θεῷ ἵνα ἀποκατασταθῇ ἡ χείρ μου. . . . Ἔγνων γὰρ ὅτι πονηρὸν πρᾶγμα ἐνεθυμήθην ἐνώπιον Κυρίου καὶ Ἰακωβ τοῦ πατρός μου. . . .' Note the juxtaposition! The text continues: 'Καὶ νῦν τέκνα μου ἀκούσατέ μου. . . .'

[39] There follows a list of his talents.

[40] Cf. also Zebulun's draught of fishes: 'Therefore the Lord gave me many fishes to capture' (Test. Zeb. 6:6).

L

now found at the point where a retrospect of the acts of God occurred in the Old Testament 'testament formulary.' In the Old Testament, human acts were mentioned only as a response to the acts of God, a situation almost exactly opposite to that found in the Testaments of the Twelve Patriarchs. The criterion set up in the Old Testament for the conduct of God[41] as well as for the conduct of man is conformity to the mutual relationship established by the covenant. There a man's righteousness is judged by a relational concept. Here, in the Testaments of the Twelve Patriarchs, a man is judged according to an absolute concept of virtue or vice, to which God's judgment is then added.

The fundamental difference lies in the differing interpretations of history. The nature of the Old Testament antecedent history is such that it extends to the present moment. When the covenant is ratified, the 'antecedent history' places Israel within the history of its salvation and, equally within the history of its sin. This situation in turn determines Israel's future conduct. In the Testaments of the Twelve Patriarchs, history is completely eliminated in this section of the formulary. 'Example' replaces 'antecedent history.' The stories of the patriarchs no longer constitute part of *Heilsgeschichte* by virtue of promise and fulfillment; they are merely exemplary. They can therefore be expanded and elaborated at will. And it is surely not fortuitous that at this very moment, beginning with the interpretation of names, we find the first allegorization of individual features.[42]

The Testament of Naphtali occupies a special position.[43] Naphtali, like the other patriarchs, first recounts aspects of his life, in particular the circumstances of his birth and his naming.[44] Having mentioned Balla, his mother, he discusses her parents, Rothan and Aina, as well as explaining the names given to their daughters Zelpha and Balla. In all these details, it is striking how little the narrative has to do with the rest of Test. Naph. The key word of Test. Naph. is 'τάξις.' In the section now under discussion, the closest we come to an appearance of this word is in the last sentence (2:1): 'ἔταξέ με ὁ πατήρ μου εἰς πᾶσαν ἀγγελίαν. . . .' The following section (2:2–8), however, is intimately connected with the rest of Test. Naph.

---

[41] See the definition of N. Glueck in his *Das Wort hesed* ('Beihefte zur ZAW,' 47 Berlin, 1927).

[42] The question of what circumstances and influences caused this basic change is an historical question and cannot be discussed within the framework of this study.

[43] Test. Asher and Test. Levi are similar.

[44] Test. Naph. 1:6–2:1.

'Order' ('τάξις') appears clearly in the creation of man. Gen. 1:27 is cited as a kind of 'reflex quotation': 'He created every man after his image.'[45] The motif of the potter is introduced and interpreted. As a potter knows the circumference of a vessel, we read, so God created every creature according to 'weight, measure, and rule.' The potter knows the use to which each vessel is put. Then follows the interpretation: 'So, too, the Lord knows the body,[46] how far it extends in what is good and when it begins with what is evil' (Test. Naph. 2:4). The confession 'Πάντα γὰρ ἐν τάξει ἐποίησεν ὁ Θεὸς καλά' (2:8) is then elaborated with a kind of medical onomasticon.[47] In this detail we can see once more the connection with 'wisdom.'

Here, too, then the subject matter of the 'antecedent history' is creation, which is to provide the pattern for human conduct.[48] This, however, associates Test. Naph. closely with the Manual of Discipline and the Damascus Document, the 'dogmatic sections' of which likewise take the creation as their point of departure. In them, also, the structure of human conduct is to agree with the fundamental structure of creation. It is therefore probably not accidental that at this very point the antithetical concepts 'the law of the Lord—the law of Beliar' (2:6) and 'light and darkness' (2:7) appear once more.

The Hebrew Test. Naph., found in the Chronicles of Jerahmeel,[49] draws in part upon the same material. The testament form, however, has disintegrated much more, thanks primarily to extensive interpolations of apocalyptic history. Formally, at least, the Hebrew text of Test. Naph. does not give the impression of constituting the basis of the text that has come down to us in Greek.[50]

---

[45] Test. Naph. 2:5: '"Οτι οὐκ ἔστι πλάσμα καὶ πᾶσαν ἔννοια ἣν οὐκ ἔγνω Κύριος· πάντα γὰρ ἄνθρωπον ἔκτισεν κατ' εἰκόνα ἑαυτοῦ.'

[46] σῶμα!

[47] 2:8: 'τὰς πέντε αἰσθήσεις ἐν τῇ κεφαλῇ
καὶ τὸν τράχυλον συνάψας τῇ κεφαλῇ
    προσθεὶς αὐτῇ καὶ τρίχας εἰς εὐπρέπειαν καὶ δόξαν

εἶτα καρδίαν	εἰς φρόνησιν	κοιλίαν	εἰς	διάκρισιν
στόμαχον	εἰς - - -	κάλαμον	πρὸς	ὑγείαν
ἧπαρ	πρὸς θυμόν	χολὴν	πρὸς	πικρίαν
καὶ σπλῆνα	πρὸς γέλωτα	νεφροὺς	εἰς	πανουργίαν
ψύας	εἰς δύναμιν	+ πλευρὰν εἰς τὸ καθεύδειν +		
ὀσφὺν	εἰς ἰσχύν			

καὶ τὰ ἑξῆς.'

[48] See the introduction to the ethical section, which follows: 'Οὕτως οὖν ἔστωσαν, τέκνα μου, πάντα τὰ ἔργα ὑμῶν ἐν τάξει εἰς ἀγαθόν ἐν φόβῳ θεοῦ, καὶ μηδὲν ἄτακτον ποιήσητε ἐν καταφρονήσει, μηδὲ ἔξω καιροῦ αὐτοῦ . . .' (Test. Naph. 2:9).

[49] See Charles, Greek Versions, p. 239, Appendix II.

[50] See also the introduction to the Testaments of the Twelve Patriarchs in Kautzsch, Apokryphen, vol. 2, pp. 458–59.

The introductory narrative section (chapters 1–12) of Test. Levi exhibits the same disintegration as the Hebrew Test. Naph. Here, too, the biographical introduction is almost totally unrelated to the ethical exhortation. In the narrative are set two visions of Levi, a description of the seven heavens, and the description of a consecration of priests. The visions, however, can easily be separated from their present context.[51]

II. Ethical Sections

(a) Introduction (statement of substance)

The formula introducing the ethical instruction is almost stereotyped: 'And now, my children, (hearken to me and . . .).'[52] This 'and now' sums up the preceding exemplary narrative from the life of the patriarch and lays the foundation for the exhortation to follow. Narrative and commandment are linked. The style changes from the narrative tenses of the past to the present and imperative. But the 'καὶ νῦν' at this point in the overall structure of the Testaments is one of the small features of the original formulary that have been preserved with the least change. It corresponds to the Old Testament introduction of the statement of substance by means of וְעַתָּה.[53] Now we cannot base any conclusions on a simple 'καὶ νῦν.' But in the Testaments of the Twelve Patriarchs this phrase introduces a passage whose connection with the original statement of substance is clearly discernible.[54] The introductory formulas are once again

---

[51] This was already pointed out by Schnapp, *Testamente*, pp. 15ff.

[52] Test. Reuben 2:1: 'Καὶ νῦν ἀκούσατέ μου, τέκνα μου. . . .'
Test. Simeon 3:1:   'Καὶ νῦν, τέκνα μου, ἀκούσατέ μου καὶ. . . .'
Test. Levi 13:1:   'Καὶ νῦν, τέκνα μου, ἐντέλλομαι ὑμῖν. . . .'
Test. Iss. 4:1:   'Καὶ νῦν ἀκούσατέ μου, τέκνα, καὶ. . . .'
Test. Zeb. 5:1:   'Καὶ νῦν, τέκνα μου, παραγγέλλω ὑμῖν. . . .'

[53] Josh. 24:14:   וְעַתָּה יְראוּ אֶת־יהוה

וְעִבְדוּ אֹתוֹ   בְּתָמִים וּבֶאֱמֶת

וְהָסִירוּ אֶת־אֱלֹהִים אֲשֶׁר עָבְדוּ אֲבוֹתֵיכֶם בְּעֵבֶר הַנָּהָר. . .

Cf. Deut. 4:1; 10:12.

[54] Test. Judah 13:1–2: 'Καὶ νῦν ἐντέλλομαι ὑμῖν, τέκνα μου,
ἀκούσατε Ἰούδα τοῦ πατρὸς ὑμῶν καὶ
φυλάξασθε τοὺς λόγους μου
τοῦ ποιεῖν πάντα τὰ δικαιώματα Κυρίου καὶ
ὑπακούειν ἐντολὰς Θεοῦ καὶ
μὴ πορεύεσθε (αβΑ) ὀπίσω τῶν ἐπιθυμιῶν ὑμῶν ἐν ὑπερηφανείᾳ καρδίας,
καὶ μὴ καυχᾶσθε ἐν ἔργοις καὶ ἰσχύι τῆς νεότητος ὑμῶν,
ὅτι γε τοῦτο πονηρὸν ἐνώπιον Κυρίου ἐστί. . . .'

followed by a series of imperatives[55] that command general types of conduct. Once again we find the same verbs: 'Fear ..., love ..., keep ..., take care lest ..., walk in ..., do not walk ...' etc. These verbs, in turn, can then be taken up once more before individual stipulations. Furthermore, the double structure of the statement of substance—dealing with man's relationship to God and to his neighbor—can still be seen.[56] The changes in the Testaments of the Twelve Patriarchs are externally minor, but not insignificant. Most striking is the replacement of the commandment 'not to follow after other gods' with the commandment 'not to follow after carnal desires.'[57] This gives an interesting anthropological interpretation to the Old Testament commandment.

On the other hand, qualities can almost be understood personally, as in the 'spirit of error,' etc.[58] In Test. Reuben 3:9 we read: 'And now, my children, love truth, and she will preserve you.'[59] Thus a statement is made concerning 'truth' that one might expect to be made about God.

In the Testaments of the Twelve Patriarchs, the statement of substance is further expanded by the frequent suggestion of the theme to be taken up in the instruction that follows.[60]

(b) Ethical instruction

It is important to state at the very outset that the parenetic portions of the Testaments of the Twelve Patriarchs constitute a collection of individual sayings varying in length. In this respect the Testaments resemble collections of sayings like the biblical book of the 'Proverbs of Solomon' or the book of 'Jesus Sirach.' This means that only to a limited extent can we think in terms of a clear train of thought or the development of a theme. The individual unit, the individual saying, can easily have an independent existence. The material is arranged according to a completely external principle;

---

[55] Series of infinitives are less common here (cf. above, p. 37). See, however, Test. Zeb. 5:1: 'Καὶ νῦν, τέκνα μου, παραγγέλλω ὑμῖν τοῦ φυλάσσειν τὰς ἐντολὰς τοῦ Κυρίου καὶ ποιεῖν ἔλεος ἐπὶ τὸν πλησίον, καὶ εὐσπλαγχνίαν ἔχειν πρὸς πάντας οὐ μόνον ἐν ἀνθρώποις ἀλλὰ καὶ ἐν ἀλόγοις ζῴοις.'

[56] See also Test. Zeb. 5:1; Test. Benj. 3:1ff.; cf. Test. Simeon 4:7; Test. Iss. 5:1; Test. Dan 5:3; Test. Joseph 11:1.

[57] Test. Judah 13:2: 'Καὶ μὴ πορεύεσθε (α, β, Α) ὀπίσω τῶν ἐπιθυμιῶν ὑμῶν.'

[58] See Test. Simeon 3:1; Test. Dan 2:1; Test. Gad 3:1.

[59] Cf. Test. Dan 2:1.

[60] Cf. Test. Iss. 4:1; Test. Zeb. 5:1; Test. Dan 2:1; Test. Gad 3:1; Test. Benj. 3:1–2; Test. Simeon 3:1 (in this case the catchword is φθόνος): 'Καὶ νῦν, τέκνα μου, ἀκούσατέ μου καὶ φυλάξασθε ἀπὸ τοῦ πνεύματος τῆς πλάνης καὶ τοῦ φθόνου.'

the sayings are assembled on the basis of catchwords. Such a work always presupposes literary and 'scholarly' activity. This is one of the clues that suggest in what milieu the author of the Testaments lived.[61]

When the catchwords of the individual testaments are brought together, the result is once more a short catalog of virtues and vices.[62] It is striking that not only Test. Reuben but also Test. Simeon contains a section concerning πορνεία. Test. Judah (οἶνος). Test. Naph. (τάξις), Test. Asher (διπρόσωπον), and Test. Benj. (διάνοια/διαβούλιον) differ from the rest of the Testaments in the type of catchword they use, since their catchwords do not mention a virtue or vice directly. These observations support the hypothesis that material already in existence was expanded secondarily to fill out the number of the twelve patriarchs. In addition, as we have shown, the narrative concerning the patriarch is often only loosely connected with the catchword of the Testament in question. On the other hand, the ethical section fits quite appropriately in its place in the overall structure of the individual Testament. It replaces the individual stipulations of the covenant formulary. The direct requirements of the commandments, however, give way to a 'didactic definition of certain typical modes of conduct.'[63] Virtues and vices are described, together with their consequences.[64] In other cases, we find a kind of 'warrant' describing the virtuous or wicked man.[65] The presentation is self-evident. The person addressed can clearly choose only to follow the path of virtue and shun vice. Nevertheless a specific exhortation is always appended.

---

[61] H. Thyen, *Der Stil der Jüdisch-Hellenistischen Homilie*, FRLANT (Göttingen, 1955,) p. 25: 'We must probably conceive the origin of this book in terms similar to the origin of James: a zealous attendant at synagogue preaching or a Jewish homilist has here assembled the sum of what he heard or composed concerning the history of the twelve sons of Jacob, expanded it by the addition of numerous familiar exhortations, and published it in the then popular form of a fictional testament.' That the author was merely a 'zealous attendant' is hardly likely.

[62] Test. Levi	σοφία	πορνεία	Test. Reuben and Simeon
Test. Iss.	ἁπλότης	φθόνος	Test. Simeon
Test. Zeb.	ἔλεος	φιλαργυρία	Test. Judah (from 18:2)
Test. Zeb.	εὐσπλαγχνία	θυμός ἀψεῦδος)	Test. Dan
Test. Joseph	σωφροσύνη	μῖσος	Test. Gad

cf. Test. Iss. 7:2–6.

[63] See von Rad, 'Early History,' p. 308.

[64] Examples include the description of πορνεία in Test. Reuben 4:6ff., φθόνος in Test. Simeon 5ff., and περὶ τῶν ἑπτὰ πνευμάτων τῆς πλάνης in Test. Reuben 2.

[65] Test. Benj. 6:1ff.: τὸ διαβούλιον τοῦ ἀγαθοῦ ἀνδρός; Test. Iss. 4:2ff.: ὁ ἁπλοῦς; Test. Gad 3:2–3; 5:1–2: ὁ μισῶν

The original nature of the exhortation as an interpretation of the divine commandment can still be seen in certain details. For example, a kind of divine legitimation is claimed for the description of πορνεία and its consequences.[66] A similar tendency can be seen when, in the same context, a 'scriptural proof' is added to the story of the fall of the 'giants' (Genesis 6).[67]

We shall now describe in somewhat more detail the way in which catchwords are used to link the material together, since it is also important for later texts. The catchword need not stand at the beginning of the smallest units; it can appear anywhere. In some cases, it is not even clear whether the catchword originally defined the subject matter of the unit or is merely mentioned in passing. For example, it is hard to tell whether the series in Test. Judah 18:2–6 referred originally to φιλαργυρία or πορνεία. The actual catchword in Test. Dan is θῦμος, but ψεῦδος often appears as well. In Test. Reuben, the catchword πορνεία takes first place among the 'spirits of error,' but only as one vice among many.[68] The catchword itself can appear in various forms and compounds.[69]

Different opinions can be recorded on a given question. With regard to wine, for example, we read (Test. Judah 16:2): 'If you drink wine with joy, filled with modesty and the fear of God, you will live.'[70] Another voice, however, says (Test. Judah 16:3): 'If you wish to be wise, be not at all a partisan of wine.' On this point, however, the various manuscripts differ among themselves. Manuscript d reads: 'I tell you, if it is possible, to drink no wine at all.' Manuscripts a, e, and f, however, declare laconically: 'But what shall I say to to you: do not drink at all.' The idea that 'in vino veritas' reads here (Test. Judah 16:4): 'Wine reveals the secrets of God and of men.'[71] This sounds quite positive. But the appended illustration from the

---

[66] Test. Reuben 5:3: 'ὅτι καίγε περὶ αὐτῶν εἶπέν μοι ὁ ἄγγελος τοῦ θεοῦ καὶ ἐδίδαξέ με. . . .'

[67] Test. Reuben 5:6ff.: 'Οὕτως γὰρ ἔθελξαν τοὺς 'Εγρηγόρους τοὺς πρὸ τοῦ κατακλυσμοῦ. ἐκεῖνοι γὰρ συνεχῶς ὁρῶντες αὐτὰς ἐγένοντο καὶ ἐν ἐπιθυμίᾳ αὐτῶν καὶ συνέλαβον τῇ διανοίᾳ τὴν πρᾶξιν. μετεσχηματίζοντο γὰρ εἰς ἄνδρα καὶ ἐν τῇ συνουσίᾳ τῶν ἀνδρῶν αὐτῶν συνεφαίνοντο αὐταῖς. Κἀκεῖναι δὲ ἐπιθυμοῦσαι τῇ διανοίᾳ τῆς φαντασίας αὐτῶν ἔτεκον γίγαντας. 'Εφαίνοντο γὰρ αὐταῖς οἱ 'Εγρήγοροι ἕως τοῦ οὐρανοῦ φθάνοντες.

Φυλάξατε οὖν ἀπὸ τῆς πορνείας. . . .'

[68] Cf. also Test. Joseph 10:1–2

[69] See Test. Judah: οἶνος, οἰνοχοεῖν, πάροινος, οἰνοποσία . . . Test. Dan: θυμός, θυμώδης, ὁ θυμούμενος, ἐπιθυμέω, μακροθυμία, μακρόθυμος. . . .

[70] The text follows manuscript b. See Kautzsch's translation.

[71] 'Καίγε μυστήρια Θεοῦ καὶ ἀνθρώπων ἀποκαλύπτει ὁ οἶνος.'

life of the patriarch, which tells how he revealed the commandments of God and the secrets of Jacob to the Canaanite woman, gives a negative meaning to the statement.

This method of composition shows the close ties that link the Testaments of the Twelve Patriarchs with wisdom literature.[72]

Parenesis can also make use of literary types that were originally alien to it. Test. Asher furnishes an example. Here, except for the preamble, there is no trace of the biographical introduction found in other testaments.[73] In its place, chapter 1 contains a didactic treatise on 'the *two ways* that God gave to men' (1:3). With this theme Test. Asher resembles the dogmatic section of the Manual of Discipline.[74] Here, however, the cosmological dualism is greatly attenuated. The first way is the way of good, the second the way of evil. Whoever 'inclines toward evil' and 'follows it' is 'ruled by Beliar';[75] if so, however, even the good deeds that he does are evil. The decision is apparently not made once and for all. The difference between the two ways lies in the 'two inclinations within our breast.'[76]

The catchword of the exhortation in Test. Asher is δύο. In the ethical section that follows it is taken up as διπρόσωπον. The form of the smallest units, which dominate this section of Test. Asher, is

---

[72] Cf., for instance, the collection of sayings concerning the physician in Ecclus. 83:1–15. There the opinions expressed range from 'Honor the physician with due honor, that you may have him in your need, for the Lord created him' (vv. 1–2) to 'Whoever sins before his creator shall fall into the hands of the physician' (v. 15).

[73] The beginning of the patriarch's speech reads: 'Ακούσατε, τέκνα 'Ασήρ, τοῦ πατρὸς ὑμῶν, καὶ πᾶν τὸ εὐθὲς ἐνώπιον τοῦ Θεοῦ ὑποδείξω ὑμῖν.'
According to Charles (*Greek Versions*, p. 172, n. 10), we have here a 'paronomasia' between εὐθές = יָשָׁר and אָשֵׁר = 'Ασήρ. This means there is some probability that the framework, too, was originally not written in Greek. At the beginning of Test. Asher the Hebrew original of the text appears with particular clarity; in several passages retranslation is necessary for comprehension (see the further notes by Charles).

[74] Cf. also Test. Judah 20! There we read that 'two spirits, the spirit of truth and the spirit of error, have converse with men.' In this statement the spirits can still be conceived as personal powers external to man. The larger context, however, makes it clear that this cannot be the meaning. 'What concerns truth and error is written upon the heart of man.' Here we have an obvious reference to Jer. 31:33 (see Charles, *Greek Versions*, p. 96, n. 12). Between truth and error stands a third element, 'conscience' (according to α) or 'the discernment of understanding' (according to β AS¹). The only function of 'the discernment of understanding' is 'to incline in what direction it will.' 'The spirit of truth,' however, 'bears witness and accuses.' It is interesting to observe how the passage links together an attenuated cosmological dualism, the Hellenistic concept of συνείδησις and the Old Testament idea of 'writing upon the heart.'

[75] Test. Asher 1:8.

[76] Test. Asher 1:5: 'Οδοὶ γάρ εἰσιν δύο, καλοῦ καὶ κακοῦ ἐν οἷς εἰσι τὰ δύο διαβούλια ἐν στέρνοις ὑμῶν διακρίνοντα αὐτά.' 'Διαβούλιον' is here obviously a translation of יֵצֶר. See von Rad, 'Early History,' p. 296.

peculiar. The units are relatively short, well defined, and constitute a sequence of some length. They are all identical in structure. The introduction reads: '"Εστιν ἄνθρωπος . . .' or '"Αλλος. . . .' Then follows a brief sketch of the negative and positive conduct of the man and, finally, the judgment on the case.[77] Here we can still make out the structure that we found above, in our discussion of the משפטים of the Manual of Discipline (cols. vi–vii), to be typical of legal decisions.[78] Formally, the decisions in Test. Asher resemble even more the cultic decisions given by the priests, like those presupposed in Hag. 2:12ff. Here a decision concerning what is clean and what is unclean is replaced by a decision concerning what is good and what is evil. The common element in both cases is probably the fact that a disputed question is discussed and given a definitive answer. It is conceivable that, just as the priest had formerly been approached in cultic questions, so later on the teacher was asked for a decision in ethical questions. This would account for the occurrence of a similar structure in a very different *Sitz im Leben*. In the Testaments, of course, this form itself underwent literary reworking.

III. Blessings and Curses

An eschatological section frequently concludes the Testaments of the Twelve Patriarchs. The function and significance of this section has often had insufficient recognition. It has been ventured in explanation that a prediction concerning the future is 'natural' for a dying patriarch.[79] There is a major difficulty, however: in many cases, these sections have been expanded by the addition of apocalyptic elements, and ethical instruction differs greatly from apocalyptic speculation. Other things being equal, one would trace each to a different *Sitz im Leben*.

---

[77] As a short example, we may cite Test. Asher 2:5, which reads:

"Αλλος κλέπτει
    ἀδικεῖ
    ἁρπάζει
    πλεονεκτεῖ
καὶ ἐλεεῖ πτωχούς· διπρόσωπον μὲν καὶ τοῦτο, τὸ δὲ ὅλον πονηρόν ἐστιν.
Test. Asher 4:3 is an example of a positive judgment. I consider the latter form secondary, however, since in this case there is no real decision.

[78] See especially the introduction: . . . אשר . . . האיש אשר

[79] de Jonge, *Testaments*, p. 120: 'As a rule the author puts them at the end of the individual Testaments without connecting them with the preceding passages. Yet they are an integral part of the Testaments for it is only natural that the last words of a dying patriarch contain predictions of the future as well as reminiscences of the past and exhortations for the present. . . .' 'Thus it is quite intelligible that the author incorporated passages dealing with the last days in his predominantly exhortatory book. . . .'

But even if the significance of these sections in the Testaments is minimized, they cannot be overlooked.[80] If our hypothesis is correct that the Testaments follow the pattern of the formulary as we have defined it, then the point at which the eschatological sections occur ceases to be surprising. In fact, on the basis of the texts studied so far we would expect such a section at this point.

In explanation, more detail will be presented on this point. In the Old Testament, Leviticus 26 and Deuteronomy 28ff. contain extensive series of blessings and curses that are clearly associated with the Yahweh covenant. In each case, the blessings and curses are preceded by a brief summary of the statement of substance.[81] A blessing is promised if the covenant is kept; a curse is threatened if it is broken. In its simplest form, the blessing involves primarily the gifts of 'nature': rain, bountiful harvest, fertility, health, long life; but it also includes peace and protection against enemies. The curse merely threatens the reverse of the blessings. Both blessing and curse lie in the future, as two possibilities. In this form of blessing and curse the Old Testament draws on much earlier models.

Now it is easy to see that these very passages in Leviticus and Deuteronomy were later subject to much revision and expansion. In the period when catastrophes befell Israel, the consequences of the curse were felt to have been realized.[82] In these expansions, the series of curses are used to describe the disasters of the present. It is therefore difficult to decide what is borrowed from the curse formulas and what is a description of the concrete disaster.[83] In this context, therefore, one can say that something takes place as it stands written 'in this book.'[84] Thus for later generations Moses also becomes a

---

[80] Ibid., p. 121: 'Yet we cannot say that the Testaments are an apocalytipical document, for the eschatological parts together form only a small portion of the book. . . . They do not occupy a central place in the Testaments.'

[81] Lev. 26:1–4: 'You shall make for yourselves no idols . . ., for I am Yahweh your God. . . . If you walk in my statutes and obey my commandments and do them, then I will . . . ' (there follows the promised blessing). Deut. 28:1–2: 'And if you obey the voice of Yahweh your God, being careful to do all his commandments which I command you this day, Yahweh your God will set you high above all the nations of the earth; and all these blessings shall come upon you. . . .'

[82] See the express statement in Deut. 29:24–27: 'It is because they forsook the covenant of Yahweh the God of their fathers. . . . Therefore the anger of Yahweh was kindled against this land, bringing upon it all the curses written in this book; and Yahweh uprooted them from their land in anger and fury and great wrath, and cast them into another land, as at this day.'

[83] See Steuernagel, *Deuteronomium*, ad loc.

[84] See Deut. 29:26; cf. Deut. 29:19–20; 28:61; Dan. 9:11, 13.

'prophet' who predicted disaster as a consequence of breaking the covenant.[85]

The blessing, however, is not simply annulled. Just as the curse is employed to describe disaster, so the blessing is used to describe a coming time of salvation.[86]

In these later stages of the form, blessing and curse are placed in temporal sequence. Between them comes a new element, a section concerning repentance and return to God.[87] Repentance demands a certain kind of human conduct, a return to obedience. But the annullment of the curse and the restoration of the covenant relationship lie in God's free will and are determined by his mercy alone.[88]

Now the same structure is presupposed in the eschatological sections of the Testaments of the Twelve Patriarchs. We must of course make it clear at the outset that we are not dealing here with a direct literary borrowing, but with an independent development that is nevertheless reasonable.

Test. Judah 23ff. furnishes a good example. The structure of this section can be analysed as follows:

(1) Description of the relationship to God and his commandments:

'I am caused great sadness, my children, by your unchastity, your sorcery, and your idolatry . . .' (there follows a long catalogue of sins).

(2) List of consequences of the curse:

'Therefore the Lord will visit you with plague, famine, death, the sword . . .' (there follow further items in a series of curses, including 'servitude among the heathen').

---

[85] Deut. 31:26: 'Take this "book of the law" and put it by the side of the ark of the covenant of Yahweh your God, that it may be there for a witness against you. For I know how rebellious and stubborn you are.' Deut. 31:29: 'For *I know* that after my death you will surely act corruptly, and turn aside from the way which I have commanded you; and *in the days to come* evil will befall you, because you will do what is evil in the sight of Yahweh. . . .'

[86] See Lev. 26:42, 45; Deut. 30:3–9. Deut. 30:3: 'Then Yahweh your God will restore your fortunes (וְשָׁב שְׁבוּתְךָ), and have compassion upon you, and he will gather you (וְשָׁב וְקִבֶּצְךָ). . . .' Deut. 39:9: 'Yahweh your God will make you abundantly prosperous in all the work of your hand, in the fruit of your body, and in the fruit of your cattle, and in the fruit of your ground; for Yahweh will again (יָשׁוּב) take delight in prospering you. . . .'

[87] Lev. 26:40: 'But if they confess their iniquity and the iniquity of their fathers. . . .' Deut. 30:2: 'When you return (וְשַׁבְתָּ) to Yahweh your God and obey his voice . . .'; cf. Deut. 2:29–30.

[88] See Deut. 4:31: 'For Yahweh your God is a merciful God; he will not fail you. . . .' Cf. 30:6.

(3) Conversion:

'. . . until you turn to the Lord[89] with all your heart and full of remorse, until you walk according to all the commandments of God.'

(4) Promise of salvation:

'Then the Lord will visit you with his mercy and lead you back from the captivity of the enemies (heathen)' (there follows a description of the time of salvation).[90]

The corresponding sections of the other Testaments can easily be analysed according to this structure. They all contain four points, although in some of the Testaments individual points may have extended or minimal development.

(1) Statement of the relationship to God and his commandments

Test. Asher 7:2 states simply: 'I know that you will sin.' God predicts (8:2): 'Your children will rebel against them [Judah and Levi] and will be in all kind of wickedness, evil, and depravity "from" the Lord.' Rebellion against Levi is also mentioned in Test. Reuben 6:5; Test. Simeon 5:4; and Test. Dan 5:4–7. The warning against 'schisms' in Test. Zeb. 9:1–5 probably also belongs in this context. The 'abomination of the heathen' and the 'wickedness of Sodom' are also found here (Test. Simeon 5:4; Test. Dan 5:4–7; Test. Naph. 4:1; Test. Benj. 9:1). This section is most intimately associated with the rest of the testament in Test. Iss., since it repeats ἁπλότης, the catchword of this Testament: 'Know

---

[89] This reading follows β AS¹; see Charles.

[90] From chapter 24 on the text-groups α, β, S¹ and the Armenian translation differ markedly in their formulations. The difference in content is not so great. Most scholars find considerable Christian influence in this section. It is certainly possible to understand the messianic prophecies in a Christian sense. Whether they are necessarily Christian in origin seems to me debatable (see the apparatus in Charles). In extensive portions of the text we are simply dealing with a concatenation and interpretation of Old Testament quotations in the same fashion as is found, for example, in the Damascus Document. Just as in recensions A and B of the Damascus Document, so here, too, different scriptural proofs are given in two different recensions. In 24:1, for example, α, β, and S¹ begin:
'Καὶ μετὰ ταῦτα ἀνατελεῖ ὑμῖν ἄστρον ἐξ Ἰακωβ ἐν εἰρήνη
καὶ ἀναστήσεται ἄνθρωπος ἐκ τοῦ σπέρματός μου
ὡς ἥλιος δικαιοσύνης . . .'
This is a 'reflex' of Num. 24:17 (𝔊):
'ἀνατελεῖ ἄστρον ἐξ Ἰακωβ καὶ ἀναστήσεται ἄνθρωπος ἐξ Ἰσραηλ.'
In the Damascus Document (7:18ff.), this quotation from Numbers is used in similar association with the 'day of visitation,' albeit following the text of 𝔐, in which the second part reads: מִיִּשְׂרָאֵל וְקָם שֵׁבֶט. The Armenian tradition begins: 'And after that the star of peace shall rise, of(?) the sun of righteousness.' Here we find a stronger echo of Mal. 3:20 (𝔊): 'καὶ ἀνατελεῖ ὑμῖν τοῖς φοβουμένοις τὸ ὄνομά μου ἥλιος δικαιοσύνης . . .'. In α, β, S¹ all that remains of Mal. 3:20 is the metaphor of the 'sun of righteousness'; similarly, A preserves only the mention of the 'star' from Num. 24:17.

therefore, my children, that in the last days your sons will forsake *simplicity* and cleave to avarice. And they will abandon innocence and draw near to deceit, and will forsake the commandments of the Lord and cleave to Beliar; and they will give up farming[!] and follow their evil thoughts.' We find the same verbs here as in the usual statement of substance; instead of 'forsaking Yahweh' and 'cleaving to foreign gods,' however, we read of 'forsaking simplicity and cleaving to avarice' and 'following evil thoughts.' The middle element of the series, 'forsaking the commandments of the Lord and cleaving to Beliar' resembles the Old Testament texts more closely, although it is not clear whether 'Beliar' should be understood in a personal sense.

This section is given its most extensive development in Test. Levi 14 and 16:1–2(3), where we discover finally that a whole 'catalogue of vices' can be introduced at this point. Test. Levi 16:1 states: 'I know that you will walk in error for seventy weeks.' One can think of this statement being expanded by the addition of specific content recounting what takes place in these seventy weeks. This would be the logical place for an 'apocalypse' within the structure of the Testament as a whole.

(2) List of consequences of the curse

The curse takes effect because of the sins named under point one. This cause and effect relationship is expressed not only in the formulation as a whole but even in the choice of particles.[91] The Old Testament statement that Yahweh himself is the 'avenger' of the broken covenant is preserved in its full force.[92] Exile is the consequence of the curse most frequently mentioned.[93] With it go 'devastation of the land' (Test. Judah 23:3; Test. Asher 7:2) and 'destruction of the Temple.'[94] The list of curses in Test. Judah 23:3–4 shows, however,[95] that exile is not the only form of curse. As

---

[91] Test. Reuben 6:6: 'Ὁ γὰρ Θεὸς ποιήσει τὴν ἐκδίκησιν . . .'
Test. Levi 15:1: 'Διὰ τοῦτο . . .'
Test. Levi 14:4: 'καὶ ἐπάξετε κατάραν ἐπὶ τὸ γένος ἡμῶν . . .' (α, β)
Test. Judah 22:1: ''Επάξει δὲ αὐτοῖς Κύριος . . .'
Test. Judah 23:3: ''Ανθ' ὧν ἐπάξει Κύριος ἐφ' ὑμᾶς . . .'
Test. Dan 5:8 and Test. Asher 7:6: '. . . καὶ διὰ τοῦτο . . .'
[92] But see Enoch 100:10–13; cf. above, pp. 24–25, 105–106, 113, 139.
[93] See Test. Levi 10:4; 15:1; 16:5; Test. Iss. 6:2; Test. Zeb. 9:6; Test. Dan 5:8; Test. Naph. 4:2; Test. Asher 7:2, 6. Cf. Test. Levi 26:31ff., 38, 41; Deut. 4:27; 28:36–37; 29:27; II Chron. 7:20.
[94] Test. Levi 15:1; Test. Judah 23:3. Test. Asher 7:2 has the plural τὰ ἄγια(?)!
[95] Cf. Jubilees 36:10; 1QS iv. 12ff.! See also Test. Benj. 7:2.

consequences of the curse, Test. Zeb. 9:6 mentions 'sickness and affliction of every sort'; Test. Dan 5:8 mentions 'all the plagues of Egypt . . . all evils. . . .' In Test. Reuben 6:6 an 'evil death' is threatened. The curse, in fact, must of necessity lead to complete destruction and annihilation.[96] In the latter passages (Test. Levi 16:5; Test. Zeb. 9:6; Test. Dan 5:8; Test. Naph. 4:2), a minor detail illustrates the special nature of all the concluding sections in the Testaments of the Twelve Patriarchs. We read, to our surprise, that the persons addressed will 'fall to the curse among the heathen' (Test. Levi 16:5). 'Sickness and affliction of every sort' (Test. Dan 5:8) will come upon them '*then* among the heathen.' What has happened here? In a list of curses, the most diverse consequences originally could be set down without any further attempt to link them together. They are still listed in this fashion in Test. Judah 23:3–4.[97] In the corresponding passages of the other Testaments, however, the individual consequences of the curse are now set in chronological order.[98] They take place one after another. They serve to describe the time of calamity. Since, however, the author is particularly aware of the fulfillment of the threat of exile and dispersion, he gives them an emphatic position at the beginning and has the other consequences of the curse follow in chronological order.

(3) Repentance

The 'repentance' element[99] is only slightly altered in the various Testaments. Almost without exception it consists merely of a few formalized sentences.[100] 'Repentance' is called for, without any need

---

[96] Test. Levi 16:5: 'fall before the curse'; Test. Asher 7:6: 'and shall no longer know your land, your tribe, and your language'; Test. Naph. 4:2: 'affliction, disaster, until he destroys . . .' (see Charles ad loc.).

[97] See also Test. Naph. 8:6.

[98] The same technique is found in the expansions of the curse passage in Deuteronomy 28. It is merely more striking in the Testaments of the Twelve Patriarchs. In Deuteronomy it is not so easy to determine with assurance where the text is a simple curse-series and where it is a description of actual distress

[99] See also E. K. Dietrich, *Die Umkehr im AT und im Judentum* (Tübingen, 1936) especially Teil III, 'Die Umkehr in den Apokryphen und Pseudepigraphen,' pp. 229–86 The form-critical context is not yet taken into account in this work

[100] Test. Iss. 6:3–4: '. . . . ὅπως, ἐὰν ἁμάρτωσι, τάχιον ἐπιστρέψωσι πρὸς τὸν Κύριον. Ὅτι ἐλεήμων ἐστὶ καὶ ἐξελεῖται αὐτοὺς τοῦ ἐπιστρέψαι αὐτοὺς εἰς τὴν γῆν αὐτῶν.'

Test. Zeb. 9:7: 'Καὶ μετὰ ταῦτα μνησθέντες Κύριον ὑποστρέψετε (α; β, A, and S¹ read μετανοήσετε) καὶ ἐλεήσει ὑμᾶς, ὅτι ἐλεήμων ἐστὶ καὶ εὔσπλαγχνος καὶ οὐ λογίζεται κακίαν τοῖς υἱοῖς τῶν ἀνθρώπων. . . .'

Test. Dan 5:9: 'Καὶ οὕτως ἐπιστρέψαντες πρὸς Κύριον ἐλεηθήσεσθε. . . .'

Test. Naph. 4:3: 'καὶ σμικρυνθέντες ἐπιστρέψετε καὶ ἐπιγνώσεσθε Κύριον τὸν

for explaining what is meant. This knowledge is assumed. The presupposition on which the 'reversal of the curse' is based is God's gift of salvation, since he is 'merciful, gracious, and of great goodness.' It is a striking fact that at this very point we find once more solemn confessional formulas. The significance of repentance here is almost precisely the same as that of repentance in Old Testament prophecy. According to H. W. Wolff, 'in this concept the primary point of interest is not the contrast with man's previous attitude, nor yet an emphasis on man's new attitude, but the restoration of an original status.'[101] 'In this fashion, then, the theme of "repentance" finds an appropriate place in the declaration of eschatological salvation.'[102]

(4) Promise of salvation

In these texts the section that deals with repentance passes directly into a description of the time of salvation. Form and content therefore correspond closely, on the assumption that theologically 'repentance' is inseparable from the granting of salvation.

Earlier blessings are reinterpreted in the Testaments of the Twelve Patriarchs.[103] Often only minor changes in the ancient blessing formulas are necessary. In some passages, in fact, the meaning of the expression is clear only upon comparison with the ancient blessing formula.

In the context of the great series of blessings, we read in Deuteronomy 28:12: 'Yahweh will open to you his good treasury the heavens, to give the rain of your land in its season and to bless all the work of your hands.' In Test. Judah 24:2 (Armenian version), this becomes: 'And the heavens will open, and the blessings of the holy Father will stream forth, and he will pour out the spirit of truth upon us.' The recension found in α, β, S¹ takes a further step; here

---

Θεὸν ὑμῶν καὶ ἐπιστρέψει ὑμᾶς εἰς τὴν γῆν ὑμῶν κατὰ τὸ πολὺ αὐτοῦ ἔλεος. . . .'

Test. Naph. 4:5: 'ἄχρις οὗ ἔλθη τὸ σπλάγχνον Κυρίου [ἄνθρωπος] ποιῶν δικαιοσύνην καὶ ποιῶν ἔλεος. . . .'

Test. Asher 7:7: ''Αλλ', ἐπισυνάξει ὑμᾶς (β; α reads Κύριος) ἐν πίστει διὰ τῆς εὐσπλαγχνίας αὐτοῦ καὶ δι' 'Αβραάμ καὶ 'Ισαὰκ καὶ 'Ιακώβ. . . .'

Cf. Deut. 4:30!

[101] H. W. Wolff, 'Das Thema "Umkehr" in der alttestamentlichen Prophetie,' ZThK, 48 (1951), p. 134.

[102] Ibid., p. 142.

[103] Many scholars term this process 'spiritualization.' But this term is only an inferior makeshift to describe the situation. The blessing is certainly conceived no less 'concretely.' The nature of the interpretation found here deserves closer study.

the reference to the 'Messiah' is even plainer: 'And the heavens will open *upon him*, they will pour forth the blessing of the spirit from the holy Father.'

Test. Dan 5:13 promises that 'Jerusalem will no longer be desolate, Israel will no longer be captive.' This is still to be understood concretely. In the same context, however, we also read (v. 11): 'He will carry off the captives of Beliar.'[104] Then there was added, probably even later, 'the souls of the saints.'

Only the borrowing of ancient series of blessings and curses can probably explain the statement that in the time of salvation no 'wild beasts' will afflict the devout.[105]

Salvation consists primarily in a restoration of the original relationship with God. The central statements used in the Old Testament to describe the covenant with God are taken up once more. Test. Judah 25:3 states: 'And you will be a people of the Lord.' Here, too, belong the statements that the Lord will be 'in the midst of' Israel,[106] and that God 'walks with men.'[107] At this point in particular Christian interpretation begins.[108]

A wealth of ideas and quotations from the whole Old Testament is utilized to describe the time of salvation, from the rest that the saints will find in 'Eden' (Test. Dan. 5:12), through the joy in the 'new Jerusalem' (ibid.), to the quotations from the end of Malachi (Test. Zeb. 9:8). It is impossible here to go into a detailed study of the meaning and content of these texts.[109]

The descriptions of the time of salvation are composed in the future tense. Noteworthy are the series of clauses beginning with τότε or καὶ μετὰ ταῦτα.[110] The τότε series correspond to the clauses constructed with אז in the eschatological sections of the Manual of Discipline and the Damascus Document. Here, however, the number of members in the series has increased considerably. The temporal extension observed in the curse sections occurs here also.

Some of the Testaments contain a repetition of the schema

[104] Abstract for concrete; cf. Num. 31:12; I Esdras 6:5, 8; I Macc. 9:70. See W. Bauer, *Greek-English Lexicon of the New Testament*, trans. W. F. Arndt and F. W. Gingrich (Chicago: 1957), p. 24. Cf. Test. Zeb. 9:8.
[105] Test. Iss. 7:7; Test. Naph. 8:6.
[106] Test. Dan 5:13; cf. Joel 2:27.
[107] Test. Iss. 7:7; cf. Exod. 33:16; 34:9
[108] See Test. Judah 24:1.
[109] See P. Volz, *Die Eschatologie der jüdischen Gemeinde* (Tübingen, 1934), §8, pp. 30–33. Volz assembles considerable material, but still by and large in too summary a fashion.
[110] Test. Sim. 6:2–7; Test. Benj. 10:6–9; cf. Test. Judah 24:1; Test. Zeb. 9:8.

'time of disaster—time of salvation.'[111] These assume a second apostasy. There are two possible reasons for this repetition of the schema. The reason may be literary: when the material in the Testaments was brought together, two parallel recensions were assembled and then combined in such a way that they give the impression of a chronological sequence.[112] Alternatively, the reason may be historical: the text originally concluded with the time of salvation; then, at a time when people felt they were living in a 'time of disaster' brought on by renewed apostasy the schema was repeated.[113]

In addition to an 'eschatological' blessing and curse section, Test. Naph. also has a section that represents a stage in the development of the 'blessings and curses' element that is closer to its form-critical origin. In it blessing and curse are juxtaposed without being placed in chronological sequence.[114] Blessing is promised for those who do 'what is good'; a curse is threatened for the man who does not do 'what is good.' As in the blessing and curse passages in Deuteronomy, we find here a peculiar change in person. Another odd feature in this context is the mention of (wild) beasts, which according to the blessing will fear man, but according to the curse will rule over him. Test. Naph, shows that the 'eschatological' form of the blessing and curse, as a time of salvation and a time of disaster, did not completely replace the simple form, as an either/or.

The Introductory Formulas of the Eschatological Section

Something like the following may be cited as the basic formula introducing the eschatological section in the Testaments of the Twelve Patriarchs:[115] 'The patriarch states: "I know . . . from the writings of righteous Enoch . . . that in the last days you . . . will rebel against the Lord. . . ."' There follows section one of the

---

[111] See Test. Levi 16–18; Test. Zeb. 9:9; Test. Naph. 4:4.

[112] This is suggested especially by the evidence in Test. Asher 7, where we find two parallel introductory formulas:

7:2: ''Εγὼ γὰρ οἶδα. . .'

7:5: ''Εγὼ γὰρ ἔγνων.. . .'

[113] See the use of 'πάλιν' in Test Zeb. 9:9; Test. Naph. 4:4.

[114] Test. Naph. 8:4(5), 6.

[115] See, for example, Test. Naph. 4:1: 'Ταῦτα λέγω ὑμῖν, τέκνα μου, ὅτι ἔγνων ἐν τῇ (A + ἁγίᾳ) γραφῇ 'Ενὼχ ὅτι καίγε ὑμεῖς ἀποστήσεσθε ἀπὸ Κυρίου. . . '

Test. Dan 5:6: ''Ανέγνων γὰρ ἐν βίβλῳ 'Ενὼχ τοῦ δικαίου. . . .'

Test. Dan 5:4: ''Εγὼ οἶδα ὅτι ἐν ταῖς ἐσχάταις ἡμέραις ἀποστήσεσθε τοῦ Κυρίου. . . .'

Cf. Test. Levi 14:1; Test. Judah 18:1; Test. Iss. 6:1; Test. Zeb. 9:5; Test. Gad: 8:2; Test. Asher 7:2, 5; Test. Benj. 9:1.

M

schema just described, outlining the relationship to God and to his commandments.[116]

According to the Testaments of the Twelve Patriarchs, knowledge of the last days is not 'free' prophetic knowledge. It is scriptural interpretation. According to Deuteronomy, Moses 'prophesied' the fulfillment of the curse.[117] Taken in its context, the Deuteronomy passage refers to the fulfillment of the curse as recorded in the 'book of the law.' Our study has shown that in the Testaments of the Twelve Patriarchs, too, blessing and curse are used as means to depict history and eschatology. Here the Testaments stand in a tradition that can be traced back to Deuteronomy. The fictitious nature of the Testaments of the Twelve Patriarchs probably also explains the reference to the 'writings of Enoch.' We need not conclude that this refers directly to the Enoch literature.[118] Test. Zeb. 9:4 mentions the 'writing of my fathers'; Test. Asher 7:5 (β, A) speaks of the 'heavenly tablets.' One can say with some assurance that 'the writing' or 'writings' cited by the author contained blessing and curse in their original form or interpreted historically as salvation and disaster. Here scriptural interpretation becomes prophecy.[119]

De Jonge—and Aschermann as well—calls the eschatological sections of the Testaments 'S.E.R. (= Sin, Exile, Return)—passages.'[120] As we have shown, however, such a designation does not fully characterize the nature of this section. Exile is only one of the many possible consequences of the curse. By the same token, we are not dealing with return from exile but with the return of salvation, the fulfillment of the blessing. In the total structure the concluding section takes on a function that it did not have in the original Old Testament covenant formulary. In the Old Testament, the formulary begins with an historical retrospect. The 'antecedent history' lays the foundation for the relationship with God; the law is a consequence, not a precondition, of the covenant relationship. The present can be understood only from the perspective of the past. The very form of the Testaments of the Twelve Patriarchs shows that history in this since no longer matters—otherwise the 'example' of

---

[116] See above, p. 156.

[117] Cf. Deut. 31:29

[118] See de Jonge, *Testaments*, p 84.

[119] In Test. Simeon 5:6, the blessing is referred to explicitly as prophecy: 'ὁ πατὴρ ἡμῶν προεφήτευσεν ἐν ταῖς εὐλογίαις. . . .'

[120] *Testaments*, p. 83: '. . . which are composed according to the same pattern.'

the patriarchs could not replace the 'antecedent history.' In this fashion the ethical teaching of the Testaments is removed from the framework of temporal relativism, just as law without history becomes a timeless, unalterable constant. But history does not simply vanish from the Testaments of the Twelve Patriarchs, leaving behind nothing but a practical morality. If we read the Testaments with an eye to their situation of the present, we can see, despite the veiled language, that they look upon the present as the time of disaster. For the author, however, the present is oriented toward the future, the future in which he expects salvation. Only in terms of this hope does he once more (or still?) experience history. We can say schematically that in the Old Testament the present always constitutes the end-point of past history, while here it stands at the beginning of history to come. The present is understood from the perspective of the future. It is of course proper to ask at this point to what extent one may still speak legitimately of 'history.' This question, however, would require extensive interpretation of the content of the Testaments.

EXCURSUS

Following our examination of the Testaments of the Twelve Patriarchs, we shall here point out several New Testament texts that, in my opinion, exhibit in part the same formal structure we observed in the Testaments.[1]

Rev. 3:1–6[2] is one of the seven letters, all of which share an external framework:

(a) Introduction with name of the addressee:

τῷ ἀγγέλῳ τῆς . . . ἐκκλησίας γράψον.   (3:1)

(b) Formal designation of the sender:

τάδε λέγει ὁ. . . .   (3:1b)

(c) Statement of victory: ὁ νικῶν. . . .   (3:5)

(d) Conclusion: ὁ ἔχων οὖς ἀκουσάτω.   (3:6)

Apart from its epistolary stylization, the text follows the schema observed in the eschatological portions of the Testaments of the Twelve Patriarchs. The same headings may be used for the individual points. The only difference is that in Revelation 3 threat of judgment and exhortation to repentance have been interchanged.[3]

(1) Description of the relationship to God and his commandments; in this description the relationship between God and the church addressed is developed in positive or negative terms: 'You have the name of being alive, and you are dead. . . . I have not found your works perfect in the sight of my God' (Rev. 3:1b–2).
(2) Exhortation to repentance: 'Repent' (v. 3a).
(3) Threat of curse or judgment; 'If you will not awake, I will come like a thief . . .' (v. 3b).
(4) Promise of salvation: 'They shall walk with me in white garments . . .' (v. 4).

As the basis for repentance, v. 3a states: 'Remember then what you have received and heard; keep that.' The text itself does not make completely clear what this means. In the Testaments of the Twelve Patriarchs, we find at this point as the basis for repentance a statement that the Lord is gracious, merciful, of great goodness, etc.

In other passages of the New Testament repentance can be linked

---

[1] The following discussion of New Testament texts is the product of collaboration with Dr. H. Köster.

[2] On the analysis here, see K. Baltzer, H. Köster, and Merkel, 'Offbg. Jo. 3:1–6,' *Göttinger Predigtmeditationen*, 12, Heft 1 (1957), pp. 8–9.

[3] The letters to Ephesus, Pergamon, and Thyatira can probably be analysed according to the same schema.

to a Christological confession. Col. 1:9–23, for example, can be analysed as follows:

1:9–12   is an exhortation to lead a worthy life;
1:13–20 provides a Christological basis.
> Within this section, 1:15–20 is a quotation from a hymn to Christ interspersed with interpretive phrases.
1:21–23 calls to mind the repentance that has taken place.

The most striking difference between this passage and the Testaments of the Twelve Patriarchs is the fact that here 'repentance' no longer lies in the future but has already taken place. Here 'apostasy' is in the past; the future is parousia.[4] 'God's mercy,' which makes repentance possible, has become reality in Christ. It is interesting that Christology begins at this very point.

In a similar fashion, I Peter 2:21–24, 25 also combines a hymn to Christ with a recollection of repentance.[5]

Ethiopic Enoch

Using texts from the Ethiopic Book of Enoch,[6] we shall follow a further transformation of the eschatological section. The texts show in particular that an individual element of the form can be expanded enormously.

Enoch 91 begins the fifth section of the entire book, the so-called 'Parenetic Book, the Didactic, Hortatory, and Censorious Discourses of Enoch.'[7] Methuselah assembles 'all his brothers and relatives.' Enoch then addresses the 'children of righteousness.'[8] The term of address 'beloved'[9] is followed by a series of exhortations. In form and content they are equivalent to a statement of substance (91:4):

'Love uprightness,
and walk in it,
do not approach uprightness with a divided heart,
and do not associate with those who have a divided heart,
but walk in uprightness and righteousness, my sons. . . .'

---

[4] See M. Dibelius, *An die Kolosser, Epheser, an Philemon*, HNT, 12 (3rd ed., Tübingen, 1953), p. 22 ad loc.

[5] The word used here for 'repentance' is ἐπιστρέφειν instead of μετανοεῖν, as is also usually true in the Testaments of the Twelve Patriarchs.

[6] The translation follows A. Dillmann, *Das Buch Enoch* (Leipzig, 1853) and G. Beer in Kautzsch, *Apokryphen*, vol. 2, pp. 217ff.

[7] Beer, in Kautzsch, *Apokryphen*, p. 298.

[8] Beer, ibid., following manuscript G (Charles); Dillmann reads: 'He spoke . . . concerning righteousness.'

[9] Beer, following G and M; Dillmann reads: 'my dear ones.'

Here the requirement 'to love uprightness' has replaced the requirement 'to love God.' 'Uprightness' is almost personified, as the short promise appended to the statement of substance makes even clearer: '. . . and it [uprightness or righteousness] will lead you on the good way, and righteousness will be your companion.' The passage does not go into detail concerning the 'good way.' Instead, an eschatological section follows at once (91:5–17). As is frequently the case in the Testaments of the Twelve Patriarchs, it is introduced by 'I know. . . .' The structure of the text is here no longer completely clear. We find repetitions and overlappings.[10] Here, too, as in the Testaments, we read that wickedness and judgment take place 'a second time,'[11] but there is even less motivation than in the Testaments. From another realm of apocalyptic probably comes the conception that unrighteousness and apostasy will 'increase' until 'the holy Lord' comes to judgment upon earth (91:7). This idea is based on a definite chronological schema.

Enoch 94:1–5a is an additional statement of substance. It is introduced by: '*And now* I say to you, my sons, love righteousness and walk in it.'[12] The following eschatological section that begins in 94:5b ('For I know . . .') extends to chapter 105. This extensive section is itself composed of various shorter units, all of which, however, have the same character. The long 'woe' series are their most striking characteristic. In each individual saying the 'woe cry' is followed by an invective with a description of the 'sinners'' offence and a threat.[13] The threats are closely associated with the earlier curses, but now the curse is fulfilled in the 'eschaton.' In this case, the 'beatitudes' are considerably shorter than the series of 'woes.' We find merely a summary statement (96:8): 'At that time many happy days will come for the righteous, when you [the mighty] are judged' or (99:10): 'But in those days all will be blest who accept the words of wisdom(!) and know them, and observe the ways of the Most High . . . for they will be delivered.'

Enoch 94:5ff. provides an example of yet another way in which the blessing and curse element of the original formulary can be changed. Blessing and curse are now proclaimed as promise and threat, but their fulfillment is transferred to the eschaton.

---

[10] Enoch 91:12–17 is a portion of the so-called Twelve Weeks Apocalypse (see chapter 93). The content of the section, with its description of disaster and salvation, shows once more the connection with what were originally series of blessings and curses.
[11] Enoch 91:6.   [12] See also 91:18, 19 and 94:3.   [13] See, for example, 96:6.

IV

THE COVENANT FORMULARY IN LITURGY AND PREACHING (THE *SITZ IM LEBEN*)

The texts we have studied have exhibited the remarkable stability of the literary type and its elements. How are we to explain this stability? Only to a minor extent can we think in terms of simple literary dependence of one text upon another. The changes in the individual elements are too great for this to be the case. A form-critical study must therefore attempt to give particulars concerning the common *Sitz im Leben* of these texts. This *Sitz im Leben* should also be able to explain how the schema of the literary type could come to influence texts not directly associated with the literary type of the covenant formulary.

I think it very likely that the common *Sitz im Leben* we are after is the use of the form in Jewish and Christian worship. Use in worship could explain the stability of the literary type. The discussion that follows should be read as a preliminary attempt to support this hypothesis.

1. THE LITURGICAL USE OF THE FORMULARY

Study of Jewish worship is made more difficult by the almost complete lack of direct literary evidence for its beginnings. This fact is adequately explained by the ancient principle: 'Whoever puts prayers in writing sins as though he were to burn the Torah.'[1] No earlier complete Christian liturgy is known that the so-called Clementine Liturgy from the Apostolic Constitutions viii.[2]

Two texts, I think, are important in this connection:

(a) The liturgy in IQS i. 18–ii. 18

Here we must return once more to this text from the Manual of Discipline. As we have shown, it preserves almost in its entirety the

---

[1] See I. Elbogen, *Der jüdische Gottesdienst* (4th ed., Hildesheim, 1962), p. 7. See also I. Elbogen and E. Lohse, 'Synagogaler Gottesdienst,' in *Die Religion in Geschichte und Gegenwart* (3rd ed., Tübingen, 1958), Bd. 2, cols. 1756ff., esp. col. 1759.4.

[2] H. Thyen, *Der Stil der Jüdisch-Hellenistischen Homilie* (FRLANT, N.F. 47, Göttingen, 1955), pp. 28ff. See also the article 'Gottesdienst,' sections IV (Riesenfeldt) and V (Kretschmar), in *Die Religion in Geschichte und Gegenwart* (3rd ed., Tübingen, 1958).

formulary of a covenant renewal.[3] The structure of the liturgy can be outlined as follows:

Invocation and Praise of God:

When they enter into the covenant   i. 18–19[4]
the priests and Levites shall praise
the God of salvation and all the works of his truth.

Response of the Community:

And all who enter into the covenant   i. 19–20
shall say after them,
'Amen, Amen.'

Antecedent history

(Recounting of God's saving acts):

Then the priests shall recount the demonstrations   i. 21–22
of God's righteousness in his mighty acts
and proclaim all his merciful faithfulness
towards Israel.

Confession of sins:

And the Levites shall recount the wrongdoings   i. 22–23
of the Israelites and all their guilty transgressions
and their sins
under the dominion of Belial.

Response of the Community:

Those who enter into the covenant shall confess after them: i. 24–25
'We have done wrong, [we have sin]ned,
we have done evil,
we and [our fa]thers before us,
by walking [   ], and God is righteous,
who has carried out his judgment upon us and our fathers;
but his merciful faithfulness has [preserved] us
throughout all ages.'

Blessing:

Then the priests shall bless all the men of God's lot,   ii. 1
who walk perfectly in all his ways,
saying:
'May he bless you with all that is good and keep you
from all evil, and may he illuminate your heart with

---

[3] See above, p. 49.
[4] The translation follows Bardtke, *Handschriften*, p. 87; Molin, *Söhne*, pp. 19–20; Brownlee, *Manual*, pp. 8–9. For the Hebrew text, see below, pp. 189ff.

knowledge of life and be gracious to you with
knowledge of eternity, may he lift up his merciful
countenance upon you for eternal peace.'

Curse:

Then the Levites shall curse all the men of   ii. 4
the lot of Belial, answering and saying:
'Be accursed in all the impious works
of your guilt. May God make you a terror
by the hand of all avengers and command after
you by the hand of all who recompense actions.
Be accursed without mercy, because your
works are dark; be confounded in the
darkness of the eternal fire. May God not be
gracious to you when you call, and may he not grant
forgiveness of your sins. May he lift up the countenance of his
wrath for the vengeance you deserve, and may there be no
salvation for you in the mouth of those who
"cleave to the fathers".'

Response of the Community:

All who enter into the covenant shall say after   ii. 10
those who bless and after those who curse,
'Amen, Amen.'

The covenant renewal is characterized by a confession of sins
interpolated in the simple covenant formulary. This confession
contains as its primary element an acknowledgment that God is
'righteous,' i.e., that he has acted according to the terms of the
covenant. It is striking that the liturgy in the Manual of Discipline
does not precede the blessing and curse with a promise that the
covenant will be granted once more, since we would expect such a
promise at this point in the structure as a whole.[5]

The distinction between confession with elements of praise[6] and
recounting of God's saving acts[7] is well marked in the liturgical
directions. The recounting of 'demonstrations of God's righteousness' corresponds precisely to the nature and function of the 'antecedent history.' The texts we have studied have shown, however, that
this section can be extended 'backwards,' as it were, by the addition
of statements concerning the creation and hymnic predications
of God.[8]

[5] See above, pp. 49–50.
[6] 1QS i. 18: הכוהנים והלויים מברכים את אל ישועות
[7] 1QS i. 21: ... והכוהנים מספרים את עדקות אל
[8] See above, pp. 100–101.

This liturgy from the Manual of Discipline can be compared with a portion of the so-called Clementine Liturgy.

(b) The Clementine Liturgy[9]

In the 'Preface,' the 'Mass of the Faithful' contains an 'antecedent history' in the classic manner. It begins:[10] 'Truly meet and right it is to praise you above all, the God who truly is. . . .'[11] There follow hymnic predications of God.[12] The formula 'All things you have brought into being out of non-being through your only-begotton Son'[13] is here once more made to refer unambiguously to the creation and not, as in II Clem. 1:8, to the redemption of mankind. There follows in12:9 ff. a section praising God for his creation.[14] Once more an onomasticon serves as the guideline by which the individual phrases are brought together.[15] The creation of the world is followed by the creation of man. The rest of the traditional outline of *Heilsgeschichte*[16] extends to the conquest of Jericho. It concludes: 'For all this, glory be to you, almighty Lord.' The praise of the angels is recalled, whereupon 'all the people' respond with the Trisagion.[17] Following the structure of the Old Testament formulary, we could designate this the assent of the people, who agree that they have themselves experienced God's saving acts.

---

[9] The text will be found in H. Lietzmann, *Liturgische Texte VI: Die Klementinische Liturgie aus den constitutiones apostolicorum VIII* ('Kleine Texte für Vorlesungen und Übungen,' 61, Bonn, 1910). The translation follows R. Storf, *Griechische Liturgien* (Kempten, 1912).

[10] Is it fortuitous that the instructions for this action read: 'The elders shall take their positions at his right hand and at his left like pupils about a teacher'? Storf (*Griechische Liturgien*, p. 42) translates 'οἱ πρεσβύτεροι' here with 'priests'! See Lietzmann, *Liturgische Texte VI*, p. 12 ad loc.

[11] Const. Ap. 12:6: '"Ἄξιον ὡς ἀληθῶς καὶ δίκαιον πρὸ πάντων ἀνυμνεῖν σε τὸν ὄντως ὄντα θεὸν τὸν πρὸ τῶν γενητῶν ὄντα. . . .'
Cf. 1QS iii. 15: מאל הדעות כול הווה ונהייה ולפני היותם הכין
[12] Cf. 1QS i. 18–19.

[13] Lietzman, *Liturgische Texte VI*, 12:7, p. 13, line 8.

[14] Ibid., 12:8, end (p. 13, line 21): '. . . καὶ μετὰ ταῦτα πάντα ποιήσας δι' αὐτοῦ τὸν φαινόμενον τοῦτον κόσμον καὶ πάντα τὰ ἐν αὐτῷ.'

[15] In its pure form, it goes something like this: heaven, earth, firmament, night, day, light, darkness, sun, moon, water, air, fire, sea, land, abyss, salt water, rivers, streams, springs, plants, animals, serpents, birds, years, months, days, solstices, rain clouds, winds, all plants and herbs. Cf. G. von Rad, 'Hiob 38 und die altägyptische Weisheit,' in his *Gesammelte Studien*, p. 264.

[16] Cf. 1QS i. 21ff.

[17] 'Καὶ πᾶς ὁ λαὸς ἅμα εἰπάτω·
"Ἅγιος, ἅγιος, ἅγιος Κύριος Σαβαώθ,
πλήρης ὁ οὐρανὸς καὶ ἡ γῆ τῆς δόξης αὐτοῦ·
εὐλογητὸς εἰς τοὺς αἰῶνας. ἀμήν.'
Lietzmann, *Liturgische Texte VI*, 12:27, p. 17, lines 13ff. Cf. 1QS i. 19–20.

If we take the Old Testament formulary as our model and go on to inquire into the nature of the section that follows, we could first of all call it the statement that the covenant has been broken, as the following sentence suggests:[18]

'When, despite the law of nature, despite the admonition of the law, the reproaches of the prophets, the guidance of the angels, they transgressed the law of nature and the law of scripture, and forgot the flood, the destruction of Sodom, the plagues of the Egyptians, and the defeats suffered by the inhabitants of Palestine, and were on the point of all perishing at once. . . .'

It would be easy to alter the style of this section so as to transform it into a confession of sins.[19] It would then comprise two points: forgetting the acts of God and transgression of the law. As a consequence, the curse of complete destruction threatens, because 'wrath rests upon all.'[20] In this analysis we have tried to ignore the present context. When we take this into account, however, we see a completely different picture. The context makes it clear that the curse threatened for breaking the covenant has not in fact come to pass:

'You, his God and Father, he appeased and reconciled with the world and freed from the wrath that rested upon all, when he was born of a virgin. . . .'[21]

In other words, at this very point in the liturgy there begins a confession of God's saving act in Christ.[22] Christ's life, passion, death, and resurrection are recited in outline.

This section concludes with the words of institution of the Lord's Supper. It is appropriate to the structure of this section and not merely quotation of a formula when the statement is made (at the breaking of the bread!): 'This is the mystery of the new covenant . . . .'[23] Structurally, the liturgy can be termed a 'Christian covenant renewal.'

In their literary form, the two liturgies cited are separated by some five hundred years.[24] In both cases, however, we can think in

---

[18] Ibid., 12:30, p. 17, lines 22–27. See Storf, *Griechische Liturgien*, p. 48.

[19] See 1QS i. 22–23.

[20] Lietzmann, *Liturgische Texte VI*, 12:31; Storf, *Griechische Liturgien*, p. 49. 'ἡ ἐπικειμένη ὀργὴ τοὺς πάντας' ('τῆς ἐπικειμένης ὀργῆς. . . .').

[21] Lietzmann, *Liturgische Texte VI*, 12:31, pp. 17–18; Storf, *Griechische Liturgien*, pp. 48–49.

[22] See also above, pp. 42 and 50, on סְלִיחָה. Cf. J. J. Stamm, *Erlösen und Vergeben im AT* (Bern, 1940).

[23] 'Τοῦτο τὸ μυστήριον τῆς καινῆς διαθήκης. . . .' Lietzmann, *Liturgische Texte VI*, 12:36, p. 19, line 2.

[24] The Clementine Liturgy probably comes from the 'church province of Syria (Antiochene Patriarchate), towards the end of the fourth century' (see J. Beckmann, *Quellen zur Geschichte des christlichen Gottesdienstes* [Gütersloh, 1956], p. 18).

terms of forms preserved in liturgies over considerable periods of time. This means that literarily late texts can easily reflect earlier forms of worship.

2. The Use of the Formulary in Preaching

The use of the formulary in preaching is a further factor that can help explain the stability of the form. In the discussion that follows we shall devote special attention to the place within the total structure of worship occupied by preaching patterned on the formulary or at least influenced by it. Here again we cannot go beyond making preliminary observations.

(a) The so-called Second Epistle of Clement is the 'earliest Christian sermon that has been preserved.'[25] Our study has shown that the structure of this sermon is based on the formulary. As has been mentioned, the text of II Clement shows where this sermon came in the course of worship. It was 'intended by its author to be read publicly during worship immediately after the Scripture reading (19:1).'[26]

(b) One of the earliest connected descriptions of Christian worship is found in Justin's First Apology, chapter 67. There we read:[27]

> 'And on the day named after the sun there takes place an assembly at a specified place of all who dwell in the city and in the country. And the memoirs of the Apostles or the writings of the Prophets are read, as much as there is time for. When the reader has ended, the president delivers an address in which he admonishes the people and exhorts them to emulate these excellent teachings.[28] Then we all stand up together and pray; and, as we have already stated, after the prayers bread, wine, and water are brought forward, and the president pronounces prayers and thanksgivings, as much as he is able, and the people assent by saying "Amen." And now what has been blessed is distributed to all, and it is brought to those who are not present by deacons. . . .'

The place of the sermon in the total structure of worship is clear. Especially noteworthy is the association of reading from Scripture, preaching, and the meal. The description of the sermon delivered by the 'president' corresponds only in part to the content of II Clement, which still maintains the original connection between

---

[25] Bihlmeyer, *Apostolischen Väter*, p. xxix.
[26] Ibid.
[27] The translation follows P. Cordshagen in E. Hennecke, *Neutestamentliche Apokryphen*, p. 605.
[28] 'εἶτα παυσαμένου τοῦ ἀναγινώσκοντος ὁ προεστὼς διὰ λόγου τὴν νουθεσίαν καὶ πρόκλησιν τῆς τῶν καλῶν τούτων μιμήσεως ποιεῖται.'

God's saving acts and the response of human conduct (3:3–4):

'This, then, is our reward, when we confess through whom we have been saved. But how shall we confess him? By doing what he says and not disregarding his commandments.'[29]

On the other hand, the phrase 'τῆς τῶν καλῶν τούτων μιμήσεως' in Justin would be most appropriate in texts like the Testaments of the Twelve Patriarchs, where the ethical sections are concerned with μίμησις of the lives of the patriarchs.

(c) The so-called Mass of the Catechumens in the Clementine Liturgy begins:

'After the reading of the Law and the Prophets and our letters, of the Acts (of the Apostles) and the Gospels, the ordained leader greets the church[30] with the words, "The grace of our Lord Jesus Christ, the love of God the Father, and the fellowship of the Holy Spirit be with you all." And all shall answer, "Amen." After the greeting, let him speak words of exhortation to the people. When he has ended his discourse . . . let all stand up together. . . .'[31]

Next come prayers and the dismissal of the various classes within the church: catechumens, energumens, baptizands, and penitents. Finally the 'Mass of the Faithful' begins.

Here the Greek terms for the sermon are 'λόγοι παρακλήσεως'[32] and 'ὁ τῆς διδασκαλίας λόγος.'

(d) Finally, we shall make reference to a text from the Acts of John. The origin and date of this work are obscure.[33] Its unique theological features need not concern us here. The important fact, first of all, is that this text still shows the connection between preaching and the Eucharist in a very primitive form.

According to Hans Lietzmann,[34] 'the text depicts a Sunday worship service around 106–110. First comes a parenetic sermon that ends as a prayer of the Apostle, who is approaching death, for the community he will leave behind. Then John asks for bread to be brought and pronounces the following thanksgiving prayer (εὐχαρίστησεν οὕτως). . . .' Only bread is mentioned here in the Eucharist.

---

[29] The translation follows H. von Schubert in Hennecke, *Neutestamentliche Apokryphen*, p. 591.

[30] Lietzmann, *Liturgische Texte VI*, p. 3: 'ὁ χειροτονηθεὶς τὴν ἐκκλησίαν.'

[31] The translation follows Storf, *Griechische Liturgien*, p. 32.

[32] Cf. Acts 13:15.

[33] See Hennecke, 'Einleitung zu den Johannesakten,' in his *Neutestamentliche Apokryphen*, pp. 171ff.

[34] *Messe und Herrenmahl* (3rd ed., Berlin, 1955), pp. 240–41.

The nature of the 'parenetic sermon' can be defined more precisely. We shall first reproduce the text in outline.[35]

'On the following day, which was a Sunday, when all the brethren were assembled, he began to address them: "Brethren, fellow slaves, fellow heirs and partners in the kingdom of the Lord!

   I. *You know the Lord,*
      how many powers he has given you through me, how many wonders, how many healings, signs, what gifts, doctrines, administrations, comforts, services, knowledge, glory, grace, endowments, faith, communion, *sheer gifts, which, as you see with your own eyes, were given to you by him,* such as have neither been seen by these eyes nor heard by these ears.

  II. *Therefore*
      be steadfast in him,
      remember him in all you do, since you know why the Lord arranged the secret decision of his salvation, which he planned for mankind.
      He himself beseeches and exhorts you through me, since he would remain without injury, without suffering blasphemy, persecution, and torture, but he knows the blasphemy you do him,
      and knows dishonor, persecution, and torture
      when you transgress his commandments.
      Therefore
      our God shall not be grieved. . . .
      He shall be pleased with us,   because we live uprightly,
                        rejoice,   because we lead a pure life,
                        be glad,   because we lead an honorable life.
            May he be untroubled,   because we live soberly,
                      full of joy,   because we support each other,
                    may he smile,   because we show ourselves temperate,
                    and rejoice,   because we love him.
      This, brethren, I preach to you,
      and hasten now to the work that lies before me,
      which henceforth will be perfected by the Lord.
      For what else might I say to you?
      You have our God's surety.
      You have the pledges of his goods.
      You have his certain presence.

 III.
      (*a*) *Now if you* no longer sin,
            he will absolve you of what you did for lack of knowledge.
      (*b*) *But if you,*
            having known him and experienced his mercy,
            return once more to the same way of life,
            then your former sins *will be* reckoned against you,
            and you *will* have no portion in him,
                        find no pity before his face."
And when he had spoken thus to them, he prayed in this fashion: . . .
And he broke the bread and gave it to all of us. . . .'

---

[35] The translation follows Hennecke, *Neutestamentliche Apokryphen*, pp. 189–90. The structure and emphasis are the author's.

The original formulary can be discerned in this text in strikingly complete form. Part I, the 'antecedent history,' consists almost entirely of a series of catchwords. But it is easy to imagine that each of these catchwords was expanded in more detail. The nature of the 'signs' and 'wonders,' for example, would be told. At this very point we find once more the formula: 'as you see with your own eyes.'[36] The introduction ('You know the Lord') and such concepts as 'doctrines,' 'knowledge,' 'glory,' 'grace,' and 'faith' provide an equally close association with texts in which the 'antecedent history' can no longer actually be called 'history,' but has dogmatic and didactic character. The ethical section (II) begins, as is often the case, with general commandments: 'Therefore be steadfast in him, remember him. . . .' It also contains a series of commandments requiring a 'devout way of life.' The content of the 'blessings and curses' in part III is somewhat vague, but they are easily recognizable by their form, especially by the introductory 'If . . . then . . .' followed by the future tense.

It remains to add that in this sermon, according to the text, we are dealing with a 'testament.' This is clear from its very words: 'I hasten now to the work that lies before me, which henceforth will be perfected by the Lord. . . .' According to the context, this sentence refers to the miraculous death of John, which is reported immediately after the Eucharist.

We can therefore suggest that preaching structured after the form of the original covenant formulary was a part of worship. We have also been able to determine with some assurance its place in the course of worship. This preaching was intimately associated with the Eucharist.[37]

---

[36] Cf. Josh. 24:17: 'For it is Yahweh our God who . . . did those great signs in our sight. . . .' See Deut. 4:34; 6:22; 11:7; 29:2; 7:19.

[37] On this point, see also G. Bornkamm, *Das Ende des Gesetzes*, München, 1952, p. 123. Concerning the place of I Corinthians in public worship, Bornkamm writes: 'Paul concludes I Corinthians with a series of liturgical formulas: (1) an invitation to exchange the sacred kiss; (2) an anathema upon whoever does not love the Lord; (3) the 'maranatha';(4) a promise of the grace of the Lord Jesus, which is clearly distinguished from the concluding assurance of the Apostle's personal love (I Cor. 16:20–24). We may say even more precisely that the formulas just mentioned come from the liturgy of the Lord's Supper, which, according to the convincing hypothesis of R. Seeberg, H. Lietzmann, and others, took place in the common assembly after the public reading of the letter from the Apostle.'

C

SUMMARY

Our study has shown that the 'covenant formulary' worked out on the basis of Old Testament texts can also be found in Jewish and Christian texts. Our point of departure for this demonstration was 1QS iii–iv.26. In a series of texts the internal structure was not immediately evident, so that in some cases scholars had even denied that there was a clear arrangement of ideas. In these cases application of the form-critical method revealed a rational structure. 'Smallest units' originally belonging to various literary types can be arranged in larger units with an over-all structure by comparison with the formulary.

The degree to which the various texts resemble the hypothesized literary type of the covenant formulary can vary. In some texts, the literary type can be traced down to the individual details of formulation; in others, the form has undergone major changes, so that only a basic schema is preserved. This basic schema can probably explain the sequence that has been observed in many texts: dogmatic section—ethical section—eschatological section.[1]

In our study, we began by letting questions of content take second place to formal considerations. It turned out that texts differing markedly in content are related through possession of an identical structure.

In contrast to the situation in the Old Testament, we can observe a further differentiation of the literary type of the covenant formulary. Our study reveals four different ways in which the formulary can be used:

(1) in the liturgy;
(2) in preaching;
(3) as a community rule;
(4) as a purely literary form.

In the Old Testament, these possibilities remain almost completely

---

[1] The concluding position of the eschatological section is striking, especially in the Christian texts. This section often bears the major emphasis, and would thus be expected to come first, or at least after the dogmatic section. Now, however, it often follows ethical instructions that are not of great importance and go into considerable detail. The sequence, however, can be explained by the exigencies of the form. The eschatological section developed formally from what had originally been the 'blessings and curses' section.

undifferentiated, and are not yet separated as to function. Deutero-nomy, for example, exhibits obvious similarities to the covenant formulary. In its present ltierary form, it is stylized as the testament of Moses. In addition to the extensive body of legal material, it contains elements that can be termed liturgical and parenetic.

Among the texts studied, 1QS i. 18–ii. 10(18) and the Clementine Liturgy provide examples of the use of the formulary in the *liturgy*. II Clement is best termed an example of *preaching*; the corpus of the Manual of Discipline and the Didache are examples of *community rules*. The form has become *literature* above all in Jubilees and the Testaments of the Twelve Patriarchs.

Our study has also shown that even in these texts outside the Old Testament the boundaries between the four possible uses can be fluid. The Damascus Document contains a 'community rule.' Its first section, however, is stylized in the form of direct personal address. The Letter of Barnabas is an epistle, predominantly literary. It is nevertheless stylistically similar to a sermon.

By illustrating the use of the form in the liturgy and in preaching, we have attempted to discover more concerning the *Sitz im Leben* of the literary type. Its use in worship, preaching, and liturgy can probably account for the remarkable stability of the form.

At this point, however, more study is needed. An attempt should be made to discover why no formal difference is found whether we are dealing—as in II Clement—with a sermon in the course of Christian worship or—as in the Acts of John—with the special case of the preaching of a gnosticizing group. A text like the Manual of Discipline belongs in the realm of Palestinian Judaism; the Testa-ments of the Twelve Patriarchs reveal unmistakable Hellenistic influences. Besides the literary and form-critical questions, one should also inquire into the historical relationships that lie behind the similarities of the tradition.

The structure of the covenant formulary has been shown to be present in these texts with more or less certainty. This can help us interpret these texts. It is more difficult to provide a strict demon-stration that the form was still consciously being used in what, from the point of view of the Old Testament, were late stages of develop-ment. Formulas no longer understood can easily be preserved for long period of time. We must still ask whether the literary type is still alive after the Old Testament or has already atrophied. We must certainly always think in terms of more or less conscious borrowing.

N

In my opinion, however, there are reasons for thinking that the form was still to be consciously employed later.

In the first place, it should be stated once more that direct literary dependence among the texts studied is scarcely conceivable. It cannot even obtain for individual elements of the form. The observed similarities are similarities of literary type.

In addition, our study devoted special attention to the question of deriving terms for the individual elements of the form from the texts themselves. For this purpose introductory and concluding formulas were cited, together with liturgical directions and instructions for the officials to whom was probably entrusted special responsibility for the maintenance of the tradition.

Some of the texts showed that even the original relationship of the individual elements to each other was still understood. The commandments, for example, even in late texts follow expressly from the relationship with God established by the 'antecedent history.'

A final argument for the survival of the literary type beyond the Old Testament is the observation that it can continue to undergo transformations that make sense. This point has been made several times in the course of examining individual texts. Here we shall summarize once more the most important transformations of the individual elements of the literary type.

The 'antecedent history' was originally a recounting of the 'demonstrations of God's righteousness' toward Israel down to the present. At first, מֵעוֹלָם is understood historically. Even in the Old Testament, however, we find a tendency to incorporate the creation into the 'antecedent history.' In the late texts history tends more and more to recede into the background, while statements concerning the creation increase in scope and importance. Salvation now becomes known through God's creation and preservation of the world. Going beyond the Old Testament, we next find statements concerning the 'nature of God.' The 'antecedent history' develops into a 'dogmatic section.' At the same time certain speculative influence become noticeable. The reduced importance attached to confession of God's acts in history cannot simply be dismissed as a 'mistake.' It is a heavy burden for men no longer to perceive such action of God in history. At this point the Christian message begins. It can once more speak of an 'antecedent history' in the strict sense, since it confesses God's act in Christ.

The Testaments of the Twelve Patriarchs represent a completely

SYNOPSIS

Old Testament Covenant Formulary	Jewish and Christian Texts	Manual of Discipline	Damascus Document	Letter of Barnabas	Didache	II Clement	Jubilees
Antecedent History	I. Dogmatic Section	iii. 15–iv. 1	1–6:11	(2:4–4)[1] 5–17	—	1–2	21:2–4
Statement of Substance	II. Ethical Section	iv. 2–6, 9–11	6:11–7:4	18–20	II. (a) Statement of Substance 1:2	II. (a) 3–4:2	II. (a) 21:5
Individual Stipulations					(b) Individual Stipulations 2:1–5:2	(b) 4:3–6:6	(b) 21:6–20 (Corpus)
Blessings	III. (a) Blessings	iv. 6b–8	7:4–6	21:1a	6:2a		21:24
Curses	(b) Curses	iv. 12–14	B 19:5–6[1]	21:1b	(6:2b?)[1]	6:7–7:6	21:22
	(c) Eschatological Section	iv. 15–26	B 20:25ff.[1]	21:3	16		
	Corpus of Legal Stipulations	v–ix(?)[1]	9:1–16:20		6:3–15		21:6–20

[1] See above, ad loc.

different direction in which the 'antecedent history' element can develop. Here all true contact with history is lacking. 'Antecedent history,' as we have seen, becomes a 'model,' and is thereby moralized.

In the ethical section of the formulary, commandments like those found in the Decalogue are replaced by catalogues of virtues and vices. The basic commandment, 'to walk according to God's ways,' develops, under various influences, into a 'doctrine of the two ways.'

The corpus of individual commandments can be expanded into a 'community rule.' The Jewish and Christian texts differ least from each other in their ethical sections.

The original element of 'blessings and curses' undergoes the most far-reaching transformations. These begin in the Old Testament, but are developed further. Blessings and curses were originally two equally open possibilities. In the Old Testament, they were first of all historicized, so that the present became the fulfillment of the blessing, while the curse was threatened in case the covenant was broken. Later this relationship was reversed. The present was perceived as the time of the curse, while salvation was expected in the future. Between the time of disaster and the time of salvation comes 'repentance.' This structure is retained in the texts outside the Old Testament. These texts differ according to where they locate their own present: in the time of disaster or at the beginning of the time of salvation. 'Repentance' can be in the past or lie in the future. Even in the Jewish texts we may find an eschatological interpretation of the time of salvation. Especially in this part of the formulary apocalyptic speculation begins.

According to the Christian texts, the possibility of 'repentance' depends on God's having acted in Christ, 'mercifully, graciously, and with great goodness.'

To put the matter in a word, we may say that in their formal structures the old and the new covenant do not differ. The new element in the new covenant is its new historical foundation.

SUPPLEMENT TO PART ONE

The Hittite treaties are cited according to the following sigla:

From Weidner, *Politische Dokumente*:

W 1 = Treaty between Šuppiluliumaš, king of Ḫatti, and Mattiwaza, king of Mitanni. Pp. 2ff.

W 2 = Treaty between Mattiwaza, king of Mitanni, and Šuppiluliumaš, king of Ḫatti. Pp. 36ff.

W 3 = Treaty between Šuppiluliumaš, king of Ḫatti, and Tetti, king of Nuḫašši. Pp. 58ff.

W 4 = Treaty between Šuppiluliumaš, king of Ḫatti, and Aziru, king of Amurru. Pp. 70ff.

W 5 = Treaty between Muršiliš II, king of Ḫatti, and Duppi-Tešup, king of Amurru. Pp. 76ff.

W 6 = Treaty between Muršiliš II (Muwatalliš), king of Ḫatti, and Rimi-šar-ma, king of Ḫalap (Aleppo). Pp. 80ff.

W 7 = Treaty between Muwatalliš, king of Ḫatti, and Šunaššura, king of Kizwatna. Pp. 88ff.

W 8 = Treaty between Ḫattušiliš III, king of atti, Ḫand Ramses II, king of Egypt. Pp. 112ff.

W 9 = Treaty between Ḫattušiliš III, king of Ḫatti, and Bentešina, king of Amurru. Pp. 124ff

W 10 = Treaty between a king of Ḫatti and Lab'u and the citizens of Tunip. Pp. 136 ff.

From Friedrich, *Staatsverträge*:

F 1 = Treaty between Muršiliš II and Duppi-Tešup of Amurru. Teil 1, pp. 4ff.

F 2 = Treaty between Muršiliš II and Targašnalliš of Ḫapalla. Teil 1, pp. 52ff.

F 3 = Treaty between Muršiliš II and Kupanta-ᵈKAL of Mirā and Kuwaliya. Teil 1, pp. 106ff.

F 4 = Fragments of the treaty between Muršiliš II and Manapa-Dattaš of the land of the river Šeḫa. Teil 2, pp. 4ff.

F 5 = Treaty between Muwattališ and Alakšanduš of Wiluša. Teil 2, pp. 50ff.

F 6 = Treaty between Šuppiluliumaš and Ḫukkanāš and the citizens of Ḫayaša. Teil 2, pp. 106ff.

In this study the siglum of the treaty is followed, wherever necessary, by the § number of the editor. Next comes, in Roman numerals, thy column (ro. = recto; vo. = verso), followed, in Arabic numerals, be the line(s). Square brackets [ ] designate a gap in the text, parentheses ( ) an addition made by the editor.

The treaty between Muršiliš II and Duppi-Tešup of Amurru, from Friedrich, *Staatsverträge*, Teil 1, pp. 5ff.:

A. § 1 1 [Thus] (says) the sun Muršiliš, the great king, the king of the l[and of Ḫa]t[ti, belove]d of the weather god, the son of Šuppil[uliumaš, the great king, the king of the land of Ḫatti, the hero].

§ 2 2 Aziraš was your grandfather, Duppi-Tešup. [He re]be[lled] against my father,

3 [and?] my father made him subject to him once more. When the kings of Nuḫašši and the king of the land of Kinza rebelled against [my father],

4 your grandfather Aziraš did not rebel against my father:

5 as he was a friend, he remained a friend. When my father did battle against his enemies,

6 your grandfather Aziraš likewise did battle against the enemies of my father. Aziraš protected the power(?) [of my father?],

B. § 1 1 [Thus (speaks) the] sun Murš[iliš, the great king, the king of the land of Ḫatti, the hero, beloved of the weather god,]

2 [the son of Šup]piluliu[maš, the great king, the king of the land of Ḫatti, the hero].

§ 2 3 Aziraš [was] your [grandfather, Duppi-Tešup . . . he became subject to my father. But when]

4 the kings of the land of Nuḫašši [and the king of the land of Kinza] came (and) [rebelled against my father],

5 Aziraš did not re[bel. . . When my father did battle against his enemies,]

6 Aziraš also [did battle against] them. [Aziraš] protected [my(?) father himself(?)],

A.   7 he did not provoke my father to anger; and my father protected Az[ir]aš together with his land,

8 he sought [n]o kind of violence against Aziraš together with his land.

9 300 (half shekels) of pure first-class gold, which my father had assessed against your grand[father] as tribute,

10 he paid to him every year. He never refused (it), he never

11 provoked him to anger.

§ 3 12 When my father had gone to his reward, I took my seat up[on the throne] of my father.

13 As your grandfather Aziraš [had been] inclined toward my father, so was he inclined to[ward me].

§ 4 [When] the kings of Nuḫašši

14 and the king of Kinza [rebelled] a second time ag[ainst m]e, your grandfather Aziraš

7 my(?) father [. . . my father protected Aziraš together with his land]

8 and [undertook no] evil against him [. . . not at]

9 all did he provoke [him to anger . . . 300 (half shekels) of pure gold, the tribute that my father]

10 had imposed on him, which [he gave] to him [regularly . . .

§ 3 But when]

11 my father became a god, [I took my seat upon the throne of my father.]

12 But [as] Aziraš [had been towards my father, so was he towards me.]

§ 4 13 [When the kings of Nuḫašši and the king of Kinza,] however, came again (and) [rebelled against *me*],

14 Aziraš [and DU-Tešup did] to them . . . ,

A. 15 and your father DU-Tešup together with the kings of [Nuḫašši . . .] . . . , they protected the power of my father,

16 and they likewise protected my power [. . . When] Az[iraš] (was) an old man,

17 he could no longer take the field against the enemy. Just as he had fought against the enemy [previously(?) with foot-soldiers (and) chariotee]rs,

18 so likewise DU-Tešup fought wi[th foot-soldiers (and) charioteers of the land of A]murru against the enemy.

19 The [sun . . .] Aziraš. . . .

[GAP]

D. § 7 11 [Wh]en, however, your father had died, ac[cording to the word of your father] I did not

12 repudiate you. Because your father

13 had often named [yo]ur [na]me(?) before the . . . ,

14 therefore I concerned myself about you. You, however,

15 were afflicted with suffering and disease.

16 [And] although you were sick, I the sun nevertheless

17 appointed you [to] the very position of your father, and to you

18 I made (your) [sist]er⟨s⟩(??), your brothers, and the land of Amurru take an oath.

§ 8 19 Now after I the sun, according to the word of your father, concerned myself about you

20 and appointed you to the position of your father,

21 behold, I made you take an oath to the king of the land of Ḫatti, the land of Ḫatti,

22 and to my sons (and) my grandsons.

23 Now keep the oaths of the king and protect the power of the king; I the sun will

24 protect you, Duppi-Tešup. And when you marry your wife

25 and beget an heir, then later(?) in the land of Amurru he himself will

26 be king. And just as I the sun protect you, so I will also protect your son.

27 But you, Duppi-Tešup, protect the king of the land of Ḫatti,

28 the land of Ḫatti, my sons (and) my grandsons throughout
the future.

29 And the tribute levied upon your grandfather and your
father—

30 300 half shekels of pure first-class gold, of full value,

31 together with (precious) stones they paid to the land of
Ḫatti—that

32 you shall pay also.
And do not set your eyes upon another;

33 your fathers payed tri[but]e

34 to the land of Egypt, but you [shall not pay tribute].

E   8 [. . .] wage war [. . .]

E   9 [. . .] and to(?) you [. . .]

Column ii   (Beginning broken)

§ 9   1 [. . .] . . . [. . .]

2 [. . . you take the field against th]at [enemy]

3 [If you with . . .] ca[mp]

4 [(and) charioteers do] no[t faithfully against the] enemy [in
question]

5 [do battle] and sp[eak] as follows:

6 '[*I* (am)] a man [of (my) oath]; and [may either they]

7 defeat [the enemy or] may the enemy [defeat] them';

8 [or] (if) you [dis]patch a [single] man against the one in
question

9 [and] caution(?) [him as fol]lows:

10 'See, the army (and) charioteers of the [land of Ḫat]ti

11 are coming; now be [on your guard]!'

12 then you will be breaking the oaths.

§ 10   13 Just as I [the s]un protect you, Duppi-T[ešup],

14 (so) you shall provide military aid for the sun and the land
of [Ḫatti]. Now if

15 in the land of Ḫatti any [evil] talk ap-

16 pears, so that [someone] is rebelling against the su[n], and
you

17 hear [it, then] help [with] your [footsoldiers] (and) your
charioteers

18 and place yourself at the disposal of the [king of the land
of Ḫat]ti as an auxiliary levy(?).

19 But if it is not possible for you to [he]lp,

20 then dispatch either [your] son [or] your brother to the king
of the land of Ḫatti

21 together with your footsoldiers (and) your [charioteers] as
auxiliaries.

22 But if you do not dispatch [your son] (or) your brother with
your soldiers (and) your charioteers

23 to the king of the land of [Ḫatt]i as auxiliaries,

24 [then] you will be transgressing the divine oaths.

§ 11 25 But if someone afflicts you, Duppi-Tešup, in a matter
26 or if someone rebels against you,
27 but you cry out to the king of the land of Ḫatti, then to you
28 the king of the land of Ḫatti will dispatch footsoldiers (and) charioteers as auxiliaries.

. . . .

29 then you will be transgressing the divine oaths.
§ 12 30 If the people of Ḫatti send out footsoldiers (and) charioteers for Duppi-Tešup
31 and to them, because they are going up into the cities,
32 Duppi-Tešup provides food (and)
33 drink regularly, and it undertakes against Duppi-Tešup
34 an evil matter—a campaign of plunder against his land or against his cities,
35 or (an attempt) to displace Duppi-Tešup in the land of Amurru
36 from the kingship—,
37 then it will be transgressing the oath.
§ 13 38 The prisoners of the land of Nuḫašši and the prisoners of the land of Kinza, which
39 my father carried off and which I carried off, if from me
40 any of these prisoners escapes and he comes to you
41 and you do not seize him
42 and do not return him to the king of the land of Ḫatti
43 and spea[k] instead to him as follows: '[Up,] go
44 where you (desire to) go; but I must not
45 know you,' then you will be transgressing the oaths.
§ 14 46 If in your presence, Duppi-Tešup, anyone pronounces(?) evil
47 words concerning the king or concerning the land of Ḫatti,
48 do not keep him secret from the king.
49 Or if to you the sun
Column iii
1 speaks any words in secret; 'These matters
2 or this matter carry out!' whatever of these matters
3 cannot be carried out, present it at once there
4 on the spot as a petition: 'This matter
5 I cannot do and cannot carry out';
6 and (then) ⟨do?⟩ it as the king shall determine(?).
7 But if a matter to be carried out you
8 do not carry out and you . . . the king
9 or a word that the king
10 [s]ays to you in secret you do not
11 keep, then you will be transgressing the oaths.
§ 15 12 If any land or a fugitive
13 sets out and seeks to go to the land of Ḫatti
14 and travels through your land,
15 set them unharmed on the (right) way,

16 show (them) the way to the land of Ḫatti and speak to them
17 friendly words; do not send them anywhere else to another.
18 But if you do not set them on the (right) way
19 and do not give them passage to the land of Ḫatti,
20 but turn their eyes aside to the mountains
21 or speak evil words in their presence,
22 then you will be transgressing the oaths.

§ 16 23 Or if the king of the land of Ḫatti is oppressing any land
with battle
24 but lets them (escape)
25 and they come into your land,
26 and if it pleases(?) you to take something (from them),
27 then request it from the king of Ḫatti; your h[and, however,]
28 you shall not put forth(?) (for it). If, however, on your own
29 you put forth(?) [your hand] (for it) or con[ceal] it [. . .]

§ 17 30 Furthermore: if a fugi[tive come into your land],
31 seize him [   ]
32 [I]f it [
33 [as a fugi]tive [
(End of the column broken off)

Column iv

§ 18 1 Kulitta, ZABABA of Ḫatti,
2 ZABABA of Ellaịa, ZABABA of Arziịa,

3 Iịarriš, Zampanaš,

§ 19 4 Ḫantidašuš of Ḫurma, Aparaš
5 of Šamuḫa, Kataḫḫaš of Ankuịa, [the 'queen']
6 of Gatapa, Ammammaš of Taḫurpa,
7 Ḫallaraš of Dunna, GAZBA
8 of Ḫupišna, Tapišuịa of Išḫ[upitt]a,
9 BELTI of Lānda, Kunniiaịan[niš]
10 of Lānda, NIN-PISAN-PISAN of Ki[nza],
11 [Mount] Lablana, Mount Šariịana,
12 [Mount P]išaiša, the gods of the Lulaḫḫi, the gods of the
Ḫabiri,
13 [EREŠKI]GAL, the male gods (and) female gods of Ḫatti,
14 [the male gods] (and) female gods of Amurru, the ancient
gods
15 [all togethe]r, Naraš, Napšaraš,
16 [Mink]i, Tuḫuši, Ammunki, Ammizzadu,
17 [ALA]LU, ANU, ANTU, Apantu, ENLIL,
18 [NINLIL], the mountains, rivers, wells, the great sea, heaven
and earth,
19 [winds], clouds (shall be) to this treaty
20 [and] oath witnesses.

§ 20 21 [Thes]e words of the treaty and of the oath,
22 [which upon] this tablet are written, if Duppi-Tešup

23 [these words] of the treaty and of the oath
24 [does not keep], may these oaths destroy Duppi-Tešup
25 [together with his person], his wife, his son, his grandson, his house,
26 [his city, his land, and wit]h his possessions.
§ 21 27 [And if Duppi-Tešup keeps] these [words]
28 [of the treaty and of the oath, which] upon th[is] tablet
29 [are written, then] may
30 [these oaths together wi]th his person, his wife,
31 [his son, his grandson . . .], your(!) house,
32 [your city, your land, your . . . , your servants protect you].
C 11 [ ] ended.

The treaty between Šuppiluliumaš and Niqmadu of Ugarit, from Nougayrol, *Palais royal IV*, pp. 48ff., text no. 17.340.[1] Duplicate(?): 17.369A, bilingual seal of Šuppiluliumaš, type 1, center recto ('cushion'[1] tablet):

Thus (says) the sun Šuppiluliumaš, the great king, king of the land of Ḫatti, the hero: When Ituraddu, king of Mukiš, Addunirari, king of Nuḫašši, and Agittešub, king of Ni'i, rebelling against the sun, the great king their master, were at war (with him), [5] they assembled their soldiers, took some cities from Ugarit, oppressed Ugarit, the people of Niqmadu, king of Ugarit, took booty, and destroyed Ugarit.

Then Niqmadu, king of Ugarit, [10] betook himself to Šuppiluliumaš, the great king, to tell him: 'May the sun, the great king my master deliver me from the hands of the enemy. I am the servant of the s[un], the great king my master. Towards the enemy of my master I am an enemy, [and] towards the friend of my master (I am) a friend. (These) kings are oppressing me.'

[15] The great king heard these words of Niqmadu: Šuppiluliumaš the great king then sent some of the king's sons and his nobles together with soldiers [and chariot]s to Ugarit, and they chased the enemy soldiers [out] of Ugarit.

[20] [All] the booty that they had taken they offered [to] Niqmadu, [and Niqmad]u, k[ing of Ug]arit paid homage grandly to the sons of the king and to the nobles [. . .]: silver, gold, copper, [in his turn(?) he] offered to them. Then, he came [to] Alalaḫ [. . .] before the sun, the great king his master, [and he spoke in these t]erms to the sun, the great king his master: (following lines extensively damaged) . . . .

]Pugul'i [. . . Šet]a, Ya'aniya [up to Mount—] Deer-Field, together with Mount Ḫadamgi, [5'] [. . .]itkitiya, Paništa'i, Nakḫati, [Ḫal]pi, Mount Nana, Šalma, Gulbata, [Z]amirit, Mara'ili, Ḫimu[l]i.

Thus Šuppiluliumaš, the great king, the king of the land of Ḫatti, the hero, has assigned these [boundaries], cities, mountains, to Niqmadu, [10'] [king of] Ugarit, by seal, as well as his sons and his sons' sons, for ever.'

[1] Reproduced by kind permission of the Imprimerie Nationale.

'Niqmadu is thus enemy towards my enemy, and friend towards my friend.' To the sun, the great king his master, he is completely devoted, and he will maintain the agreement of friendship with the land of Ḫatti. [15'] Thus the sun, the great king, has known the loyalty of Niqmadu.

Whoever shall alter the words of this tablet of the agreement, the thousand gods shall know him.

Adad of heaven, the sun of heaven, Adad of Ḫatti, the sun of Arinna, Ḫebat of Kizzuwatni, [20'] Ištar of Alalaḫ, Ningal of Nubanni, Adad of Mount Ḫazi (in truth, they shall know him).

THE LITURGY FROM THE MANUAL
OF DISCIPLINE
(1QS i. 18–ii. 18)[1]

Invocation and Praise of God

1QS i. 18–19   ובעוברם בברית
יהיו הכוהנים והלויים מברכים את אל ישועות
ואת כל מעשי אמתו

Exod. 34:6–7   וַיִּקְרָא יְהֹוָה יְהֹוָה אֵל רַחוּם וְחַנּוּן

אֶרֶךְ אַפַּיִם וְרַב־חֶסֶד וֶאֱמֶת:
נֹצֵר חֶסֶד לָאֲלָפִים
נֹשֵׂא עָוֹן וָפֶשַׁע וְחַטָּאָה
וְנַקֵּה לֹא יְנַקֶּה פֹּקֵד
עֲוֹן אָבֹת עַל־בָּנִים
וְעַל־בְּנֵי בָנִים
עַל־שִׁלֵּשִׁים
וְעַל־רִבֵּעִים:

Neh. 9:5–6   וַיֹּאמְרוּ הַלְוִיִּם... קוּמוּ בָּרֲכוּ אֶת־יְהֹוָה אֱלֹהֵיכֶם
מִן־הָעוֹלָם עַד־הָעוֹלָם
וִיבָרְכוּ
שֵׁם כְּבוֹדֶךָ וּמְרוֹמַם עַל־כָּל־בְּרָכָה וּתְהִלָּה:
אַתָּה־הוּא יְהֹוָה לְבַדֶּךָ
אַתָּ עָשִׂיתָ אֶת־הַשָּׁמַיִם שְׁמֵי הַשָּׁמַיִם וְכָל־צְבָאָם
הָאָרֶץ וְכָל־אֲשֶׁר עָלֶיהָ
הַיַּמִּים וְכָל־אֲשֶׁר בָּהֶם
וְאַתָּה מְחַיֶּה אֶת־כֻּלָּם
וּצְבָא הַשָּׁמַיִם לְךָ מִשְׁתַּחֲוִים:

Ps. 106:48   בָּרוּךְ־יְהֹוָה אֱלֹהֵי יִשְׂרָאֵל מִן־הָעוֹלָם וְעַד הָעוֹלָם
(Cf. Ps. 135:5–7)

Response of the Community

1QS i. 19–20   וכול העוברים בברית אומרים אחריהם אמן אמן
Ps. 106:48   וְאָמַר כָּל־הָעָם   אָמֵן

[1] An attempt has been made to insert into the liturgy parallel texts representing the elements of a covenant renewal. For a discussion, see above, p. 49; for a translation of the liturgy, see pp. 168–69.

Antecedent History
(Recounting of God's saving acts)

והכוהנים מספרים את צדקות אל במעשי גבורתום	1QS i. 21–22
ומשמיעים כול חסדי רחמים על ישראל	(cf. Exod. 34:10; Ps. 105:12–44; Ps. 135:8–12)
אַתָּה־הוּא יְהוָה הָאֱלֹהִים	Neh. 9:7ff.
אֲשֶׁר בָּחַרְתָּ בְּאַבְרָם וְהוֹצֵאתוֹ מֵאוּר...	
וְכָרוֹת עִמּוֹ הַבְּרִית...	Antecedent
וּבְרַחֲמֶיךָ הָרַבִּים לֹא־עֲשִׂיתָם כָּלָה וְלֹא עֲזַבְתָּם	history through
כִּי אֵל־חַנּוּן וְרַחוּם אָתָּה:	v. 31
מִי יְמַלֵּל גְּבוּרוֹת יְהוָה יַשְׁמִיעַ כָּל־תְּהִלָּתוֹ:	Ps. 106:1–3

Confession of Sins

והלויים מספרים את עוונות בני ישראל	1QS i. 22–23
וכול פשעי אשמתם וחטאתם	
בממשלת בליעל [ ]	
...כִּי עַם־קְשֵׁה־עֹרֶף הוּא	Exod. 34:9
...כִּי עֲוֹנֹתֵינוּ רָבוּ לְמַעְלָה רֹאשׁ	Ezra 9:6–7
וְאַשְׁמָתֵנוּ גָדְלָה עַד לַשָּׁמָיִם:	
מִימֵי אֲבֹתֵינוּ אֲנַחְנוּ בְּאַשְׁמָה גְדֹלָה	
עַד הַיּוֹם הַזֶּה	
...וְ ( ) מְלָכֵינוּ שָׂרֵינוּ כֹּהֲנֵינוּ וַאֲבֹתֵינוּ	Neh. 9:34ff.
לֹא עָשׂוּ תּוֹרָתֶךָ....	(cf. Dan. 9:4–19; Ps. 106:4–46)

(In Exod. 34:9*b*; Neh. 9:32; Dan. 9:17–19; Ps. 106:47, 4 there follows a prayer for God's mercy.)

Response of the Community

העוברים בברית מודים אחריהם לאמור	1QS i. 24–25
נעווינו [ ]נו הרשענו	
אנו [אב]ותינו מלפנינו בלכתנו....	
וַיַּעַן שְׁכַנְיָה...וַיֹּאמֶר לְעֶזְרָא	Ezra 10:2
אֲנַחְנוּ מָעַלְנוּ בֵאלֹהֵינוּ....	

Blessing

1QS ii. 1   והכוהנים מברכים את כול אנשי גורל אל
ההולכים תמים בכול דרכיו

ואומרים....

Curse

1QS ii. 4   והלויים מקללים את כול אנשי גורל בליעל
וענו ואמרו....

Response of the Community

1QS ii. 10   וכול העוברים בברית אומרים אחר המברכים
והמקללים

אמן אמן

BIBLIOGRAPHY

Achelis, Hans. "Apostolische Kirchenordnung," in *Realenzyklopädie für Protestantische Theologie und Kirche*. 3. Aufl. Leipzig, 1896. Bd. 1, pp. 730–34.

Albright, William F. "The Hebrew Expression for 'Making a Covenant' in Pre-Israelite Documents," *Bulletin of the American Schools of Oriental Research*, 121 (1951), pp. 21–22.

Alt, Albrecht. *Kleine Schriften zur Geschichte des Volkes Israel*. 3 vols. München: Beck, 1953–59. Partially available in English as *Essays on Old Testament History and Religion*, trans. R. A. Wilson. Oxford: Blackwell, 1966.

Altaner, Berthold. *Patrology*, trans. H. C. Graef. New York: Herder, 1960.

Aschermann, Hartmut. *Die paränetischen Formen der Testamente der 12 Patriarchen und ihr Nachwirken in der frühchristlichen Mahnung. Eine formgeschichtliche Untersuchung*. Unpublished dissertation, Berlin, 1955.

Audet, Jean-Paul. *La Didachè, Instructions des Apôtres*. ("Études Bibliques") Paris: Gabalda, 1958.

Auer, F. "Das AT in der Sicht des Bundesgedankens". in *Lex tua veritas, Festschrift H. Junker*. Trier: Paulinus, 1961. Pp. 1–15.

Baltzer, Klaus. "Das Bundesformular, sein Ursprung und seine Verwendung im Alten Testament," *Theologische Literaturzeitung*, 83 (1958), cols. 585 ff.

Baltzer, Klaus. *Offenbarung Johannes 3:1–6* ("Göttinger Predigtmeditationen," 12 Jhg., Heft 1.) Göttingen: Vandenhoeck & Ruprecht, 1957.

Bardtke, Hans. *Die Handschriftenfunde am Toten Meer*. 2. Auflage. Berlin: De Gruyter, 1953.

Barthélemy, D., and J. T. Milik. *Qumran Cave I*. ("Discoveries in the Judaean Desert," 1.) Oxford: Oxford University Press, 1955.

Batten, Loring W. *A Critical and Exegetical Commentary on the Books of Ezra and Nehemiah*. ("International Critical Commentary," 11.) Edinburgh: Clark, 1913.

Bauer, Hans. "Ein aramäischer Staatsvertrag aus dem 8. Jahrhundert v. Chr. Die Inschrift der Stele von Sudschin," *Archiv für Orientforschung*, 8 (1932/33), pp. 1–16.

Bauer, Walter. *A Greek-English Lexicon of the New Testament*. Translated by W. F. Arndt and F. W. Gingrich. Chicago: University of Chicago Press, 1957.

—. *Der Wortgottesdienst der ältesten Christen*. ("Sammlung gemeinverständlicher Vorträge und Schriften aus dem Gebiet der Theologie und Religionsgeschichte," Nr. 148.) Tübingen: Mohr, 1930.

Baumgärtel, Friedrich. "Zur Liturgie in der 'Sektenrolle' vom Toten Meer," *Zeitschrift für die alttestamentliche Wissenschaft*, 65 (1953), pp. 263 ff.

Baumgartner, W. "Die literarischen Gattungen in der Weisheit des Jesus Sirach," *Zeitschrift für die alttestamentliche Wissenschaft*, 34 (1914), pp. 161–98.

o

Beckmann, Joachim. *Quellen zur Geschichte des christlichen Gottesdienstes.* Gütersloh: Bertelsmann, 1956.

Beer, Georg. *Exodus.* ("Handbuch zum AT," Reihe 1, Bd. 3.) Tübingen: Mohr, 1939.

Begrich, Joachim. "Berit: ein Beitrag zur Erfassung einer alttestamentlichen Denkform," *Zeitschrift für die alttestamentliche Wissenschaft,* N. F. Bd. 19 (1944), pp. 1–11.

Behm, S. "διαθήκη," in G. Kittel, editor, *Theological Dictionary of the New Testament.* Translated by G. W. Bromley. Grand Rapids: Eerdmans, 1964– . Vol. 2, pp. 127–37.

Bengtson, H. *Die Verträge der griechisch-römischen Welt von 700 bis 338 v. Chr.* ("Die Staatsverträge des Altertums," 2.) München: Beck, 1962.

Bentzen, Aage. *Daniel.* ("Handbuch zum AT," Reihe 1, Bd. 19.) 2nd ed. Tübingen: Mohr, 1952.

—. *Introduction to the Old Testament.* 2nd ed. Copenhagen: Gad, 1948–49.

—. *Die Josianische Reform und ihre Voraussetzungen.* Copenhagen: Gad, 1926.

Benzinger, I. *Die Bücher der Chronik.* ("Kurzer Hand-Commentar zum AT," Abt. 20.) Tübingen: Mohr, 1901.

—. *Die Bücher der Könige.* ("Kurzer Hand-Commentar zum AT," Abt. 9.) Freiburg: Mohr, 1899.

Bertholet, Alfred. *Deuteronomium.* ("Kurzer Hand-Commentar zum AT," Abt. 5.) Freiburg: Mohr, 1899.

—. *Die Bücher Esra und Nehemia.* ("Kurzer Hand-Commentar zum AT," Abt. 19.) Tübingen: Mohr, 1902.

Beyerlin, Walter. *Die Kulttraditionen Israels in der Verkündigung des Propheten Micha.* ("Forschungen zur Religion und Literatur des Alten und Neuen Testaments," 72.) Göttingen: Vandenhoeck & Ruprecht, 1959.

—. *Origins and History of the Oldest Sinaitic Traditions.* Translated by S. Rudman. Oxford: Blackwell, 1966.

Bickerman, Elias. "Couper une alliance," *Archives d'Histoire du Droit Oriental,* 5 (1950/51), pp. 133–56.

Bihlmeyer, Karl. *Die apostolischen Väter.* ("Sammlung ausgewählter kirchen- und dogmengeschichtlicher Quellenschriften," Reihe 2, Heft 1, Teil 1.) Neubearbeitung der Funkschen Ausgabe. 2nd ed. Tübingen: Mohr, 1956.

Blank, Sheldon H. "The Curse, the Blasphemy, the Spell and the Oath," *Hebrew Union College Annual,* 23:1 (1950/51), pp. 73–95.

Boecker, H. J. "Anklagereden und Verteidigungsreden im AT," *Evangelische Theologie,* 20 (1960), pp. 398–412.

—. *Redeformen des Israelitischen Rechtslebens.* Neukirchen: Verlag des Erziehungsvereins, 1964.

Bonsirven, J. *La Bible Apocryphe.* Paris: Fayard, 1953.

—. *Textes rabbiniques des deux premiers siècles chrétiens.* Roma: Pontificio Istituto Biblico, 1955.

Borger, Riekele. "Zu den Asarhaddon-Verträgen aus Nimrud," *Zeitschrift für Assyriologie,* 54 (1961), pp. 173–96.

—. "Die Inschriften Asarhaddons, König von Assyrien," in *Archiv für Orientforschung, Beiheft 9* (1956), pp. 107 ff.

—. "Mesopotamien in den Jahren 629–621 v. Chr.," *Wiener Zeitschrift für die Kunde des Morgenlandes*, 55 (1959), pp. 62–76.

—and W. G. Lambert. "Ein neuer Era-Text aus Ninive," *Orientalia*, 27 (1958), pp. 137–49.

Bornkamm, Günther. *Das Ende des Gesetzes*. ("Beiträge zur evangelischen Theologie," 16.) München: Kaiser, 1962.

Bousset, W. *Die jüdische Apokalyptik*. Berlin: Reuther, 1902.

—. "Ein aramäisches Fragment des Testamentum Levi," *Zeitschrift für die neutestamentliche Wissenschaft*, 1 (1900), pp. 344–46.

—. *Eine jüdische Gebetssammlung im siebenten Buch der apostolischen Konstitutionen*. ("Nachrichten der königlichen Gesellschaft der Wissenschaften zu Göttingen," Phil.-hist. Klasse, Heft 1, pp. 435–89.) Berlin: Weidmann, 1915.

—. "Die Testamente der 12 Patriarchen," *Zeitschrift für die neutestamentliche Wissenschaft*, 1 (1900), pp. 141–86, 187–209.

Braun, F. M. "Les Testaments des XII Patriarches et le problème de leur origine," *Revue Biblique*, 67 (1960), pp. 516–49.

Brockelmann, Carl. *Hebräische Syntax*. Neukirchen: Verlag des Erziehungsvereins, 1956.

Brownlee, William. *The Dead Sea Manual of Discipline*. ("Bulletin of the American Schools of Oriental Research, Supplementary Studies," 10–12.) New Haven: American Schools of Oriental Research, 1951.

Buber, Martin. *Two Types of Faith*. Translated by N. P. Goldhawk. London: Routledge, 1951.

—. *Königtum Gottes: Das Kommende*. 2nd ed. Berlin: Schocken, 1936.

Bultmann, Rudolf. *History and Eschatology*. ("Gifford Lectures.") Edinburgh: Edinburgh University Press, 1955.

—. *Der Stil der Paulinischen Predigt und die kynisch-stoische Diatribe*. ("Forschungen zur Religion und Literatur des Alten und Neuen Testaments.") Göttingen: Vandenhoeck & Ruprecht, 1910.

Burrows, Millar. *The Dead Sea Scrolls of St. Mark's Monastery*. Vol. 2. New Haven: American Schools of Oriental Research, 1951.

Caspari, W. *Die Samuelbücher*. ("Kommentar zum AT," Bd. 7.) Leipzig: Deichert, 1926.

Cazelles, Henri. "Le Deutéronome," in *La Sainte Bible de Jérusalem*, 2nd ed. Paris: Editions du Cerf, 1958.

—. *Études sur le code de l'alliance*. Paris: Letouzey & Ané, 1946.

—. "Jérémie et le Deutéronome," *Recherches de sciences réligieuses*, 39 (1951), pp. 5–36.

—. "Loi israelite," in *Dictionnaire de la Bible*, Supplément 5, pp. 497–530. Paris: Letouzey & Ané, 1957.

Charles, R. H. *The Greek Versions of the Testaments of the XII Patriarchs*. Oxford: Oxford University Press, 1908.

Conybeare, Fred C. "The Testaments of the Twelve Patriarchs," *Jewish Quarterly Review*, 5 (1893), pp. 375–97.

Coppens, Joseph. "La Nouvelle Alliance en Jer. 31:31–34," *Catholic Biblical Quarterly*, 25 (1963).

Corssen, P. "Zur lateinischen Didascalia apostolorum," *Zeitschrift für die neutestamentliche Wissenschaft*, 1 (1900), pp. 339–43.

Cowley, A. E. *The Hittites*. ("Schweich Lectures," 1918). London, Oxford University Press, 1920.

Cross, Frank Moore. *The Ancient Library of Qumran*. ("Haskell Lectures," 1956/57.) New York: Doubleday, 1958.

Cullmann, Oscar. *Urchristentum und Gottesdienst*. ("Abhandlungen zur Theologie des Alten und Neuen Testaments," Bd. 3.) Zürich: Zwingli, 1956.

Davies, William. *Torah in the Messianic Age and/or the Age to Come*. ("Journal of Biblical Literature, Monograph Series," 7.) Philadelphia: Society of Biblical Literature, 1952.

Deissler, Alfons. "Micha 6:1-8. Der Rechtsstreit Jahwes mit Israel um das rechte Bundesverhältnis," *Trierer theologische Zeitschrift*, 68 (1959), pp. 229–34.

Delitzsch, Friedrich. *Assyrisches Handwörterbuch*. Leipzig: Hinrichs, 1896.

Dentan, Robert, C., editor. *The Idea of History in the Ancient Near East*. ("American Oriental Series," 38.) New Haven: Yale University Press, 1955.

Dibelius, Martin. *An die Kolosser, Epheser, und Philemon*. ("Handbuch zum NT," Bd. 12.) Tübingen: Mohr, 1953.

—. *Botschaft und Geschichte*. Bd. 2. Tübingen: Mohr, 1956.

—. *Der Hirt des Hermas*. ("Handbuch zum NT," Ergänzungsband, Die Apostolischen Väter, 4.) Tübingen: Mohr, 1923.

—. *Die Pastoralbriefe*. ("Handbuch zum NT," Bd. 13.) Tübingen: Mohr, 1955.

Dietrich, E. K. *Die "Umkehr" im AT und im Judentum*. Tübingen: Mohr, 1936.

Dillmann, A. *Das Buch Henoch*. Leipzig: Vogel, 1853.

Driver, Godfrey R., and John C. Miles. *The Assyrian Laws*. Oxford: Clarendon, 1935.

—. *The Babylonian Laws*. 2 vols. Oxford: Clarendon, 1952–55.

Driver, Samuel R. *A Critical and Exegetical Commentary on Deuteronomy*. ("International Critical Commentary," 5.) 3rd ed. Edinburgh: Clark, 1902.

Duhm, Bernhard. *Das Buch Jeremia*. ("Kurzer Hand-Commentar zum Alten Testament," Abt. 11.) Tübingen: Mohr, 1901.

Dumermuth, F. "Zur deuteronomischen Kulttheologie und ihren Voraussetzungen," *Zeitschrift für die alttestamentliche Wissenschaft*, 70 (1958), pp. 59–98.

Dupont-Sommer, André. "Le Livre des Hymnes découverts près de la Mer Morte (1 QH)," *Semitica*, 7 (1957).

—. "Trois stèles araméennes provenantes de Sfiré: un traité de vassalité du VIIIe siècle avant J.-C.," *Revue d'Archéologie et d'Histoire*, 10 (1960), pp. 21–54.

Dupont-Sommer, André, and Jean Starcky. "Une inscription araméenne inédite de Sfiré," *Bulletin du Musée de Beyrouth*, 13 (1956), pp. 23–41.

—. "Une stèle araméenne inédite de Sfiré (Syrie) due VIIIᵉ siècle avant J.-C." *Comptes Rendus de l'Académie des Inscriptions et Belles-Lettres*, 1957, pp. 245–49.

—. "Un traité araméen du VIIIᵉ siècle avant J.-C.," *ibid.*, 1958, pp. 177–82. See also: International Congress of Orientalists. *Akten des 24. Internationalen Orientalisten-Kongresses*, pp. 238–40. Wiesbaden: Deutsche Morgenländische Gesellschaft, 1959.

Eichrodt, Walther. *Theology of the Old Testament*. Translated by J. A. Baker. 2 vols. Philadelphia: Westminster, 1961–67.

Eißfeldt, Otto. "Die älteste Erzählung vom Sinaibund," *Zeitschrift für die alttestamentliche Wissenschaft*, 73 (1961).

—. *Hexateuch-Synopse*. Leipzig: Hinrichs, 1922.

—. *Die Komposition der Samuelisbücher*. Leipzig: Hinrichs, 1931.

—. *Das Lied Moses, Dt. 32:1-43 und das Lehrgedicht Asaph Ps. 78 samt einer Analyse der Umgebung des Mose-Liedes*. ("Berichte der Sächsischen Akademie der Wissenschaften," Phil.-Hist. Klasse, 104/5.) Berlin: Akademie, 1958.

—. *The Old Testament: An Introduction*. Translated by P. R. Ackroyd. New York: Harper, 1965.

Elbogen, Ismar. *Der jüdische Gottesdienst in seiner geschichtlichen Entwicklung*. ("Schriften hrsg. von der Gesellschaft zur Förderung der Wissenschaft des Judentums.") 4th ed. Hildesheim: Olms, 1962.

—. "Synagogaler Gottesdienst," in *Die Religion in Geschichte und Gegenwart*, 3rd ed., Bd., 2, cols. 1756–61. Tübingen: Mohr, 1958.

Elliger, Karl. *Das Buch der zwölf Kleinen Propheten*, II. ("Das Alte Testament Deutsch," Teilbd. 25.) 2nd ed. Göttingen: Vandenhoeck & Ruprecht, 1951.

Engisch, Karl. *Einführung in das juristische Denken*. Stuttgart: Kohlhammer, 1956.

Eppel, Robert. *Le piétisme juif dans les Testaments des douze patriarches* ("Études d'histoire et de philosophie réligieuses publiées par la Faculté de Théologie Protestante de l'Université de Strasbourg," No. 22.) Strasbourg: Imprimerie Alsacienne, 1930.

Fascher, Erich. "Testament" (Altes und Neues), A. Prolegomena, in *Paulys Realenzyklopädie*, neue Bearbeitung von G. Wissowa, Reihe 2, Halbbd. 9, cols. 856 ff. Stuttgart: Metzler, 1934.

Fensham, F. C. "Clauses of Protection in Hittite Vassal-Treaties and the Old Testament," *Vetus Testamentum*, 13 (1963), pp. 133–43.

—. "Common Trends in Curses of the Near Eastern Treaties and kudurru-Inscriptions Compared with Maledictions of Amos and Isaiah," *Zeitschrift für die alttestamentliche Wissenschaft*, 75 (1963), pp. 155–75.

—. "Maledictions and Benedictions in Ancient Near Eastern Vassal-Treaties and the OT," *Zeitschrift für die alttestamentliche Wissenschaft*, 74 (1962), pp. 1–9.

—. "The Possibility of the Presence of Casuistic Legal Material at the

Making of the Covenant at Sinai," *Palestine Exploration Quarterly*, 93 (1961), pp. 143–46.

—. "The Treaty between Solomon and Hiram and the Alalakh Tablets," *Journal of Biblical Literature*, 79 (1960), pp. 59–60.

Finkelstein, Louis. "The Book of Jubilees and the Rabbinic Halaka," *Harvard Theological Review*, 16 (1923), pp. 39–61.

Fitzmyer, Joseph A. "The Aramaic Suzerainty Treaty from Sefire in the Museum of Beirut," *Catholic Biblical Quarterly*, 20 (1958), pp. 444–76.

Fohrer, Georg. "Der Vertrag zwischen König und Volk in Israel," *Zeitschrift für die alttestamentliche Wissenschaft*, 71 (1959), pp. 1–22.

Fonesca, L. G. da. "ΔΙΑΘΗΚΗ Foedus aut Testamentum?" *Biblica*, 8 (1927), pp. 31–50; 161–81; 291–319.

Forrer, F. O. "The Hittites in Palestine," *Palestine Exploration Quarterly*, 68 (1936); 69 (1937).

Freydank, H. "Eine hethitische Fassung des Vertrages zwischen dem Hethiterkönig Šuppiluliuma und Aziru von Amurru," *Mitteilungen des Instituts für Orientforschung*, 7 (1960), pp. 356–81.

Fried, S. A. *Die Gesetzesschrift des Königs Josia*. Leipzig, 1903.

Friedrich, Johann. *Die Staatsverträge des Hatti-Reiches in hethitischer Sprache*. ("Mitteilungen der Vorderasiatisch-Ägyptischen Gesellschaft," 31 and 34:1.) 2 vols. Leipzig, 1926–30.

Frost, Stanley B. *Old Testament Apocalyptic*. London: Epworth, 1952.

Fuchs, Ernst. *Hermeneutik*. Bad Cannstatt: Müllerschön, 1954.

Fuente, García de la. "Los contratos en el AT comparados con los de Egipto, Asiria y Babilonia," *Estudios Bíblicos*, 14 (1955), pp. 223–54.

Galling, Kurt. *Die Bücher der Chronik, Esra, Nehemia*. ("Das Alte Testament Deutsch," Bd. 12.) Göttingen: Vandenhoeck & Ruprecht, 1954.

—. *Die Erwählungstraditionen Israels*. ("Beihefte zur Zeitschrift für die alttestamentliche Wissenschaft," Bd. 48.) Gießen: Töpelmann, 1928.

Gelb, Ignace J. Review of D. J. Wiseman, "The Vassal Treaties of Esarhaddon," *Iraq*, 20 (1958), in *Bibliotheca Orientalis*, 19 (1962), pp. 159–62.

Gerstenberger, Erhard. *Wesen und Herkunft des sogenannten apodiktischen Rechts im AT*. Dissertation, Bonn, 1961.

Gese, Hartmut. "Der Davidsbund und die Zionserwählung," *Zeitschrift für Theologie und Kirche*, 61 (1964), pp. 10–26.

Gesenius, Wilhelm. *Hebrew Grammar*. Revised by E. Kautzsch, translated by A. E. Cowley. 2nd English ed. Oxford: Clarendon, 1910.

Gevirtz, Stanley. "West-Semitic Curses and the Problem of the Origins of Hebrew Law," *Vetus Testamentum*, 11 (1961), pp. 137–58.

Glueck, Nelson. *Das Wort hesed*. ("Beihefte zur Zeitschrift für die alttestamentliche Wissenschaft," 47.) Berlin: Töpelmann, 1927.

Gössman, P. F. *Das Era-Epos*. Würzburg: Paulinus, 1955.

Goetze, Albrecht. *Kleinasien*. ("Handbuch der Altertumswissenschaft," Abt. 3, Teil 1, Bd. 3:1.) 2nd ed. München: Beck, 1957.

—. Review of H. Otten, *Keilschrifttexte aus Boghazköi*, in *Journal of Cuneiform Studies*, 11 (1957), pp. 110–12.

Goodspeed, E. J., editor. *Die ältesten Apologeten.* Göttingen: Vandenhoeck & Ruprecht, 1914.

—. "The Didache, Barnabas and the Doctrina," *Anglican Theological Review,* 27 (1945), pp. 228–47.

Greßmann, Hugo. *Die Anfänge Israels.* ("Die Schriften des Alten Testaments in Auswahl," Abt. 1, Bd. 2.) 2nd ed. Göttingen: Vandenhoeck & Ruprecht, 1922.

Groß, Heinrich. *Der Sinai-Bund als Lebensform des auserwählten Volkes im AT.* ("Trierer Theologische Studien," 15.) Trier: Paulinus, 1962.

Güterbock, Hans G. *Authority and Law in the Hittite Kingdom.* ("Supplements to the Journal of the American Oriental Society," 17.) New Haven: American Oriental Society, 1954.

Gunkel, Hermann. *Einleitung in die Psalmen.* Zu Ende geführt von J. Begrich. ("Göttinger Handkommentar zum AT," Ergänzungsbd. to Abt. 2.) Göttingen: Vandenhoeck & Ruprecht, 1933; reissued 1966.

Gunneweg, Antonius H. J. "Sinaibund und Davidsbund," *Vetus Testamentum,* 10 (1960), pp. 335–41.

Gurney, Oliver R. "Hittite Prayers of Mursili II," *Annals of Archeology and Anthropology,* 27 (1940), pp. 3–163.

Habermann, A. M. *'Edah we-'Eduth. Three Scrolls from the Judaean Desert.* Jerusalem: Mahbaroth le-Sifruth, 1952.

Haelvoet, M. *La théophanie du Sinai. Analyse littéraire des recits d'Ex. XXIX—XXXIV.* ("Analecta Lovaniensia Biblica et Orientalia," 2:39. Louvain, 1953.

Hallo, William W. *Early Mesopotamian Royal Titles.* ("American Oriental Series," 43.) New Haven: American Oriental Society, 1957.

Harrelson, Walter. "Worship in Early Israel," *Biblical Research,* 3 (1958), pp. 1–14.

Harvey, Julien. "Le 'Rîb-Pattern', réquisitoire prophétique sur la rupture de l'alliance," *Biblica,* 43 (1962), pp. 172–96.

Heinemann, G. *Untersuchungen zum apodiktischen Recht.* Dissertation, Hamburg, 1958.

Hempel, Johannes. *Die althebräische Literatur und ihr hellenistisch-jüdisches Nachleben.* ("Handbuch der Literaturwissenschaft," Bd. 22.) Wildpark-Postdam: Athenaion, 1930.

—. "Die israelitischen Anschauungen von Segen und Fluch im Lichte altorientalischer Parallelen," *Zeitschrift des Deutschen Morgenländischen Gesellschaft,* 79 (1925). Reprinted in his *APOXYSMATA.* ("Beihefte zur Zeitschrift für die alttestamentliche Wissenschaft," 81.) Berlin: Töpelmann, 1961.

—. *Die Schichten des Deuteronomiums.* ("Beiträge zur Kultur- und Universalgeschichte," Heft 33.) Leipzig: Voigtländer, 1914.

Hennecke, Edgar. *Neutestamentliche Apokryphen.* 2nd ed. Tübingen: Mohr, 1924.

Herrmann, S. "Die Königsnovelle in Ägypten und in Israel," *Wissenschaftliche Zeitschrift der Karl Marx-Universität Leipzig.* 1954, pp. 33–44.

Hertzberg, H. W. *Die Bücher Josua, Richter, Ruth.* ("Das Alte Testament Deutsch," Bd. 9.) Göttingen: Vandenhoeck & Ruprecht, 1953.

Hesse, F. "Wurzelt die prophetische Gerichtsrede im israelitischen Kult?" *Zeitschrift für die alttestamentliche Wissenschaft,* 65 (1953), pp. 45–53.

Hillers, Delbert R. *Treaty Curses and the Old Testament Prophets.* ("Biblica et Orientalia," 16.) Roma: Pontificio Istituto Biblico, 1964.

Hinke, W. M. J. *A New Boundary Stone of Nebuchadrezzar I. from Nippur.* ("The Babylonian Expedition of the University of Pennsylvania," vol. 4.) Philadelphia: University of Pennsylvania Press, 1907.

Hoftijzer, J. *Die Verheissungen an die drei Erzväter.* Leiden: Brill, 1956.

Hölscher, Gustav. *Geschichtsschreibung in Israel.* ("Skrifter utg. av Kgl. Human. Vetenskapssamfundet," 50.) Lund: Gleerup, 1952.

—. "Komposition und Ursprung des Deuteronomiums," *Zeitschrift für die alttestamentliche Wissenschaft,* 40 (1922), pp. 161–255.

Holladay, William L. *The Root Šûbh in the OT with Particular Reference to its Usages in Covenant Contexts.* Leiden: Brill, 1958.

Holzinger, H. *Das Buch Exodus.* ("Kurzer Hand-Commentar zum AT," Abt. 2.) Tübingen: Mohr, 1900.

—. *Das Buch Josua.* ("Kurzer Hand-Commentar zum AT," Abt. 6.) Tübingen: Mohr, 1901.

Horst, Friedrich. *Das Privilegrecht Jahwes.* ("Forschungen zur Religion und Literatur des Alten und Neuen Testaments," 45.) Göttingen: Vandenhoeck & Ruprecht, 1930.

—. "Die Doxologien im Amosbuch," *Zeitschrift für die alttestamentliche Wissenschaft,* 47 (1929), pp. 45 ff.

—. "Segen und Fluch," in *Die Religion in Geschichte und Gegenwart,* 3rd ed., Bd. 5, cols. 1649–51. Tübingen: Mohr, 1961.

—. *Die 12 Kleinen Propheten (Nahum bis Maleachi).* ("Handbuch zum AT," Reihe 1, Bd. 14.) 2nd ed. Tübingen: Mohr, 1954.

Hospers, J. H. *De numeruswisseling in het boek Deuteronomium.* Utrecht, 1947.

Hrozny, B. *Hethitische Könige.* ("Boghazkoi-Studien," Heft 5.) Leipzig: Hinrichs, 1920.

Huffmon, Herbert B. "The Covenant Lawsuit in the Prophets," *Journal of Biblical Literature,* 78 (1959), pp. 285–95.

Hunkin, G. W. "The Testaments of the Twelve Patriarchs," *Journal of Theological Studies,* 16 (1915), pp. 80–97.

Hyatt, James P. "Torah in the Book of Jeremiah," *Journal of Biblical Literature,* 60 (1941), pp. 381–96.

Imschoot, P. van. "L'alliance dans l'Ancien Testament," *Nouvelle Revue Théologique,* 74 (1952), pp. 785–805.

—. *Théologie de l'Ancien Testament.* Vol. 1. Paris, 1954.

James, M. R. "Notes on Apocrypha," *Journal of Theological Studies,* 16 (1915), pp. 403–13.

Janssen, Enno. *Juda in der Exilszeit.* ("Forschungen zur Religion und Literatur des Alten und Neuen Testaments," N. F. 51.) Göttingen: Vandenhoeck & Ruprecht, 1956.

Jaubert, Annie. *La notion d'alliance dans le judaïsme aux abords de l'ère chrétienne.* ("Patristica sorbonensia," 6.) Paris: Editions du Seuil, 1963.

Jenni, Ernst. *Das Wort 'olam im AT.* Berlin: Töpelmann, 1953.

Jepsen, Alfred. "Berith. Ein Beitrag zur Theologie der Exilszeit," in *Verbannung und Heimkehr*; *Festschrift Rudolph.* Tübingen: Mohr, 1961. Pp. 161–79.

—. *Die Quellen des Königsbuches.* Halle: Niemeyer, 1953.

—. *Untersuchungen zum Bundesbuch.* ("Beiträge zur Wissenschaft vom Alten und Neuen Testament," Folge, 3, Heft 5.) Stuttgart: Kohlhammer, 1927.

Johnson, Norman B. *Prayer in the Apocrypha and Pseudepigrapha.* ("Journal of Biblical Literature, Monograph Series," vol. 2.) Philadelphia: Society of Biblical Literature, 1948.

Jonge, M. de. *The Testaments of the Twelve Patriarchs.* Assen: Van Gorcum, 1953.

Junker, Hubert. "Die Entstehungszeit des Ps. 78 und des Deuteronomiums," *Biblica*, 34 (1953), pp. 487–500.

Kaiser, Otto. "Wort des Propheten und Wort Gottes," in *Tradition und Situation; Festschrift Weiser.* Göttingen: Vandenhoeck & Ruprecht, 1963. Pp. 75–92.

Karge, Paul. *Die Geschichte des Bundesgedankens im Alten Testament.* ('Alttestamentliche Abhandlungen', 2) Münster: Aschendorff, 1910.

Kautzsch, E. *Die Apokryphen und Pseudepigraphen des Alten Testaments.* 2 vols. Tübingen: Mohr, 1900. Reprinted, Hildesheim: Olms, 1962.

—. *Die Heilige Schrift des Alten Testaments.* 4. Auflage, hrsg. von A. Bertholet. 2 vols. Tübingen: Mohr, 1922–23.

Kittel, Rudolf. *Die Bücher der Könige.* ("Handkommentar zum AT," Abt. 1, Bd. 5.) Göttingen: Vandenhoeck & Ruprecht, 1900.

Klein, G. *Der älteste christliche Katechismus und die jüdische Propaganda-Literatur.* Berlin: Reimer, 1909.

Kline, Meredith G. "Dynastic Covenant," *Westminster Theological Journal*, 23 (1960), pp. 1–15.

—. *The Treaty of the Great King: the Covenant Structure of Deuteronomy.* Leiden: Brill, 1963.

—. "The Two Tables of the Covenant," *Westminster Theological Journal*, 22 (1959), pp. 133–46.

Klostermann, August. *Der Pentateuch.* Leipzig: Deichert, 1893.

Koch, Klaus. *Sdq im Alten Testament.* Dissertation, Heidelberg, 1953.

Koehler, Ludwig. *Lexicon in Veteris Testamenti libros.* Leiden: Brill, 1953.

—. *Hebrew Man.* Translated by P. R. Ackroyd. Nashville: Abingdon, 1956.

—. *Theologie des Alten Testaments.* ("Neue theologische Grundrisse.") Tübingen: Mohr, 1935, reprinted 1947. 3rd, revised edition. Tübingen: Mohr, 1953.

König, Eduard. *Das Deuteronomium.* ("Kommentar zum AT," Bd. 3.) Leipzig: Deichert, 1927.

Köster, Helmut. "Segen und Fluch (im NT)," in *Die Religion in Geschichte und Gegenwart*, 3rd ed., Bd. 5, cols. 1651–52. Tübingen: Mohr, 1961.

—. *Synoptische Überlieferung bei den Apostolischen Vätern.* ("Texte und Untersuchungen zur Geschichte der altchristlichen Literatur," Bd. 65.) Berlin: Akademie, 1957.

Korošec, Viktor. "Les Hittites et leurs vassaux syriens à la lumière des nouveaux textes d'Ugarit (Le Palais Royal d'Ugarit IV)," *Revue Hittite et Asianique,* 18 (1960), pp. 65–79.

—. *Hethitische Staatsverträge, ein Beitrag zu ihrer juristischen Wertung.* ("Leipziger rechtswissenschaftliche Studien," Heft 60.) Leipzig: Weicher, 1931.

—. "Quelques remarques juridiques sur deux traités internationaux d'Alalak," in *Droits de l'antiquité et sociologie juridique; mélanges Lévy-Bruhl.* ("Publications de l'Institut de droit romain de l'Université de Paris," 17.) Paris: Sirey, 1959. Pp. 171–78.

—. "Staatsverträge in keilschriftlicher Überlieferung," in International Congress of Orientalists. *Akten des XXIV. Internationalen Orientalisten-Kongresses.* Wiesbaden: Deutsche Morgenländische Gesellschaft, 1959.

Kraetzschmar, R. *Die Bundesvorstellung im Alten Testament in ihrer geschichtlichen Entwicklung.* Marburg: Elwert, 1896.

Kraus, Hans Joachim. *Gottesdienst in Israel.* ("Beiträge zur evangelischen Theologie.") München: Kaiser, 1954. 2nd ed., 1962. English: *Worship in Israel.* Translated by G. Buswell. Richmond: John Knox, 1966.

—. *Die Königsherrschaft Gottes.* ("Beiträge zur historischen Theologie," Bd. 13.) Tübingen: Mohr, 1951.

—. *Die prophetische Verkündigung des Rechts in Israel.* ("Theologische Studien," 51.) Zollikon: EVZ, 1957.

Kruse, H. "Novi foederis hora natalis," *Verbum Domini,* 37 (1959), pp. 257–75; 321–35.

Kübler, B. "Testament" (juristisch), in *Pauly's Realenzyklopädie,* neu bearbeitet von G. Wissowa, Reihe 2, Halbbd. 9, col. 966. Stuttgart: Metzler, 1934.

Kuhn, Karl Georg. "Die Sektenschrift und die iranische Religion," *Zeitschrift für Theologie und Kirche,* 49 (1952), pp. 296–316.

—. "Die beiden Messias Aarons und Israels," *Theologische Literaturzeitung,* 79 (1954), cols. 760–61.

Kutsch, Ernst. *Das Herbstfest in Israel.* Dissertation, Mainz, 1955.

—. "תקרא," *Zeitschrift für die alttestamentliche Wissenschaft,* 65 (1953), pp. 247 ff.

Lefévre, A. "Malédiction et bénédiction," in *Dictionnaire de la Bible,* Supplément 5, pp. 746–51. Paris: Letouzey & Ane, 1957.

Lehmann, Manfred R. "Abraham's Purchase of Machpelah and Hittite Law," *Bulletin of the American Schools of Oriental Research,* 129 (1953), pp. 15–17.

Leipoldt, Johannes. *Der Gottesdienst der ältesten Kirche.* Leipzig: Dörffling, 1937.

Lempp, Walter. *Bund und Bundeserneuerung bei Jeremia.* Dissertation, Tübingen, 1955.

Leslau, Wolf. *Falasha Anthology.* ("Yale Judaica Series," vol. 6.) New Haven: Yale University Press, 1951.

Letteris, Mei Halevi. *Das hebräische Alte Testament nach der Masora.* Wien, 1885.

Lewy, Immanuel. "The Puzzle of Dt. XXVII. Blessings Announced but Curses Noted," *Vetus Testamentum,* 12 (1962), pp. 207–11.

L'Hour, J. "L'Alliance de Sichem," *Revue biblique,* 69 (1962), pp. 5–36, 161–84, 350–68.

Lietzmann, Hans. *Die Didache.* ("Kleine Texte für Vorlesungen und Übungen," Nr. 6.) 5th ed. Berlin: De Gruyter, 1948.

—. *Liturgische Texte VI: Die Klementinische Liturgie aus den constitutiones apostolorum VIII.* ("Kleine Texte für Vorlesungen und Übungen," Nr. 61.) Bonn: Marcus & Weber, 1910.

—. *Messe und Herrenmahl.* ("Arbeiten zur Kirchengeschichte," Bd. 8.) 3rd ed. Berlin: De Gruyter, 1955.

Lohfink, Norbert. "Der Bundesschluß im Lande Moab," *Biblische Zeitschrift,* N. F. 6 (1962), pp. 32–56.

—. "Darstellungskunst und Theologie in Dtn. 1:6—3:29," *Biblica,* 41 (1960), pp. 105–34.

—. "Die deuteronomistische Darstellung des Übergangs der Führung Israel von Mose auf Josue," *Scholastik,* 37 (1962), pp. 32–44.

—. *Das Hauptgebot. Eine Untersuchung literarischer Einleitungsfragen zu Dtn. 5—11.* ("Analecta biblica," 20.) Roma: Pontificio Istituto Biblico, 1963.

—. "Wie stellt sich das Problem Individuum–Gemeinschaft in Dt. 1:6—3:29?" *Scholastik,* 35 (1960), pp. 403–407.

McCarthy, Dennis J. *Treaty and Covenant.* ("Analecta biblica," 21.) Roma: Pontificio Istituto Biblico, 1963.

Malamat, A. "Doctrines of Causality in Hittite and Biblical Historiography, a Parallel," *Vetus Testamentum,* 5 (1955), pp. 1–12.

Manson, T. W. "Some Reflections on Apocalyptic," in *Aux sources de la tradition chrétienne. Mélanges offerts à M. Maurice Goguel.* ("Bibliothèque thèologique.") Neuchatel: Delachaux & Niestlé, 1950. Pp. 139–45.

Martin-Achard, Robert, "La nouvelle alliance selon Jérémie," *Revue de Théologie et de Philosophie,* 12 (1962), pp. 81–92.

Meißner, B. *Babylonien und Assyrien, I.* ("Kulturgeschichtliche Bibliothek," Reihe 1, Bd. 3–4.) 2 vols. Heidelberg: Winter, 1920–25.

Mendenhall, George E. *Law and Covenant in Israel and the Ancient Near East.* Pittsburgh: Biblical Colloquium, 1955. Reprinted from *Biblical Archaeologist,* 17 (1954), pp. 26–46, 49–76.

—. "Puppy and Lettuce in Northwest-Semitic Covenant Making," *Bulletin of the American Schools of Oriental Research,* 133 (1954), pp. 26–30.

Mercati, G. "Note on the Manuscripts of the Apostolic Constitutions Used in the Editio Princeps," *Journal of Theological Studies,* 15 (1914), pp. 453–54.

Meyer, Arnold. *Das Rätsel des Jacobusbriefes.* ("Beihefte zur Zeitschrift für die neutestamentliche Wissenschaft," 10.) Gießen: Töpelmann, 1930.

Meyer, G. *Zwei neue Kizzuwatna-Verträge.* ("Mitteilungen des Instituts für Orientforschung," Bd. 1.) Berlin: Akademie der Wissenschaften, 1953.

Michaelis, W. " ὁδός," in G. Kittel, editor, *Theological Dictionary of the New Testament*, translated by G. W. Bromiley, vol. 5, pp. 42 ff. Grand Rapids: Eerdmans, 1968.

Milik, J. T. "Le Testament de Lévi en araméen," *Revue biblique*, 62 (1955), pp. 398–406.

Milton, John P. *God's Covenant of Blessing.* Rock Island: Augustana, 1961.

Minchin, Basil. *Covenant and Sacrifice.* London: Longmans, 1958.

Minette de Tillesse, G. "Sections 'tu' et sections 'vous' dans le Deutéronome," *Vetus Testamentum*, 12 (1962), pp. 29–87.

Mørstad, E. *Wenn du der Stimme des Herrn, deines Gottes, gehorchen wirst. Die primären Einführungen zu Dtn. 28:3–6 und 16–19.* Oslo: Land og Kirke, 1960.

Molin, Georg. *Die Söhne des Lichts.* Wien: Herold, 1954.

Montgomery, James A. *Critical and Exegetical Commentary on the Book of Kings.* ("International Critical Commentary," 9.) Edinburgh: Clark, 1951.

Moran, William L. "The Ancient Near Eastern Background of the Love of God in Deuteronomy," *Catholic Biblical Quarterly*, 25 (1963), pp. 77–87.

—. "De foederis mosaicae traditione," *Verbum Domini*, 40 (1962), pp. 3–17.

—. "Moses und der Bundesschluß am Sinai," *Stimmen der Zeit*, 170 (1961/ 62), pp. 120–33.

Mowinckel, Sigmund. *Le Décalogue.* ("Études d'Histoire et de Philosophie Religieuses," Nr. 16.) Paris, 1927.

—. *Psalmenstudien II. Das Thronbesteigungsfest Jahwäs und der Ursprung der Eschatologie.* ("Vitenskapsselkapets Skrifter," Hist. Fil. Kl. Nr. 6.) Kristiana: Dybwad, 1922.

—. *Psalmenstudien V. Segen und Fluch in Israels Kult und Psalmendichtung.* ("Vitenskapsselkapets Skrifter," Hist. Fil. Kl. Nr. 3.) Kristiana: Dybwad, 1923.

Muilenburg, James. "The Form and Structure of the Covenant Formulations," *Vetus Testamentum*, 9 (1959), pp. 347–65.

Munck, Johannes. "Discours d'adieu dans le NT et dans la littérature biblique," in *Aux sources de la tradition chrétienne. Mélanges offerts à M. Maurice Goguel.* ("Bibliothèque théologique.") Neuchatel: Delachaux & Niestlé, 1950. Pp. 155–70.

Munn-Rankin, J. M. "Diplomacy in Western Asia in the Early Second Millennium," *Iraq*, 18 (1956), pp. 68–110.

Murray, John. *The Covenant of Grace; a Biblico-Theological Study.* London: Tyndale, 1956.

Muss-Arnolt, W. *A Concise Dictionary of the Assyrian Language.* 2 vols. Berlin: Reuther, 1905.

Newman, Murray L. *The People of the Covenant.* Nashville: Abingdon, 1962.

Noth, Martin. *Das Buch Josua.* ("Göttinger Handkommentar zum Alten Testament," Abt. 1, Vol. 3, Pt. 1.) 2nd ed. Gettingen: Vandenhoeck & Ruprecht, 1922.

—. "Old Testament Covenant-Making in the Light of a Text from Mari," *The Laws in the Pentateuch and other Studies*. Translated by D. R. Ap-Thomas. Edinburgh: Oliver and Boyd, 1966, and Philadelphia: Fortress, 1967. Pp. 108–17.

—. "The Laws in the Pentateuch: Their Assumption and Meaning," *The Laws in the Pentateuch and other Studies*. Pp. 1–107.

—. "Der historische Hintergrund der Inschriften von sefire," *Zeitschrift des Deutschen Palästinavereins*, 77 (1961), pp. 118–72.

—. *The History of Israel*. 2nd English ed. Translated by S. Godman and P. R. Ackroyd. London: Black, 1960.

—. *The Old Testament World*. Translated by V. I. Gruhn. Philadelphia: Fortress, 1966.

—. *Das System der zwölf Stämme Israels*. ("Beiträge zur Wissenschaft vom Alten und Neuen Testament," Folge 4, Heft 1.) Stuttgart: Kohlhammer, 1930.

—. *Überlieferungsgeschichte des Pentateuchs*. Stuttgart: Kohlhammer, 1948.

—. *Überlieferungsgeschichtliche Studien*. ("Schriften der Königsberger Gelehrten Gesellschaft," Geisteswiss. Kl., Jg. 18, Heft. 2.) 2nd ed. Tübingen: Mohr, 1957.

—. *Die Ursprünge des alten Israel im Lichte neuer Quellen*. ("Sitzungsberichte der Arbeitsgemeinschaft für Forschung des Landes Nordrhein-Westfalen," 94.) Köln: Westdeutscher Verlag, 1961.

—. *Das zweite Buch Mose*. ("Das Alte Testament Deutsch," 2.) Göttingen: Vandenhoeck & Ruprecht, 1959. English: *Exodus*. Translated by J. S. Bowden. Philadelphia: Westminster, 1962.

Nougayrol, Jean. *Le palais royal d'Ugarit. Textes accadiens et hourrites des archives est, ouest, et centrales*. ("Mission de Ras Shamra," 6.) Paris: Imprimerie Nationale, 1955.

—. *Le palais royal d'Ugarit IV. Textes accadiens des archives sud (archives internationales)*. ("Mission de Ras Shamra," 9.) Paris: Imprimerie Nationale, 1956.

Nowack, Wilhelm. *Die Bücher der Chronik und Esra, Nehemia und Esther*. ("Handkommentar zum AT," Abt. 1, Bd. 6.) Göttingen: Vandenhoeck & Ruprecht, 1902.

—. "Das Bundesbuch," in *Beiträge zur alttl. Wissenschaft Karl Budde überreicht*. ("Beihefte zur Zeitschrift für die alttestamentliche Wissenschaft," 34.) Gießen: Töpelmann, 1920.

—. "Deuteronomium und Regum," in *Vom alten Testament; Karl Marti zum 70. Geburtstage gewidmet*. ("Beihefte zur Zeitschrift für die alttestamentliche Wissenschaft," 41.) Gießen: Töpelmann, 1925. Pp. 221 ff.

Östborn, Gunnar. *Tora in the Old Testament*. Lund: Gleerup, 1945.

Oesterley, W. O. E. *The Jewish Background of the Christian Liturgy*. Oxford: Clarendon, 1925.

Oestreicher, Theodor. *Das deuteronomische Grundgesetz*. ("Beiträge zur Förderung christlicher Theologie," Bd. 27, Heft 4.) Gütersloh: Bertelsmann, 1923.

Ortmann, Heinz. *Der Alte und der Neue Bund bei Jeremia.* Dissertation, Berlin, 1940.

Otten, Heinrich. "Ein althethitischer Vertrag mit Kizzuwatna," *Journal of Cuneiform Studies,* 5 (1951), pp. 129–32.

—. "Die inschriftliche Funde; Bericht über die Ausgrabungen in Boğazköy im Jahre 1954," *Mitteilungen der Deutschen Orient-Gesellschaft,* 88 (1955), pp. 33–36.

Pedersen, Johannes. *Der Eid bei den Semiten in seinem Verhältnis zu verwandten Erscheinungen, sowie die Stellung des Eides in Islam.* ("Studien zur Geschichte und Kultur des islamischen Orients," Heft 3.) Straßburg, 1914.

—. *Israel, its Life and Culture.* 2nd ed. 2 vols. London: Oxford, 1963–64.

Pfeiffer, Robert H. *History of New Testament Times.* New York: Harper, 1949.

—. *Introduction to the Old Testament.* New York: Harper, 1941.

Philonenko, Marc. "Les interpolations chrétiennes des Testaments des Douze Patriarches et les Manuscrits de Qumrân", *Revue d'Histoire et de Philosophie Religieuses,* 38 (1958), pp. 309–43; 39 (1959), pp. 14–38.

Pirenne, J. "La politique d'expansion hittite, envisagée à travers les traités de vassalité et de protectorat," *Archiv Orientálni,* 18 (1950), pp. 373–82.

Preuschen, Erwin. "Die armenische Übersetzung der Testamente der zwölf Patriarchen," *Zeitschrift für die neutestamentliche Wissenschaft,* 1 (1900), pp. 106–40.

—. "Die lateinische Übersetzung der 'zwei Wege', " *ibid.,* p. 307.

Pritchard, James B., editor. *Ancient Near Eastern Texts Relating to the Old Testament.* 2nd ed. Princeton: Princeton University Press, 1955.

Procksch, Otto. *Das nordhebräische Sagenbuch, die Elohimquelle.* Leipzig: Hinrichs, 1906.

Puukko, Antti F. *Die altassyrischen und hethitischen Gesetze und das Alte Testament.* ("Studia orientalia," 1.) Helsinki: Societas orientalis fennica, 1925.

Quell, Gottfried. "The Old Testament Concept 'berit'," in G. Kittel, editor, *Theological Dictionary of the New Testament.* Translated by G. W. Bromiley. Grand Rapids: Eerdmans, 1964–. Vol. 2, pp. 106–27.

Rad, Gerhard von. *Studies in Deuteronomy.* Translated by D. Stalker. ("Studies in Biblical Theology," 9.) Chicago: Regnery, 1953.

—. *Das formgeschichtliche Problem des Hexateuchs.* ("Beiträge zur Wissenschaft vom Alten und Neuen Testament," Folge 4, Heft 26.) Stuttgart: Kohlhammer, 1938.

—. *Das Geschichtsbild des chronistischen Werkes.* ("Beiträge zur Wissenschaft vom Alten und Neuen Testament," Folge 4, Heft 3.) Stuttgart: Kohlhammer, 1930.

—. "Das judäische Krönungsritual," *Theologische Literaturzeitung,* 72 (1947), cols. 211 ff.

—. "Die levitische Predigt in den Büchern der Chronik," in *Festschrift Otto Procksch zum 60. Geburtstag.* Leipzig: Deichert, 1934. Pp. 113–24.

—. "Der Lobpreis Israels," in "*Antwort*"; *Karl Barth zum 70. Geburtstag*. Zürich: Evangelischer Verlag, 1956. Pp. 676 ff.

—. *The Problem of the Hexateuch and Other Essays*. Translated by E. W. T. Dicken. Edinburgh: Oliver and Boyd, 1963.

Ranoszek, R. "Traktat króla hetyckiego Arnuwandasa z krajem Ismirika," *Comptes rendues des séances de la Société des Sciences et des Lettres de Varsovie*, 32 (1939), pp. 25–30.

Resch, G. "Das hebräische Testament Naphtali," *Theologische Studien und Kritiken*, 1899, pp. 206–36.

Reventlow, Henning, Graf. *Das Amt des Propheten bei Amos*. ("Forschungen zur Religion und Literatur des Alten und Neuen Testaments," 80.) Göttingen: Vandenhoeck & Ruprecht, 1962.

—. *Gebot und Predigt im Dekalog*. Gütersloh: Mohn, 1962.

—. "Kultisches Recht im Alten Testament," *Zeitschrift für Theologie und Kirche*, 60 (1963), pp. 267–304.

Rhodokanakis, Nikolaus. *Altsabäische Texte I*. ("Sitzungsberichte der Akademie der Wissenschaften Wien," Phil.-hist. Klasse, Bd. 206.) Wien: Hölder, 1930.

Riemschneider, M. *Die Welt der Hethiter*. ("Große Kulturen der Frühzeit.") Stuttgart: Kilpper, 1954.

Riesenfeld, H. "Gottesdienst im NT," in *Die Religion in Geschichte und Gegenwart*, 3rd ed., vol. 2, cols. 1761–63. Tübingen: Mohr, 1958.

Rießler, Paul. *Altjüdisches Schrifttum ausserhalb der Bibel*. Augsburg: Filser, 1928.

Robinson, Theodore H. *Die zwölf Kleinen Propheten (Hosea bis Micha)*. ("Handbuch zum Alten Testament," Reihe 1, Bd. 14.) 2nd ed. Tübingen: Mohr, 1954.

Rönsch, Hermann. *Das Buch der Jubiläen*. Leipzig: Füss, 1874.

Rosenthal, Franz. "Notes on the Third Aramaic Inscription from Sefíre-Sûjîn," *Bulletin of the American Schools of Oriental Research*, 158 (1960), pp. 28–31.

Rost, Leonhard. *Die Damaskusschrift*. ("Kleine Texte für Vorlesungen und Übungen," 167.) Berlin: De Gruyter, 1933.

—. "Sinaibund und Davidsbund," *Theologische Literaturzeitung*, 72 (1947), cols. 129–34.

—. *Die Vorstufen von Kirche und Synagoge im Alten Testament*. ("Beiträge zur Wissenschaft vom Alten und Neuen Testament," Folge 4, Heft 24.) Stuttgart: Kohlhammer, 1938.

—. "Die Wohnstätte des Zeugnisses," in *Festschrift Friedrich Baumgärtel zum 70. Geburtstag*. ("Erlanger Forschungen," Reihe A, Bd. 10.) Erlangen: Universitätsbund, 1959. Pp. 158–65.

—. "Zur Struktur der Gemeinde des Neuen Bundes im Lande Damaskus," *Vetus Testamentum*, 9 (1959), pp. 393–98.

Rothstein, Johann W. *Kommentar zum 1. Buch der Chronik*. Abgeschlossen von Johannes Hänel. ("Kommentar zum Alten Testament," Bd. 18, Teil 2.) Leipzig: Schobl, 1927.

Rudolph, Wilhelm. *Der Aufbau von Exodus 19—24*. ("Beihefte zur

Zeitschrift für die alttestamentliche Wissenschaft," 66.) Gießen: Töpelmann, 1936.

—. *Chronikbücher*. ("Handbuch zum Alten Testament," Reihe 1, Bd. 21.) Tübingen: Mohr, 1955.

—. *Esra und Nehemia samt 3. Esra.* ("Handbuch zum Alten Testament," Reihe 1, Bd. 20.) Tübingen: Mohr, 1949.

—. *Jeremia.* ("Handbuch zum Alten Testament," Reihe 1, Bd. 12.) Tübingen: Mohr, 1958.

Šanda, Albert. *Die Bücher der Könige.* ("Exegetisches Handbuch zum Alten Testament.") 2 vols. Münster: Aschendorff, 1911–12.

Schaeder, Hans H. *Esra der Schreiber.* ("Beiträge zur historischen Theologie," Bd. 5.) Tübingen: Mohr, 1930.

Scharbert, Josef. "'Fluchen' und 'Segen' im Alten Testament," *Biblica*, 39 (1958), pp. 1–26.

—. "Formgeschichte und Exegese von Ex. 34:6 f und seinen Parallelen," *Biblica*, 38 (1957), pp. 130–50.

—. *Heilsmittler im Alten Testament und im Alten Orient.* ("Quaestiones disputatae," 23/24.) Freiburg: Herder, 1964.

Schedl, Claus. "Bund und Erwählung," *Zeitschrift für katholische Theologie*, 80 (1958), pp. 495 ff.

Scheil, V. *Textes Elamites-Anzanites.* ("Mémoires de la délégation en Perse," 11.) Paris, 1911.

Schmidt, Hans. "Bund" I. Im Alten Testament, in *Die Religion in Geschichte und Gegenwart*, 1st ed., vol. 1, cols. 1432ff. Tübingen: Mohr, 1909.

—. *Die Psalmen.* ("Handbuch zum Alten Testament," Reihe 1, Bd. 15.) Tübingen: Mohr, 1934.

Schmitt, Götz. *Der Landtag von Sichem.* ("Arbeiten zur Theologie," Reihe 1, Heft, 15.) Stuttgart: Calwer, 1962.

Schnapp, Friedrich. *Die Testamente der zwölf Patriarchen.* Halle: Niemeyer, 1884.

Schreiber, R. *Der neue Bund im Spätjudentum und Christentum.* Dissertation, Tübingen, 1954/55.

Seebass, Horst. *Der Erzvater Israel und die Einführung der Jahweverehrung in Kanaan.* ("Beihefte zur Zeitschrift für die alttestamentliche Wissenschaft," 98.) Berlin: Töpelmann, 1966.

Sekine, Masao. "Davidsbund und Sinaibund bei Jeremia," *Vetus Testamentum*, 9 (1959), pp. 47-57.

Simpson, Cuthbert A. *The Early Traditions of Israel.* Oxford: Blackwell, 1948.

Sjöberg, Erik. *Gott und die Sünder im palästinischen Judentum.* ("Beiträge zur Wissenschaft vom Alten und Neuen Testament," Folge 4, Heft 27.) Stuttgart: Kohlhammer, 1939.

Smend, Rudolf. *Die Bundesformel.* ("Theologische Studien," 68.) Zürich: EVZ Verlag, 1963.

Smith, Henry P. *A Critical and Exegetical Commentary on the Books of Samuel.* ("International Critical Commentary," 8.) Edinburgh: Clark, 1912.

Soden, Wolfram von. *Grundriß der akkadischen Grammatik*. ("Analecta orientalia," 33.) Roma: Pontificio Instituto Biblico, 1952.

Soggin, Juan Alberto. "Kultätiologische Sagen und Katechese im Hexateuch," *Vetus Testamentum*, 10 (1960), pp. 341–47.

Sollberger, Edmond. *Corpus des inscriptions "royales" présargoniques de Lagaš*. Genève: Droz, 1956. Pp. 9 ff.

Sommer, Ferdinand. "Die Aḫḫijavâ-Urkunden," *Abhandlungen der Bayerischen Akademie der Wissenschaften*, Phil.-hist. Abteilung, Neue Folge 6 (1932), p. 390.

Stamm, Johann J. *The Ten Commandments in Recent Research*. Translated by M. E. Andrew. ("Studies in Biblical Theology," 2nd series, no. 2.) Naperville: Allenson, 1967.

—. "Dreißig Jahre Dekalogforschung," *Theologische Rundschau*, 27 (1961), pp. 189–239; 281–305.

—. *Erlösen und Vergeben im Alten Testament*. Bern: Haupt, 1940.

Stendahl, Krister. *The School of St. Matthew*. Philadelphia: Fortress, 1968.

—. *The Scrolls and the New Testament*. New York: Harper, 1957.

Steuernagel, Carl. *Das Deuteronomium*. ("Göttinger Handkommentar zum Alten Testament," Abteilung 1, Bd. 3, Teil 1.) Göttingen: Vandenhoeck & Ruprecht, 1923.

—. *Das Buch Josua*. ("Göttinger Handkommentar zum Alten Testament," Abteilung 1, Bd. 3, Teil 2.) Göttingen: Vandenhoeck & Ruprecht, 1923.

Storf, Remigius. *Griechische Liturgien*. Mit Einleitungen von Theodor Schermann. ("Bibliothek der Kirchenväter," 5.) Kempten: Kösel, 1912.

Sugi, I. "Der Vertrag des Tudḫalijaš IV. mit IŠTAR-muwaš von Amurru," *Orient*, 1 (1960), pp. 1-22.

Thompson, John A. "Covenant Patterns in the Ancient Near East and their Significance for Biblical Studies," *Reformed Theological Review*, 18 (1959), pp. 65–75.

Thureau-Dangin, Francois. *Die sumerischen und akkadischen Königsinschriften*. ("Vorderasiatische Bibliothek," Bd. 1, Abteilung 1.) Leipzig: Hinrichs, 1907.

Thyen, Hartwig. *Der Stil der jüdisch-hellenistischen Homilie*. ("Forschungen zur Religion und Literatur des Alten und Neuen Testaments," Neue Folge 47.) Göttingen: Vandenhoeck & Ruprecht, 1955.

Torrey, Charles C. *The Lives of the Prophets, Greek Text and Translation*. ("Journal of Biblical Literature Monograph Series," 1.) Philadelphia: Society of Biblical Literature, 1946.

Tsevat, Matitiahu. "The Neo-Assyrian and Neo-Babylonian Vassal Oaths and the Prophet Ezekiel," *Journal of Biblical Literature*, 78 (1959) pp. 199–204.

Vogt, Ernst. "Nova inscriptio aramaica saec. 8 A.C.," *Biblica*, 39 (1958), pp. 269–74.

—. "Vox 'berit' concrete adhibita illustratur," *Biblica*, 36 (1955), pp. 565–66.

P

Volz, Paul. *Die Eschatologie der jüdischen Gemeinde.* Tübingen: Mohr, 1934.
—. *Der Prophet Jeremia.* ("Kommentar zum Alten Testament," Bd. 10.) Leipzig: Deichert, 1922.
Waterman, Leroy. *Royal Correspondence of the Assyrian Empire,* II. ("University of Michigan Studies," Humanistic Series, vols. 17–20.) Ann Arbor: University of Michigan Press, 1930–31.
Weidinger, Karl. *Die Haustafeln.* ("Untersuchungen zum Neuen Testament," Heft 14.) Leipzig: Hinrichs, 1928.
Weidner, Ernst F. "Assurbanipal in Assur," *Archiv für Orientforschung,* 13 (1939-41), Tafel xiv and p. 215, n. 69.
—. *Politische Dokumente aus Kleinasien; die Staatsverträge in akkadischer Sprache aus dem Archiv von Boghazkoi.* ("Boghazkoi-Studien," Heft 8 and 9.) Leipzig: Hinrichs, 1923.
—. "Der Staatsvertrag Aššurnirâris von Assyrien mit Matti'ilu von Bît-Agusi sowie der Vertrag Samsi-Adads V. mit Marduk-zakir-sumi I. und der Vertrag Asarhaddons mit Ba'al von Tyrus," *Archiv für Orientforschung,* 8 (1932/33), pp. 17–27.
Weise, Manfred. *Kultzeiten und kultischer Bundesschluß in der "Ordensregel" vom Toten Meer.* ("Studia post-biblica," 3.) Leiden: Brill, 1961.
Weiser, Artur. *Das Buch des Propheten Jeremia, Kap. 25:15—52:34.* ("Das Alte Testament Deutsch," Bd. 21.) Göttingen: Vandenhoeck & Ruprecht, 1955.
—. *Das Buch der zwölf Kleinen Propheten I.* ("Das Alte Testament Deutsch," Bd. 24.) Göttingen: Vandenhoeck & Ruprecht, 1949.
—. *The Psalms.* Translated by H. Hartwell. ("The Old Testament Library.") Philadelphia: Westminster, 1962.
Wellhausen, Julius. *Die Composition des Hexateuchs und der historischen Bücher des Alten Testaments.* 2nd edition. Berlin: Reimer, 1889.
—. *Geschichte Israels.* Berlin: Reimer, 1878.
Wernberg-Møller, Preben. *The Manual of Discipline.* Grand Rapids: Eerdmans, 1957.
Whitley, Charles F. "Covenant and Commandment in Israel," *Journal of Near Eastern Studies,* 22 (1963), pp. 37–48.
Whittaker, Molly. *Die Apostolischen Väter I: Der Hirt des Hermas.* ("Die griechischen christlichen Schriftsteller der ersten Jahrhunderte," Bd 48.) Berlin: Akademie, 1956.
Wibbing, Siegfried. *Die Tugend- und Lasterkataloge im Neuen Testament.* Dissertation, Heidelberg, 1955.
Widengren, Geo. *The Ascension of the Apostle and the Heavenly Book.* ("Uppsala Universitets Årsskrift," 1950:7.) Uppsala: Lundequist, 1950.
—. "King and Covenant," *Journal of Semitic Studies,* 2 (1957), pp. 1-32.
—. *Sakrales Königtum im Alten Testament und im Judentum.* ("Franz Delitzsch Vorlesungen," 1952.) Stuttgart: Kohlhammer, 1955.
Windisch, Hans. *Der Barnabasbrief.* ("Handbuch zum Neuen Testament," Ergänzungsband, Die Apostolischen Väter, 3.) Tübingen: Mohr, 1920.
—. *Die Katholischen Briefe.* ("Handbuch zum Neuen Testament," Bd. 15.) 3rd ed. Tübingen: Mohr, 1951.

Wiseman, Donald J. *The Alalakh Tablets*. ("Occasional Publications of the British Institute of Archaeology at Ankara," No. 2.) London: British Institute of Archaeology, 1953.

—. "Esarhaddon's Treaties with the Medes," in International Congress of Orientalists. *Akten des XXIV. Internationalen Orientalisten-Kongresses München 1957.* Wiesbaden: Deutsche Morgenländische Gesellschaft, 1959.

—. "The Vassal-Treaties of Esarhaddon," *Iraq*, 20 (1958), pp. 1 ff.

Wolff, Hans Walter. "Jahwe als Bundesvermittler," *Vetus Testamentum*, 6 (1956), pp. 317–20.

—. "Das Kerygma des Deuteronomistischen Geschichtswerkes," *Zeitschrift für die alttestamentliche Wissenschaft*, 73 (1961), pp. 171–86.

—. "Das Thema 'Umkehr' in der alttestamentlichen Prophetie," *Zeitschrift für Theologie und Kirche*, 48 (1951), pp. 129–48.

—. "'Wissen um Gott' bei Hosea als Urform von Theologie," *Evangelische Theologie*, 12 (1952/53), pp. 533–54.

Woude, Adam. S. van der. *Uittocht en Sinai.* Nijkerk, 1960.

Wright, George Ernest. "The Lawsuit of God. A Form-Critical Study of Deuteronomy 32," in *Israel's Prophetic Heritage*; *Essays in Honor of James Muilenburg.* New York: Harper, 1962. Pp. 26–67.

Würthwein, Ernst. "Der Ursprung der prophetischen Gerichtsrede," *Zeitschrift für Theologie und Kirche*, 49 (1952), pp. 1-16.

Zimmerli, Walther. *Erkenntnis Gottes nach dem Buch Ezekiel.* ("Abhandlungen zur Theologie des Alten und Neuen Testaments.") Zürich: Zwingli, 1954.

—. "Das Gesetz im Alten Testament," *Theologische Literaturzeitung*, 85 (1960), pp. 481–98.

—. "'Ich bin Jahwe," in *Geschichte und Altes Testament*; *Festschrift A. Alt.* ("Beiträge zur historischen Theologie," 16.) Tübingen: Mohr, 1953.

—. "Sinaibund und Abrahambund. Ein Beitrag zum Verständnis der Priesterschrift," *Theologische Zeitschrift*, 16 (1960), pp. 268–80.

—. "Das zweite Gebot," in *Festschrift Alfred Bertholet zum 80. Geburtstag.* Tübingen: Mohr, 1950. Pp. 550–63.

Zulay, Menahem. *Zur Liturgie der babylonischen Juden.* ("Bonner orientalistische Studien," 2.) Stuttgart: Kohlhammer, 1933.

INDEX OF PASSAGES